As a woman living in a relationship not recognised by law, and publishing under a male pseudonym, George Eliot was one of the most controversial and at the same time most successful writers of the Victorian period. Today she is considered not only a key figure among Victorian women writers, but also one of the most influential contributors to the tradition of modern fiction in English; her novels, including *The Mill on the Floss* and *Middlemarch*, are firmly established as major literary classics.

This guide to George Eliot's enduringly popular work offers:

- an accessible introduction to the contexts and many interpretations of Eliot's texts, from publication to the present;
- an introduction to key critical texts and perspectives on the life and work of Marian Evans (the woman behind the pseudonym), situated in a broader critical history;
- cross-references between sections of the guide, in order to suggest links between texts, contexts and criticism;
- suggestions for further reading.

Part of the **Routledge Guides to Literature** series, this volume is essential reading for all those beginning detailed study of George Eliot and seeking not only a guide to her works but also a way through the wealth of contextual and critical material that surrounds them.

Educated at Łódź, Poland, and Worcester College, Oxford, **Jan Jędrzejewski** is Head of English at the University of Ulster. He has published *Thomas Hardy and the Church* (1996), essays on Victorian literature, Irish literature, and Anglo-Polish literary relations, and editions of Hardy and Le Fanu.

Routledge Guides to Literature

Routledge Guides to Literature offer clear introductions to the most widely studied authors and texts. Each book engages with texts, contexts and criticism, highlighting the range of critical views and contextual factors that need to be taken into consideration in advanced studies of literary works. The series encourages informed but independent readings of texts by ranging as widely as possible across the contextual and critical issues relevant to the works examined, rather than presenting a single interpretation. Alongside general guides to texts and authors, the series includes 'Sourcebooks', which allow access to reprinted contextual and critical materials as well as annotated extracts of primary text.

Already available:*

George Eliot

Jan Jędrzejewski

Routledge
Taylor & Francis Group

LONDON AND NEW YORK

First published 2007
by Routledge
2 Park Square, Milton Park, Abingdon, Oxon OX14 4RN

Simultaneously published in the USA and Canada
by Routledge
270 Madison Ave, New York, NY 10016

Routledge is an imprint of the Taylor & Francis Group, an informa business

© 2007 Jan Jędrzejewski

Typeset in Sabon and Gill Sans by RefineCatch Limited, Bungay, Suffolk
Printed and bound in Great Britain by
Antony Rowe Ltd, Chippenham, Wiltshire

British Library Cataloguing in Publication Data
A catalogue record for this book is available from the British Library

Library of Congress Cataloging in Publication Data
Jedrzejewski, Jan.
  George Eliot / Jan Jedrzejewski.
    p. cm. -- (Routledge guides to literature)
  Includes bibliographical references and index.
  1. Eliot, George, 1819–1880--Criticism and interpretation. 2. Women
and literature--England--History--19th century. I. Title.
  PR4688.J44 2007
  823'.8--dc22   2007008407

ISBN 10: 0–415–20249–3 (hbk)
ISBN 10: 0–415–20250–7 (pbk)

ISBN 13: 978–0–415–20249–7 (hbk)
ISBN 13: 978–0–415–20250–3 (pbk)

Contents

Acknowledgements

To my sister Anna

I would like to thank the University of Ulster for granting me a period of research leave to complete this study, and the University's library staff for their efficient support. I am grateful to W.J. McCormack, Ken Newton, and John Rignall for their valuable advice. My fellow series editor Richard Bradford has been generous with his time and expertise not only during the preparation of this volume, but ever since we devised these *Guides* almost a decade ago. A very special word of thanks goes to Liz Thompson and to her colleagues at Routledge for their patience and understanding.

Abbreviations, frequently cited works and cross-referencing

CH *George Eliot: The Critical Heritage*, ed. David Carroll, London: Routledge and Kegan Paul, 1971.

Cross Cross, J.W., *George Eliot's Life, as Related in Her Letters and Journals*, Edinburgh: Blackwood, 1885.

J *The Journals of George Eliot*, ed. Margaret Harris and Judith Johnston, Cambridge: Cambridge University Press, 1998.

L *The George Eliot Letters*, ed. Gordon S. Height, London: Oxford University Press, 1954–78.

All quotations from George Eliot's major fictions are taken from Penguin English Library editions, 1965–80; quotations from her other works are taken from the following editions:

> *Collected Poems*, ed. Lucien Jenkins, London: Skoob, 1989.
> *Impressions of Theophrastus Such*, ed. D.J. Enright, London: Dent, 1995.
> *'The Lifted Veil' and 'Brother Jacob'*, ed. Sally Shuttleworth, London: Penguin, 2001.
> *Selected Essays, Poems, and Other Writings*, ed. A.S. Byatt and Nicholas Warren, London: Penguin, 1990.

Cross-referencing

Cross-referencing between sections is a feature of each volume in the Routledge Guides to Literature series. Cross-references appear in brackets and include section titles, as well as the relevant page numbers in bold type, e.g. (see Life and contexts, **pp. 14–15**).

1

Life and contexts

What's in a name? Writers' names are rarely a matter of concern for literary critics – and yet in the case of George Eliot (to call her by the pseudonym under which she became famous), the sheer diversity of first names, surnames, diminutives, contractions, aliases and pen names she adopted at various periods in her life and in different contexts acquires a special significance, reflecting something very central not only to her personality as an individual, but also to her achievement as an artist. Her adoption of the surnames of her long-term partner George Henry Lewes and, subsequently, of her husband John Walter Cross was perhaps the simplest and most obvious of those decisions, reflecting her commitment to the marital or quasi-marital relationships into which she entered, whether or not they were recognised by the law. The other choices she made – dropping the final 'e' from Mary Anne, then adopting the contracted name of Marian, then reverting to Mary Ann – seem to indicate a process of soul-searching, an attempt to define and redefine herself, and to signal to others the changing nature of her understanding of her identity and her place in the world. This process is perhaps most clearly seen in the way in which she adopted – and dropped – some of the names she used in the family circle and in the company of, and correspondence with, her friends: for some time in her youth, she was 'Clematis' ('mental beauty') to her friends Maria Lewis and Martha Jackson; even more significantly, later on in her life she became 'Madonna' to Lewes, 'Mutter' to her stepsons and 'Mother' or 'Madre' to her younger friends and admirers, Elma Stuart and Emilia Pattison – all of those names carrying complex cultural and emotional associations, particularly for a woman who challenged some of the most fundamental stereotypes and assumptions the society of her time made in relation to the roles it expected women to play as 'angels in the house' – obedient wives, devoted mothers, committed Christians. She was a woman who emerged from her relatively humble Warwickshire background to become the most respected English novelist of her time; an intellectual who, despite having received only limited formal education, became one of her epoch's most erudite thinkers; a determined agnostic who, living in a predominantly Christian society, was prepared, in her personal life, to follow her own moral judgement rather than the received perceptions of morality and religion and yet acquired, through her writing, a kind of moral authority that turned her into something of a national institution, one of the most respected ethical thinkers of her age. One of the most complex personalities of the Victorian era, George Eliot embodied, in her personal life, in her career as a translator, editor and literary critic, and in her creative work, many of the paradoxes that lay at the heart of the complex and dynamic world of mid- and late nineteenth-century Britain.

Childhood and education (1819–35)

The girl who was to become George Eliot was born Mary Anne Evans on 22 November 1819 at South Farm, on the Arbury estate near the town of Nuneaton in Warwickshire. Her father, Robert Evans, was the manager of the estate; universally respected, not only by his employers, the Newdigate family, but also by members of his local community, for his integrity, his wide practical knowledge and experience, and his managerial skills, he acquired, over the years, a social status that was certainly closer to that of a middle-class professional than that of a mere member of estate staff. Having lost his first wife, by whom he had two surviving children, Robert and Frances, he married (in 1813) Christiana Pearson, the youngest daughter of a prosperous local farmer. The family soon grew, with the birth of Christiana (in 1814), Isaac (in 1816), and Mary Anne; there were to be two more children, twin boys, but both of them died in infancy. In 1820, a few months after the birth of Mary Anne, the family moved from South Farm to a more spacious and comfortable home on the Arbury estate, Griff House; it was to become their family home until Robert Evans's retirement in 1841.

The essential peace and security of the domestic environment of Mary Anne's childhood helped to create, in the future writer's imagination, a vision of late-Georgian England as a world that, though by no means free from tensions and difficulties, ultimately offered people a sense of moral and social order, harmony, and stability. Although among her major works of fiction only *The Mill on the Floss* could be described as semi-autobiographical (see Works, **pp. 44–51**), most of the others, except *Romola* and *Daniel Deronda*, recreate the kind of late eighteenth- or, more often, early nineteenth-century environment of the Midlands of England which their author would have known either directly from her childhood or from family memories. It might still have been an England of rural parishes and small market towns, an England that travelled by coach, or on horseback, or indeed on foot, an England that preserved many of the traditional customs, attitudes and ways of living that had developed, organically, over the centuries of the country's history – but at the same time it was an England which was no longer parochial and isolated, an England which was increasingly aware that change was right around the corner, that new industries, new technologies, new ideas and, in consequence, new challenges were just about to transform the existing status quo. The fact that Griff House was no pastoral retreat but a house situated within easy distance of local coal pits and of the silk-weaving town of Nuneaton no doubt contributed to Mary Anne's awareness of the processes of economic, social and political change that were reshaping the towns and villages of Britain as the Industrial Revolution was taking its hold over the country in the early nineteenth century. George Eliot's two novels dealing with the issue of political reform, *Felix Holt* (see Works, **pp. 61–7**) and *Middlemarch* (see Works, **pp. 67–80**), no doubt owe a good deal to their author's early awareness of the tensions that characterised the public life of Britain in the late 1820s and early 1830s, culminating in the Reform Act of 1832. With its elimination of the worst abuses of the old electoral system, such as the existence of 'pocket boroughs' – parliamentary constituencies in which elections were decided through the influence of different forms of patronage – and the redistribution of seats from depopulated 'rotten boroughs' to the new industrial and commercial centres in the Midlands and the north of England, the Reform Act marked the entrance into the world of parliamentary politics of the middle classes – the very people among whom Mary Anne was growing up and whose lives were to become the subject of some of the most important of her works.

Significant as the echoes of public events may have been in the development of the future writer's awareness of social and political problems facing the country, the most important influence on her personal and intellectual development in her early years was, naturally, that of her family. The key figure for Mary Anne was certainly her father: as his youngest surviving child, she was predictably indulged and grew to treat him with love and respect that amounted almost to reverence – although the fact that she matched him in strong-mindedness meant that their relationship was not always entirely unproblematic. The significance – and complexity – of Robert Evans's influence on his daughter is reflected on the one hand in the frequency with which father–daughter relationships are focused on in her fiction, particularly in *The Mill on the Floss* (see Works, **pp. 44–51**), *Romola* (see Works, **pp. 56–61**) and *Felix Holt* (see Works, **pp. 61–7**) and, on the other hand, in the idealised portraits of Adam Bede, in the novel of that title (see Works, **pp. 36–44**), and of Caleb Garth in *Middlemarch* (see Works, **pp. 67–80**). The affection with which those characters are drawn stands in sharp contrast with the portrayal, in *The Mill on the Floss*, of Mrs Tulliver, arguably based on the novelist's mother; her rather lukewarm relationship with Maggie, the novel's semi-autobiographical protagonist, as well as the relative scarcity – or inadequacy – of mother–daughter relationships in George Eliot's other works, can well be interpreted as a reflection of the emotional distance that may have separated the future writer from her mother.

Mary Anne's relationships with her siblings were, on the other hand, close and warm. Her sister Christiana is believed to have inspired the affectionate portrayal of Lucy Deane in *The Mill on the Floss* and of Celia Brooke in *Middlemarch*; it was, however, their brother Isaac, three years Mary Anne's senior, who was the young girl's most important childhood companion and playmate. The intensity of Mary Anne's attachment to her brother can be guessed from the emotional power and spontaneity with which she was to present the relationship between Maggie and Tom Tulliver in *The Mill on the Floss* (see Works, **pp. 44–51**) and with which she was to return to the subject a few years later in the collection of sonnets entitled 'Brother and Sister' (see Works, **p. 95**). It may well be the case that her lifelong tendency to form intense friendships with men (see Life and contexts, **pp. 8–9**) might have been an attempt to reproduce the closeness and intimacy of the relationship she had with her brother.

Mary Anne's education was as good as could have been expected in view of both her social background and the general state of women's education in the early nineteenth century. Her schooling began at a local day school, which she attended together with Isaac; at five, in 1824, she joined Christiana at

Miss Lathom's boarding school in Attleborough, just a few miles away from Griff, and four years later, in 1828, both girls moved to another school, this time in nearby Nuneaton – it was there, at Mrs Wallington's, that Mary Anne was taught by Maria Lewis, who was later to become a close friend and confidante. However, Mary Anne's intelligence and curiosity soon demanded more challenging tuition than the local establishments were able to offer; in consequence, she was sent, in 1832, to a rather more upmarket school, run by Mary and Rebecca Franklin, the daughters of a Baptist minister, in the city of Coventry. The curriculum there was much broader, though it was still distinctly oriented towards the acquisition of 'accomplishments' rather than academic knowledge; it did, however, involve the study of English (including lessons in elocution), French, history, arithmetic and music – areas in which Mary Anne was to continue her self-directed studies for decades to come. It was also during her school years that she began to develop her lifelong interest in literature, concentrating at that stage on English poetry – she was particularly impressed by Milton – and on recent fiction, particularly the works of Sir Walter Scott.

The school years were of fundamental importance to Mary Anne in one other major respect – it was as a result of the influence of her teachers, both in Nuneaton and in Coventry, that she developed a profound, and lasting, interest in matters of religion. Brought up in the conventional and somewhat lukewarm tradition of mainstream Anglicanism, she encountered, first through Maria Lewis and then through the Franklins, forms of Christian belief that were, in their different ways, much more personal and much more intense than the largely unreflective, formalised, routine kind of Christianity practised in her immediate family circle.

Although, like the Evanses, a member of the Church of England, Maria Lewis was an Evangelical – a believer in an approach to religion that stressed the autonomy of the individual and the significance of personal religious experience (including personal conversion) and of direct emotional involvement in matters of faith. A type of mindset, a way of life and a system of values rather than a denomination, Evangelicalism developed, in late-eighteenth-century Britain, very much as part of the same broad movement towards the rediscovery of the spiritual essence of Christianity that had produced, earlier in the eighteenth century, the development of Methodism, and that would lead, in the second quarter of the nineteenth century, to the rise of the Tractarian Movement and the resurfacing of Roman Catholicism. Unlike the latter developments, Evangelicalism was a quintessentially Protestant phenomenon: it focused on the importance of individual conscience, and it valued Bible-based preaching above religious rituals; at the same time, however, it did have a significant social dimension, in the sense that it stressed that Christian values should permeate every aspect of life, from strict observance of the Sabbath to active engagement in the moral reformation of society – best exemplified by the role played by one of the most prominent Evangelicals, the politician and philanthropist William Wilberforce, in the campaign for the abolition of slavery.

The combined influence of Maria Lewis's Evangelical enthusiasm and earnestness, on the one hand, and of the quiet but confident spirit of Nonconformity which obtained in the Franklins' school on the other, led the young Mary Anne to develop a sense of seriousness about matters of religious belief which was to remain a characteristic feature of her intellectual and emotional make-up for the rest of her life. Quite characteristically, Mary Anne's response to Christianity was largely ethical: in line with Evangelical thinking, she focused much of her attention on seeking ways of achieving individual moral perfection through a sustained effort at self-improvement. In consequence, the young Mary Anne was becoming increasingly Puritanical in some of her attitudes – by the late 1830s, she would not only display exemplary Evangelical piety in her indifference to such vanities of life as interest in her own appearance, but she would also at one point give up, for a period of time, the reading of fiction and other forms of 'profane' literature in favour of serious works of theological and devotional nature (see L, I, 21–4). It is in many ways symbolic of her commitment to Christianity that it was with a devotional poem on death, 'Farewell', that she made, in 1840, her literary debut in the *Christian Observer*.

At Griff and Coventry (1835-49)

Mary Anne's essentially peaceful and harmonious childhood came to a rather abrupt end in the winter of 1835–6: she returned home for Christmas to find both her parents in poor health; her mother's condition – she had been suffering from breast cancer – was in fact rapidly deteriorating. Christiana Evans's death, on 3 February 1836, may not have come as a shock, but it did mean a radical change in the patterns of the Evans family life as the daughters, Christiana and Mary Anne, found themselves having to take over the responsibilities involved in the running of their father's household. Christiana was, in fact, to leave the family home at Griff before too long as well – her marriage, in 1837, to a local doctor, Edward Clarke, marked, for Mary Anne, the beginning of a period in her life during which her principal occupation was that of her father's housekeeper, companion and, eventually, nurse. It was perhaps something of a symbolic gesture that on the occasion of signing the register as her sister's bridesmaid, the future writer first used a different spelling of her name, dropping the final 'e' and in this way assuming, in a sense, not only a new family role, but almost a new identity.

Dutiful as she was in the carrying out of her domestic responsibilities, Mary Ann did not abandon her studies; on the contrary, she embarked, in the late 1830s, on an extensive programme of reading and self-education, which was soon to turn into a lifelong commitment. Although her interests were very broad, ranging from literature to geology and natural history, her main focus was, at that stage, on the study of history and theology – she was hoping to prepare a chart of ecclesiastical history, a project she abandoned when a similar publication appeared before her own had taken shape – and on learning languages: she was soon to add to her proficiency in French by acquiring a working knowledge of Italian and German.

This arrangement continued until 1841, when Robert Evans, now in his sixty-eighth year, decided to retire, transferring over to his son Isaac, who was about to be married to Sarah Rawlins, the daughter of a Birmingham merchant, both his job on the Arbury estate and, in consequence, the tenancy of Griff House. Mary Ann, in due course, accompanied her father to his chosen retirement home, a comfortable suburban villa at Foleshill, on the outskirts of Coventry.

The new environment brought with it not only a major change in Mary Ann's lifestyle but also, and very importantly, a broadening of her horizons: with her domestic responsibilities now significantly reduced, Mary Ann was able to develop a new network of social contacts which were to provide her with precisely the kind of intellectual stimulation and challenge she needed as a consequence of her expanding intellectual interests. Although her initial contacts in Coventry were the family of her former teachers, the Franklin sisters, who introduced Mary Ann to Coventry's clerical world, by far the most significant of the new acquaintances proved to be of a rather different ilk: a local manufacturer, philanthropist and writer Charles Bray, his wife Caroline (Cara) and her sister Sara Hennell. Rather unorthodox in their approach to life (Bray was something of an eccentric freethinker, and he and his wife had a more or less open marriage), but certainly open-minded and intellectually curious, they were to become not only Mary Ann's faithful – though by no means always uncritical – friends and intellectual partners but also, very importantly, her crucial point of contact with the predominantly metropolitan world of the Victorian cultural and literary establishment. It was largely owing to the opportunities that her closeness to the Bray–Hennell circle created for her that the future writer was able to transform herself, in a matter of but a few years, from an amateur provincial woman-scholar into a respected translator, journalist and editor in her own right.

The first, and in many ways the most significant, aspect of that transformation was a radical, and rather dramatic, change in Mary Ann's religious beliefs. By the early 1840s, the religious certainty of her earlier years was beginning to be undermined, largely because her interest in history and theology brought to her attention the work of biblical commentators and critics who, in a manner typical of nineteenth-century historicism and rationalism, read the Bible not so much as a holy scripture inspired by God, but as a set of texts, created over a period of time in specific historical, social and cultural circumstances and, therefore, demanding to be analysed, whether as historical documents or as works of literature, in a critical fashion, against the background of the context from which they originated and without resorting to interpretations that could not be explained in strictly rational terms. An important consequence of that approach, which was to become known as the Higher Criticism, was the tendency to read aspects of the biblical story which were incompatible with that kind of rationalist, historicist thinking – such as, most fundamentally, the story of the Resurrection – in terms of myth, legend or fiction, based, to a certain extent, on actual historical events, but not always entirely true in the literal, factual sense. This approach did not necessarily imply doubt in the existence of God, but it did question one of the central tenets of Christianity – the status of Jesus as the Son of God. This was, indeed, the main focus of one of the most important works of Higher Criticism, the German philosopher and theologian David Friedrich Strauss's *Das Leben Jesu, kritisch bearbeitet* (1835–6) – a book which was to play an important role in the development of Mary Ann's ideas and her literary career. In England, one of the earliest studies in that vein was *An Inquiry Concerning the Origin of Christianity*, published, in 1838, by none other than Charles Hennell, a brother of Sara and Cara. Focusing on the analysis of the story of Jesus, perceived in purely human rather than divine terms, Hennell's book derives from his Unitarian beliefs, involving the rejection of the doctrine of the Holy Trinity; despite its questioning of the divinity of Jesus, it remains, however, in true Unitarian spirit, deeply respectful and supportive of the moral dimension of Christian teaching.

Mary Ann first encountered Hennell's book shortly before she first met the Brays, probably some time in the autumn of 1841. It is difficult to assess the extent to which the acquaintance with the author's family actually strengthened the impact Hennell's study clearly made on her religious opinions; it does, however, appear that their newly found friendship provided her with a measure of support which helped her to articulate her changing views openly – in particular, to her conventionally Christian father. The key moment, in this respect, came in January 1842, when Mary Ann refused to accompany her father to church – although the ensuing conflict was resolved after a few months, when she agreed to outwardly conform to her father's expectations while privately maintaining her opinions, her decision to stand up against her father's authority and openly declare her unorthodox views was one of the first manifestations of the kind of moral and philosophical seriousness and integrity that were to become the trademarks of not only Mary Ann Evans the thinker, but also of George Eliot the writer.

It was certainly Mary Ann's increasing familiarity with a broad range of contemporaneous historical, philosophical and theological scholarship, as well as her commitment to the ideological and methodological principles of Higher Criticism, that facilitated her first major venture into the world of writing and publishing: in 1844, she was asked to take over from Hennell's wife Elizabeth Rebecca, known by her friends as Rufa, the task of translating into English Strauss's *Das Leben Jesu*. This huge task – the text of the translation ran, when completed, to over 1,300 pages of print – occupied her for over two years: the book was finally published in 1846, under the title *The Life of Jesus, Critically Examined*, by one of early Victorian London's more prominent liberal publishers, John Chapman. Although the name of the translator was not formally acknowledged in the text, the publication of Strauss's book did nonetheless mark the beginning of a professional relationship that was in due course to become, for Mary Ann, the route into the very heart of the dynamic and often controversial world of Victorian letters (see Life and contexts, **pp. 10–13**).

During the busy time when she was working on her translation, Mary Ann maintained close contacts with the Brays and the Hennells, accompanying them on holiday trips around Great Britain and taking an active part in their extensive social life back at home in Coventry. The guests who stayed with the Brays in their home at Rosehill included some of the most respected thinkers and writers of the time, such as the social reformer and philosopher Robert Owen, the novelist, essayist and critic Harriet Martineau and the American philosopher and essayist Ralph Waldo Emerson. It was also through the Brays that Mary Ann embarked on another path of her literary career: interested as keenly as ever in current work in history, philosophy and sociology, she began, in 1846, to publish book reviews in Charles Bray's radical newspaper, the *Herald*.

Mary Ann's reading was not, of course, restricted to serious works of theology and philosophy: her Coventry years were for her also the time of extensive literary education, which was in due course to make her by far the most erudite among the major Victorian novelists. She was very well versed in the literary tradition of English poetry: she had, from her school years, been familiar with Shakespeare and Milton, as well as with eighteenth-century poets such as Edward Young (an early favourite, whose work she was at a later stage to come to criticise in rather acerbic terms) and William Cowper, and she was profoundly influenced by the writings of the major poets of the Romantic era, among whom she felt by far the most enthusiastic about Wordsworth. She also had an extensive knowledge of narrative fiction: apart from her old childhood favourites Bunyan and Scott, she was particularly impressed by the moral focus and psychological insights of the novels of Samuel Richardson, as well as by the works of Samuel Johnson and Oliver Goldsmith, while her reading in the tradition of women's fiction included, among others, the works of Maria Edgeworth and Jane Austen. At the same time, as befitted a budding journalist who was over the following ten years to produce some of mid-nineteenth-century Britain's most important book reviews and literary-critical essays, Mary Ann kept abreast of all the major developments in current literary life; she read the works of virtually all of her major contemporaries, a number of whom were in due course to become her personal acquaintances and friends: she knew the novels of Dickens, Thackeray, the Brontës, Elizabeth Gaskell and Trollope, as well as the poetry of Tennyson, the Brownings and Arnold. Very importantly too, Mary Ann's literary interests were not restricted to writing in English: over the years, she not only maintained her fluency in French, German and Italian, but also acquired a working knowledge of Latin and Greek, as well as, at a later stage, of Spanish and Hebrew, and she read extensively in all those languages. The authors whose work she knew particularly well included Homer, the three Greek tragedians Aeschylus, Sophocles and Euripides, Horace, Virgil, Dante and Cervantes; while among the more recent and contemporaneous writers, her interest focused on the literatures of France (she was especially interested in Rousseau and, among contemporary writers, Balzac and George Sand) and, in particular, Germany: she had a profound interest in German Romanticism, in particular in the works of Goethe, Schiller, Novalis and E.T.A. Hoffman, as well as in the poetry of her near-contemporary Heinrich Heine.

For all the immersion in her intellectual pursuits, Mary Ann remained, throughout the 1840s, in a rather uncomfortable position in her personal life. With all of her siblings married and focusing on trying to get on with their conventional middle-class lives, and with her father increasingly fragile, she was becoming more and more emotionally vulnerable; the feeling of growing isolation from her immediate family circle, and from old friends such as Maria Lewis, made her look out for friendship and support elsewhere. Her female friends, particularly Sara and Cara, proved very supportive indeed; at the same time, however, they could not provide her with the kind of masculine presence, support and perhaps even guidance, which Mary Ann used, in her childhood and youth, to find in her father and brother. This kind of emotional restlessness, which the future novelist was later to recreate in a number of her novels, most prominently perhaps in *The Mill on the Floss* (see Works, **pp. 44–51**), *Romola* (see Works, **pp. 56–61**) and *Middlemarch* (see Works, **pp. 67–80**) began, in the 1840s, to generate a pattern which recurred, on numerous occasions, in her relationships with her male acquaintances, sometimes older than her and, more frequently than not, married. Herself still single and, in consequence of her broad and supposedly 'masculine' interests, increasingly unconventional for a young woman living in the early Victorian period, Mary Ann sought in her friendships the kind of intellectual and psychological intimacy that might well have appeared controversial to those around her. To what extent her contacts with people such as Hennell or his father-in-law, the physician and scholar Dr Robert Brabant, whom she visited in his house at Devizes after the Hennells' wedding in 1843, involved an element of sexual attraction is a matter of speculation; Mary Ann was certainly aware of the ambivalence of her position vis-à-vis her male friends, as she reveals in a mocking vision of herself accepting a proposal from an imaginary German professor (see L, VIII, 13–15). Whatever the nature of those friendships, it remains beyond doubt that they were to provide her with insights and inspiration which enabled her to investigate, in her novels, some of the complexities of relationships between her male and female characters, particularly those in which the women characters' emotional vulnerability expresses itself through their – sometimes misplaced – intellectual and spiritual admiration for their male counterparts. Though it is difficult to draw specific parallels, it seems clear that the presentation of characters such as Girolamo Savonarola, in Romola (see Works, pp. 56–61) or Mr Casaubon, in Middlemarch (see Works, pp. 67–80), owes something to their creator's not unproblematic search for male friendship and support.

In the late 1840s, the health of Robert Evans, now in his mid-seventies, was gradually deteriorating, which made increasing demands on Mary Ann's time and energy. She continued to nurse her father throughout the months of his final illness until his death, which came on 31 May 1849. Despite the differences in their worldview, which continued to generate tensions in their domestic life, Mary Ann remained sincerely devoted to him, which made his departure obviously painful for her in emotional terms; at the same time, however, his death did constitute for her a form of liberation from what until then had been the defining – and at the same time restrictive – context of her life, making her now, at the age of nearly thirty, free at last to embark on the kind of life she had been preparing for over the previous decade.

The years of independence (1849–54)

After the death of her father, Mary Ann found herself at a crossroads: although no longer bound by a sense of filial duty, she now had to consider a variety of other aspects of her position – including in particular her financial situation. The way in which Robert Evans's will divided his estate between his children was properly equitable, but not entirely fair perhaps, one might think, given the loyalty with which his youngest daughter had devoted herself to his care over the last few years of his life. Mary Ann's legacy was, at £2,000, the same as what each of her married sisters received, first as a dowry and then in the will; her money was to be put in trust, guaranteeing an income of around £90 a year – a sum comparable with the earnings of a junior clerk or teacher, and thus likely to be sufficient if she were to follow the conventional route and move in with one of her siblings, but certainly not substantial enough to live on should she wish to embark on an entirely independent and active life of the kind she would be likely to aspire to – particularly if she were to leave Coventry. It was therefore clear that she would need to consider some form of employment, however limited opportunities would have been for a woman of her social class in the middle of the nineteenth century. In practical terms, the possibilities that would have been realistic, in view of her background and education, would have involved some form of teaching or writing – the latter being perhaps the more likely option, in view of her earlier experience, during her Coventry years, of journalism and translation (apart from Strauss, she had also attempted a translation, from Latin, of the seventeenth-century Dutch-Jewish philosopher Baruch Spinoza's *Tractatus Theologico-politicus*, a project which remained uncompleted).

In the immediate aftermath of the death of her father, however, Mary Ann needed time away, both to recover emotionally as well as physically (she had been suffering from bad headaches, which were to become a source of constant distress for her for the rest of her life) and to consider her future. The Brays, friendly and helpful as ever, stepped in and took her for her first trip abroad, to France, northern Italy and Switzerland. They travelled through Paris, Avignon, Marseilles, Nice, Genoa and Milan to Geneva, where Mary Ann decided to remain for some time, while her friends departed on their return journey to England. She stayed first at a relatively upmarket pension, Campagne Plongeon, where she was one of a very heterogeneous group of people, many of them political refugees seeking, in tolerant Switzerland, a safe haven in the aftermath of the European revolutions of 1848. The letters she wrote about her fellow guests to the Brays provide clear evidence of the powers of observation and character analysis that foreshadow the subtlety of social and psychological insight that was to become one of the defining features of her novels (see *L*, I, 289–313 and VIII, 18–20). After a few months, she moved in, as a lodger, with the family of the D'Albert Durades, both painters several years her senior, who accepted her very much as a member of the family and became lifelong friends. In Julie D'Albert Durade Mary Ann found a surrogate mother figure, whom she actually addressed as 'Maman', while her husband François, another of Mary Ann's father/brother figures, was to become not only a trusted friend, with whom she remained in correspondence for the rest of her life, but also her authorised French translator; in addition, he may also have provided the inspiration for the creation of the character of Philip Wakem in *The Mill on the Floss* (see Works, **pp. 44–51**).

Mary Ann – or rather Marian, as she began to sign herself around that time – returned to England in the spring of 1850. She spent some time in the homes of her brother and sister, and rather more with the Brays at Rosehill, but before too long she decided to move to London, to live in the boarding house owned by her old acquaintance John Chapman (see Life and contexts, **p. 7**), who was at that stage the editor, and was soon (1851) to become the owner, of the *Westminster Review*, one of the most important and influential of Victorian periodicals. The publisher and his erudite lodger quickly developed a close working partnership, with Marian becoming a contributor to the *Review*; as in the case of her previous friendships, the exact nature of their personal relationship remains (particularly in view of Chapman's highly unorthodox domestic arrangements, which involved a wife, Susanna, as well as a semi-official live-in governess-cum-mistress, Elisabeth Tilley) a matter of biographical speculation (see Ashton 1996: 83–6, and Hughes 1998: 145–52), but the chemistry between the two must have been strong enough for the wife and the mistress to unite their forces against the newcomer, which resulted in a somewhat farcical series of relocations into and out of the Chapman household which Marian had to undertake over the subsequent three years.

Although the friendship with Chapman was not to survive the test of time, his attractive, flamboyant, but ultimately egocentric personality was to influence the presentation of some of George Eliot's more colourful male characters, with Tito Melema in *Romola* perhaps best encapsulating Chapman's mixture of charm, dilettantism and selfishness (see Works, **pp. 56–61**).

Whatever the complexities of Marian's domestic arrangements, the friendship with Chapman produced one fundamentally important result: following his purchase of the *Westminster Review*, she became, *de facto*, its editor, with Chapman remaining in overall control as the public face of the enterprise and its (often rather less than successful) business manager. The significance of this new role for the development of Marian's literary career can hardly be overestimated: the *Westminster Review*, with its tradition of intellectual radicalism going back to its early nineteenth-century founders, James Mill and Jeremy Bentham, was one of the most respected and influential of nineteenth-century journals and therefore a uniquely powerful forum for the discussion of the most significant cultural, literary, political and scientific issues shaping the intellectual life of mid-Victorian Britain. Like other major reviews of the time, such as the *Athenaeum*, the conservative *Quarterly Review* and the liberal *Edinburgh Review*, the *Westminster Review* was a characteristic example of that particular type of periodical, in many ways unique to the nineteenth century and reflective of the specifically Victorian type of mindset. Taking as their starting point, in most cases, the discussion of recent publications covering a variety of subjects from sociology to natural history and from geology to national and international politics, Victorian reviews provided their readers with substantial digests of key developments in current thought, produced by writers who were often outstanding experts in their respective fields and thus offering comprehensive and yet relatively compact introductions to a broad spectrum of problems shaping the intellectual life of the period. The diversity of subjects discussed in the reviews is well illustrated by the range of material covered by the *Westminster Review* during the time of Marian's editorship. The ten issues she edited, between January 1852 and April 1854, included, among others, articles on current issues in British, European and world politics, from the situation in Russia to slavery in America, as well as on science and natural history, from the future of geology to the biology of shellfish. Very prominent, as could have been expected given Marian's interests, was the coverage of history, philosophy and religion, with extensive articles on major historical figures such as Mary Stuart, on contemporary thinkers, for example the German philosophers Arthur Schopenhauer and Johann Gottlieb Fichte, and on a variety of subjects relating to theology, religious history and the sociology of religion, from early Christianity to the state of religion in modern Italy, and from John Knox to the Mormons. Articles on literary subjects included studies of Shelley and Balzac, as well as contemporaneous authors, such as Charlotte Brontë, Elizabeth Gaskell, William Makepeace Thackeray and Matthew Arnold; in addition, each issue featured a comprehensive summary account of current literary developments in England, America, Germany and France. The list of contributors was most impressive as well: it included, apart from Chapman and Marian herself, her old acquaintance Harriet Martineau and her brother the philosopher James Martineau, the philosophers John Stuart Mill and Herbert Spencer, the historians John Mitchell Kemble and James Anthony Froude, the lawyer, writer and translator Theodore Martin, the journalist and literary scholar Henry Morley, the biologist Thomas Henry Huxley, the exiled leader of the Italian nationalist movement Giuseppe Mazzini, and others. Marian's editorial role, which involved the planning of the contents of the review, negotiations with contributors, etc., meant that she was now, at last, very much in the centre of the intellectual life of Victorian Britain.

One of the consequences of Marian's arrival on the intellectual scene of mid-nineteenth-century London was a rapid expansion of her circle of acquaintances. Although the friendship with the Brays and the Hennells had over the years brought her into contact with a number of the leading luminaries of the day, it was not until she settled in London that she was able to build her own independent social life, reflecting her own diverse sympathies, interests and personal preferences. Thus, for example, the close bond she formed in the early 1850s with two of her new women friends, Bessie Rayner Parkes (later Belloc) and Barbara Leigh Smith (later Bodichon), both radical feminists and campaigners for women's rights, helped to stimulate the future novelist's complex response to one of the key social and political issues of the mid- and late nineteenth century – the question of the legal, social, educational, professional and political position of women. Although George Eliot was never to become a feminist novelist in the same way in which, for example, Charlotte Brontë had been before her, the theme of women's role in social and family life was to feature prominently throughout her œuvre (see Criticism, **pp. 129–34**), from *The Mill on the Floss* (see Works, **pp. 44–51**) and *Romola* (see Works, **pp. 56–61**) to the key novels of the 1870s, *Middlemarch* (see Works, **pp. 67–80**) and *Daniel Deronda* (see Works, **pp. 80–8**).

Meeting new people and making new friends was, of course, just one of the aspects of Marian's experience of the social life of the metropolis. The vibrant capital of the world's most powerful nation, the London of the 1850s was arguably the most dynamic and advanced city in the world, its global dominance confirmed by the success of the Great Exhibition of 1851; with its scholarly institutions, galleries and theatres offering a diverse programme of events, a keen autodidact of Marian's intellectual interests and artistic tastes was never short of opportunities for education and entertainment. She duly made use of those opportunities; she went to public lectures on geometry and the natural sciences, explored the British Museum's collections of antiquities, visited exhibitions at the Royal Academy and joined her Coventry friends on a visit to the Crystal Palace to see the Great Exhibition. It was also during her London years that Marian was first able to indulge her taste for music and drama: she attended concerts and developed a lifelong taste for the theatre and, particularly, the opera.

Marian's increasingly active participation in the professional, social and cultural life of London's intellectual establishment was important in one other respect, not insignificant for a single woman in her thirties that she was – it made her consider, in terms rather more serious than during her Coventry years, the question of her personal future. This became particularly clear when, some time in 1851, she became friendly with one of her future *Westminster Review* contributors, Herbert Spencer, who would take her to the theatre and the opera, accompany her on long walks and generally provide her with the kind of companionship which she must have missed in the absence of her old Coventry friends. Although their friendship was genuine, it was not destined to lead to a mutual commitment: while the exact nature of the relationship remained, for a long time, a matter of biographical speculation, the evidence of Marian's letters to Spencer, not disclosed until 1976, appears to prove that the emotionally reserved Spencer was not prepared to reciprocate the kind of intense affection which Marian was to prepared to give him (see *L*, VIII, 42, 56–7 and Paxton 1991: 47–8).

However complex the relations between Marian and Spencer were on a personal level, their friendship was significant for the future novelist in intellectual terms as well; it was precisely during the time of their closeness, in the early 1850s, that Spencer was developing the key concepts of his influential philosophy of evolutionism, which applied biological laws of organic development to the analysis of society and culture. With Spencer's tendency to apply his theories universally to all manifestations of human activity and Marian's more empirical concern with the individual, their views were bound to diverge: Marian could not accept, for example, Spencer's mechanistic approach to psychology and his hedonist ethics. At the same time, however, her evolutionist interpretation of social development as an organic, progressive movement leading to 'the growing good of the world' (*Middlemarch*, 896), which was to become one of the underlying assumptions of her fiction, certainly owes much of its force to her early acquaintance with Spencer's thoughts and writings.

In view of the closeness of Marian's association with Spencer, it was therefore rather ironical that it was precisely through him that she met, in October 1851, the man who was to become her long-term companion – the journalist, writer and critic George Henry Lewes. Two years older than Marian (he was born on 18 April 1817), he came from a relatively impoverished, though vaguely middle-class, family background; by the time he met her, he had already become a reasonably well-established figure in the literary circles of London, having published, apart from countless articles and reviews, a number of books in areas ranging from philosophy to fiction and from literary history to tragedy; he was also, from 1850, the literary editor of a weekly journal, the *Leader*. The sheer range of Lewes's intellectual pursuits – apart from his knowledge of literature and philosophy, he was a historian and a biographer, whose *Life of Goethe* (1855) was to become a standard biography of the German poet and novelist for decades to come, and he also had a lifelong interest in the natural sciences – made him one of the most interesting literary people of his day, despite the fact that, as a journalist and an amateur gentleman-scholar, he lacked the kind of intellectual *gravitas* the Victorians appreciated: although he was frequently invited to write for numerous periodicals, including the *Westminster Review*, he was not considered to be an author of quite the same calibre as their star contributors, such as John Stuart Mill or Thomas Carlyle. At the same time, like Marian largely self-taught – his formal education had been somewhat patchy, and he had not been to university – he had the kind of intellectual openness and readiness to take on challenges that would make him an ideal partner for Marian's intellectual ambitions.

The one difficulty lay in the fact that, like most of Marian's earlier male friends, Lewes was married – although his marital life was by no means conventional. By the time he met Marian, his ten-year-long marriage, which had produced five children (of whom three, all boys, had survived infancy), had reached a rather bizarre stage: his wife Agnes had embarked on a long-term affair with his best friend and co-editor of the *Leader*, Thornton Hunt – himself a married man with a steadily growing family. When the first of Agnes's four children by Hunt was born, in 1850, Lewes registered the boy as his own, which made it legally impossible for him to sue for divorce on the grounds of his wife's adultery. In consequence, in the early 1850s Lewes's personal situation was highly complex, and his marital and economic status rather ambivalent: technically a married man with considerable financial responsibilities for his – and his wife's – growing young family, he was in practical terms a single man, free to seek female company should he feel inclined to do so.

As Marian's friendship with Lewes was becoming increasingly close as time progressed – they began to see each other regularly in 1853, to facilitate which she moved out of the Chapmans' house into independent lodgings – the situation presented her with a major dilemma. Although the atmosphere within the free-thinking literary circles of Victorian London was by no means prudish, as demonstrated by the unorthodox domestic arrangements of the Chapmans, the Hunts and the Leweses, the public opinion of the time still demanded – and very explicitly so – that outward signs of propriety and respectability in all matters sexual should be strictly maintained, whatever might be going on behind closed doors. In addition, the standards of sexual propriety were radically different for men and for women: while men were relatively free to pursue their sexual interests, as long as they did so in a reasonably discreet fashion, women were expected to remain chaste, as any outward breach of that principle resulted in automatic branding of the culprit as a 'fallen woman' and in social ostracism. Marian's position as a single woman living an independent life and earning her own living through writing and editing might have been unusual but, as things stood when Lewes arrived on the scene, it was still socially acceptable: whatever liaisons she might or might not have got involved in previously, they had never become public knowledge and therefore had not compromised her position. However, with Lewes unable to marry her legally, a decision to live with him openly would not only constitute a challenge to the received sexual morality of the day, and to the inflexibility of the rules of family law with regard to marriage and divorce, but also, for Marian much more than for Lewes, would become a form of social suicide – a conscious abdication of her status as a 'respectable' woman and consequently, an acceptance of a life of isolation and loneliness. Most importantly, a union with Lewes was likely to bring about estrangement from her family – with her brother Isaac becoming increasingly conventional in his attitudes, there was little hope that he would take the kind of tolerant view of the matter that Marian could expect of her more liberal friends in Coventry and London.

Whatever the consequences of her decision, Marian was, however, prepared to face them – helped, not least, by the reassurance she found in the reading and translation, for publication by Chapman, of the German philosopher Ludwig Feuerbach's study *Das Wesen des Christenthums* (1841). This work, belonging very much to the tradition of Higher Criticism (see Life and contexts, **pp. 6–7**), encapsulated many of the ideas Marian was herself considering in the 1850s; the most important of these was the perception of religion as an essentially human concept, a distillation of the most positive values, aspirations and potentialities of humankind. A logical conclusion of the acceptance of that philosophy was a consideration of all moral decisions exclusively in the light of their impact on other people; the concepts of good and evil were effectively identified, respectively, with altruism and egoism, and the measure of morality was not the conformity to some predefined, God-given law, but the extent to which an individual carried out his or her duty towards others. This stress on the central role of the fundamental values of humanity as the cornerstone of individual and social morality brought Marian close to the doctrine of the religion of humanity – one of the central tenets of Positivism, an influential philosophical movement originated in France by the sociologist August Comte and concerned primarily with the evolution and progression of human thought and its various manifestations towards the scientific ideal of objectivity and perfection. Although Marian had been familiar with the philosophy of Positivism since her Coventry years, and although she was in due course to form close friendships with some of Britain's most prominent Positivist thinkers, such as Richard Congreve and Frederic Harrison, she never adopted the dogmatic position towards which Comte's philosophy developed as the nineteenth century progressed, with its pantheon of secular saints, ranging from Homer to Shakespeare, from Archimedes to Gutenberg, and from Julius Caesar to King Frederic the Great of Prussia, and with quasi-religious observances based on various forms of Roman Catholic worship. Marian's interest in Positivism remained, throughout her life, primarily ethical: her humanist moral vision was to become not only the fundament of Marian's own life but also the key element of the moral message of the novels she was, as George Eliot, to produce over the next quarter of a century (see Criticism, **pp. 137–42**); the ideas of the religion of humanity feature particularly prominently in the idealised treatment of the motif of redemption in *Silas Marner* (see Works, **pp. 51–6**) and *Romola* (see Works, **pp. 56–61**).

Once the decision to live with Lewes was made, all that remained for Marian to do was to wind up her outstanding commitments in London so that they could both leave England, together, for Germany – the idea was partly to make the period of transition as inconspicuous as was in the circumstances possible and partly to facilitate Lewes's research towards his biography of Goethe. Before departure, Marian saw through the press the last of 'her' issues of the *Westminster Review*, as well as her translation of Feuerbach, which came out in July 1854, under the title *The Essence of Christianity* – the only work she was ever to see in print signed with her own name. There was no occasion – not surprisingly given the circumstances – for extended goodbyes: on 20 July, having sent just a very brief farewell note to her Coventry friends, Marian joined Lewes on a boat bound for Antwerp to start a new life on the Continent, this time no longer as Marian Evans (though she continued to use the old name for some time in her letters to friends), but as Marian (Evans) Lewes.

The budding novelist (1854–9)

Marian and Lewes travelled, via Antwerp, Brussels, Liège, Cologne (where they had a short meeting with David Friedrich Strauss) and Frankfurt to Weimar, the small German town made famous by its association with Goethe, whose home it had been for the last fifty years of his life. After three months in Weimar, where their circle of acquaintances included two of the best-known composers and pianists of the day, the Hungarian Ferenc Liszt and the Russian Anton Rubinstein (both of whom are likely to have inspired the creation of Klesmer in *Daniel Deronda* – see Works, **pp. 80–8**), the Leweses continued on to Berlin, where they stayed for four months, returning to England in March 1855. This lengthy journey was the first of a number of extended trips abroad which they were to make over the next twenty years. All of those visits to the Continent followed a similar pattern, involving a combination of sightseeing, theatre, music, social life – which would often be less problematic than at home, given the rather more relaxed Continental attitudes with regard to their unorthodox marital status – as well as extensive study (mainly, though by no means exclusively, of the literature, art and history of the countries they visited) and writing: until Marian established herself as a novelist, they had to rely on a regular flow of articles and reviews, mainly for the *Westminster Review* and the *Leader*, to ensure that their financial situation, made more difficult by the costs of the education of Lewes's sons and by the demands of Agnes Lewes's growing family, remained stable. As a result, the Leweses' travels tended, at least until Marian established herself as a highly successful professional novelist, to be very much working visits rather than holidays – but they nonetheless proved, particularly for Marian, very inspirational: Continental Europe was to provide the setting for a number of her works, from those set entirely outside of England, such as *Romola* (see Works, **pp. 56–61**) and the long dramatic poem *The Spanish Gypsy* (see Works, **pp. 93–4**), to those, such as *Middlemarch* (see Works, **pp. 67–80**) and *Daniel Deronda* (see Works, **pp. 80–8**), in which foreign locations provide important counterpoints to their predominantly English settings. Even more importantly perhaps, Marian's knowledge of languages and her extensive reading of the work of Continental European writers made her, in comparison with most of her Victorian contemporaries, much more aware of the directions in which European literature and culture were moving in the mid-nineteenth century; in fact, it was certainly to the reading of leading Continental novelists such as Balzac and Turgenev that she owed much of the aesthetic seriousness with which, rather unlike some of her English fellow practitioners of the genre, she treated the novel as a literary form.

The Leweses' first visit to Germany was, of course, important in one other respect: it gave them a chance to escape the attention of the gossipmongers of the London literary world, for whom their decision to live together was obviously a source of major controversy. The reactions of Marian's friends varied: while Bray and Chapman (not surprisingly perhaps given the highly unusual character of their own domestic arrangements) as well as Rufa Hennell, Bessie Parkes and Barbara Leigh Smith were supportive of her decision to set up home with Lewes, Sara Hennell and, in particular, Cara Bray viewed it in much more critical terms. Although their friendship did survive in the long term, despite, for example, a year-long break in Marian's correspondence with Cara, they were never to be quite as close as they used to be in the old days at Rosehill. Marian would never pay another visit to Coventry, and the frequency of her meetings with Sara and Cara decreased quite dramatically – a measure of the emotional and indeed intellectual distance that was gradually getting in the way of their relationship.

The question of how to convey the message about Lewes to Marian's family was rather more complex: she did not, at first, notify any of her siblings of her changed circumstances, and she remained in regular contact with her widowed sister Christiana, visiting her and her family – on her own, needless to say – at Christmas 1855. It was not until 1857, nearly three years after she and Lewes began living together, that she first mentioned her new life in letters to her brother (see *L*, III, 331–2) and her half-sister Fanny (see *L*, III, 333); Isaac's response, quite predictably given his conventional views, was not only to break off all contacts with Marian (financial arrangements to do with her father's legacy were from then on dealt with via a solicitor) but also to put pressure on Christiana and Fanny to do likewise. They both obeyed him, although Christiana was to break the silence in 1859, a short time before her death. However, at that point she was too ill to be visited, and so Marian was never to see her – or indeed any of her other siblings – again. The Evans chapter of her life had now been well and truly closed.

That is, however, to anticipate. After their return from Germany, the Leweses settled in East Sheen, an outer suburb south-west of central London, in the first of a succession of houses they lived in, in Richmond and Wandsworth, before moving back to town in 1860. Marian's work continued steadily: she was focusing, on the one hand, on a translation, from Latin, of another work of Baruch Spinoza, *Ethics*, which, although completed, remained unpublished until as recently as 1981 – and, on the other hand, on further contributions to the *Westminster Review*, the *Leader* and the *Saturday Review*. The subjects of her articles, many of which derived from her recently acquired first-hand knowledge of German life and culture, ranged, as ever, very widely, from contemporary literature (reviews of Charles Kingsley, Tennyson, Browning, Ruskin and others, and a series of essays on the German poet Heinrich Heine) to a study on 'The Future of German Philosophy', and from a critique of Evangelical piety in 'Evangelical Teaching: Dr Cumming' (see Works, **p. 91**) to a sociological analysis of contemporary German society in 'The Natural History of German Life' (see Works, **pp. 92–3**). Perhaps the most important of the essays published during the fruitful period of 1855–56 was, however, 'Silly Novels by Lady Novelists', a biting critique of the sentimentality, verbosity and ignorance of much of contemporary women's fiction (see Works, **p. 92**). It is in many ways symptomatic that this was one of the last of Marian's major critical works; her attention was clearly beginning to move to another area of literary activity, as within a fortnight of the completion of that essay, in September 1856, she embarked, with Lewes's encouragement, on a new project – the first of her short stories, 'The Sad Fortunes of the Reverend Amos Barton' (see Works, **pp. 33–4**).

The writing proceeded fast: after six weeks, the manuscript was ready to be dispatched, by Lewes, to the Edinburgh publisher John Blackwood, the editor of the influential *Blackwood's Edinburgh Magazine*. Lewes did not reveal to Blackwood the identity of the author, stating instead that the story – the first of a series – had been written by a friend who had asked him to contact Blackwood on his behalf (see *L*, II, 269); no doubt part of the reason for that camouflage was to ensure that the story was judged on its merit, and not in the light of Marian's compromised social position. Blackwood's reaction was swift and encouraging, to the extent that he undertook to publish the story in his *Magazine* without seeing further samples of the author's work (see *L*, II, 275). 'Amos Barton' duly appeared, in two instalments, in January and February 1857, marking the beginning of Marian's lifelong association with Blackwood's publishing house and with John Blackwood personally. He was not only to publish all her major works except *Romola* (see Life and contexts, **pp. 21–2**), but also to become a trusted friend and literary adviser, whose role in the nurturing of Marian's literary career was second only to Lewes's. It was in writing to Blackwood on 4 February 1857 that she signed herself, for the first time, as George Eliot, 'George' after Lewes's first name, and 'Eliot' because it was 'a good mouth-filling, easily pronounced word' (Cross, I, 431).

The support of both her partner and her publisher helped Marian to get on with the writing of the two remaining stories of the projected series. 'Mr Gilfil's Love-Story' (see Works, **pp. 34–5**) was written between October 1856 and April 1857 and published, in four parts, from March to June 1857, to be followed by 'Janet's Repentance' (see Works, **pp. 35–6**), written between May and October 1857, and published, in five parts, from July to November that year. Throughout that time, the true identity of the author remained a closely kept secret, even if perceptive readers might well have noted – and speculated upon – the anonymous author's evident familiarity with the world of the Midlands of England in which the action of the stories is set. With the publication of *Scenes of Clerical Life* in book form due to follow, Blackwood himself was glad enough to preserve Marian's – or rather, as far as he was concerned, George Eliot's – anonymity for commercial reasons: in view of the suspicions he is likely to have begun to entertain about the authorship of the stories (the identity of George Eliot was not revealed to him until February 1858), the publication of the collection as the work of a hitherto unknown male author was likely not only to increase the interest of the reading public but also to prevent any negative impact on sales that would have come from the association of the stories with Marian's 'scandalous' life (see *L*, III, 222–3). This concern was linked, to a very considerable extent, to the influence that was exerted on the Victorian publishing trade by circulating libraries – an extensive network of subscription libraries which offered to the Victorian reading public, for a small annual fee, cheap and easy access to literature, including, in particular, contemporary fiction. One of the key aspects of the success of circulating libraries was their insistence that the books they stocked were in full compliance with the nineteenth-century ideals of decorum and taste, appropriate for perusal by all readers, including the paragons of Victorian respectability, unmarried daughters of country vicars. As a result, it would not have been unreasonable to assume that any book published under the name of Marian Evans – or Marian Evans Lewes – would be likely to be rejected by library managers as potentially suspect on the grounds of the author's supposed immorality in her personal life – with obvious financial consequences for the publisher.

Scenes of Clerical Life (see Works, **pp. 32–6**) was eventually published, in two volumes, in January 1858. The book met with generally favourable critical reception (see Works, p. 36) with broadly appreciative newspaper reviews as well as praise from a number of leading literary figures of the day to whom the author had asked Blackwood to send presentation copies. They included, among other, Charles Dickens, who was, interestingly, the only one of the early readers of the stories to suspect that their author was actually a woman. The success of the book brought Marian a substantial sum of money – more than £400 in all – which made it possible for her and Lewes to go, in the spring and summer of 1858, on a five-month visit to Germany and Austria (Munich, Vienna, Prague, Dresden and Leipzig). It also brought her a great deal of much-needed reassurance; she was now ready not only to disclose the identity of George Eliot to Blackwood but also to proceed with the writing of her next story, this time a full-length novel set, like the stories from *Scenes of Clerical Life*, in a rural community reminiscent of the world of her Midlands childhood.

Written between October 1857 and November 1858 and published in the conventional Victorian form of a three-decker (i.e., in three volumes) in February 1859, *Adam Bede* (see Works, pp. 36–44) was another major success, both with the critics and with the reading public: it went into a second edition within less than two months of publication, and it earned its author, in the first year after publication, nearly £2,000 – a clear indication that Marian was now in a position to consider herself a professional novelist. At the same time, the enthusiastic reception of the novel (see Works, p. 44) led to increased speculation about the real identity of the person calling himself/herself George Eliot; much of it focused around a certain Joseph Liggins of Attleborough – a rather unsuccessful middle-aged ex-Cambridge man, with a history of failed attempts to build up a career in teaching and in journalism. With the secret of the authorship of *Scenes of Clerical Life* and *Adam Bede* becoming known to more and more people – apart from Blackwood, Spencer had been told relatively early, and others, like Barbara Bodichon (see *L*, III, 56–7), had their suspicions (in the case of Chapman, his inquisitiveness about the matter actually prompted Marian to break off their friendship) – the author's anonymity could no longer be maintained, not least because it put a considerable strain on Marian's relationships with some of her friends, particularly her Coventry circle. By the end of June 1859 the secret was, effectively, out, and the Leweses decided not to attempt any further disguises: Marian Evans Lewes, the journalist, translator and literary critic, had become George Eliot, the professional novelist.

The professional author (1859–68)

With her literary career clearly in the ascendant, Marian was now in a position to take a more assertive stand in her negotiations with publishers: she managed, for example, to ensure that her next project, a semi-autobiographical novel which was to become *The Mill on the Floss* (see Works, pp. 44–51), would be published in volume form rather than as a serial, as Blackwood had originally suggested. Marian's unwillingness to submit herself to the constraints and pressures involved in writing for magazine publication was to do, at least in part, with her artistic temperament and with the nature of nature of the fictional worlds she created – worlds which developed in a measured, organic way and in consequence did not lend themselves easily to the kind of structural manipulation (such as balanced distribution of climactic episodes and careful handling of suspense) that the creation of a successful serial required. It was not, however, just the artistic side that mattered: with Lewes's three sons by Agnes at school in Switzerland and with a comfortable lifestyle, travel, etc., to be paid for, Marian's concerns were financial as much as artistic, and she expected, in standard circumstances, to earn more from the sales of a novel in book form than from serialisation. When the financial incentive was persuasive enough – as was, in fact, to be the case only three years later, when she was paid £7,000 for *Romola* (see Life and contexts, **pp. 21–2**) – Marian would be prepared not only to agree to provide a serial, but in doing so also to break the long-established connection with Blackwood in favour of another publisher, George Smith, and his prestigious *Cornhill Magazine*.

To be able to earn this kind of money, Marian needed, of course, to maintain the high level of productivity that characterised the first years of her writing career. The work on *The Mill on the Floss*, begun in the early months of 1859, proceeded relatively slowly at first: Marian was naturally affected by the news of the death, on 15 March, of her sister Christiana and distracted by the Liggins affair. She also took a break from work on her novel to write a short story 'The Lifted Veil' (see Works, **pp. 88–9**), which was published in July that year. Marian's concentration was not helped, either, by the fact that she and Lewes maintained their peripatetic lifestyle, making a number of trips around Britain, largely in search of locations which she could use in her novel, as well as travelling, in July, to Paris, Basle and Lucerne, in order for Lewes to visit his sons at their school at Hofwyl. When, in the autumn, their life became more settled, Marian's writing gathered pace. The book was completed in March 1860 and published the following month, another resounding critical and commercial success (see Works, **p. 51**), bringing its author, in the year of publication, more than £3,500.

In their characteristic way, the Leweses did not stay in England to savour the success of *The Mill on the Floss*; within a few days of despatching the last pages of the novel to Blackwood, they set off for Italy, via Paris. Their trip, which lasted over three months, took in all of the country's major historical cities: they travelled via Turin to Genoa, then on to Leghorn, Pisa and Rome, where they spent nearly a month visiting the city's museums and historical monuments – an echo of that visit is no doubt to be found in the presentation of Dorothea and Casaubon's honeymoon in *Middlemarch* (see Works, **pp. 67–80**). From Rome, they continued on to Naples, visiting, among other places, Pompeii and the Amalfi coast; then they headed back north, spending more than a fortnight in Florence – a visit that gave her 'the idea of writing a historical romance' (*L*, III, 339) that was to become *Romola* (see Works, **pp. 56–61**) – before setting off for Bologna, Ferrara, Padua, Venice and Milan. The rest of the journey was about seeing people: the Leweses went on to Zurich and Berne, where Marian met, for the first time, Lewes's sons; joined by the oldest of them, Charles, who had by then completed his education, they then continued on to Geneva, where they visited Marian's old friends the D'Albert-Durades (see Life and contexts, **p. 10**), and then back home to London.

With Charles from now on a permanent member of the household – he was to live with the Leweses until his marriage in 1865 – and with his brothers due to finish school in the not-too-distant future, Marian was now very firmly placed in a quasi-maternal role – the boys would call her 'Mutter' or 'Mother', rather than 'Mamma', which was how they addressed Agnes Lewes. Not being a mother herself, Marian found in Lewes's sons the kind of family she missed as a result of her decision not to have children, as well as in consequence of her estrangement from her own blood family. She appears to have genuinely enjoyed this new domestic arrangement, despite the fact that it forced her and Lewes to adopt a lifestyle that was rather more conventionally settled and family like than they had been accustomed to before: perhaps the most radical change was the decision to move back to central London, made after Charles secured, through the influence of the Leweses' friend, the novelist Anthony Trollope, a civil service job with the Post Office. With the second of the Lewes boys, Thornie (Thornton), transferring, also in 1860, from Hofwyl to a school in Edinburgh and, in consequence, spending his vacations with the Leweses in London, their home became, in some ways, a conventional mid-Victorian family household – a rather paradoxical development given the unorthodox nature of Marian's relationship with Lewes and her continued ostracisation by the majority of the London society of the day.

The focus on family life and, in particular, on the development of a quasi-parental relationship with her stepsons, which dominated Marian's life from the summer of 1860 onwards, accounts for the significance of the motifs of adoption, quasi-adoption and other variations on the theme of parenthood and quasi-parenthood in virtually all of George Eliot's later novels. Not surprisingly, it proved particularly potent in the book she embarked on writing soon after her move to London: *Silas Marner* (see Works, **pp. 51–6**), written in little more than four months between November 1860 and March 1861, offers what is perhaps the author's most powerful vision of the morally transforming power of parental – or, more properly, quasi-parental or adoptive-parental – love. Published in April 1861, the novel was reviewed, on the whole, very favourably (see Works, **pp. 55–6**), though, perhaps in view of its relative shortness and simplicity, it did not generate quite as much of an impact on the general public as had been the case with its two full-length predecessors, *Adam Bede* and *The Mill on the Floss*; it still, however, earned its author more than £5,000, substantially more than any of her earlier works.

Within less then three weeks of the publication of *Silas Marner*, the Leweses set out for the Continent again – this time specifically for Florence, where Marian intended to embark on a comprehensive study of the city, which she needed to do in preparation for the writing of the historical novel, the idea of which she had conceived on her visit there the previous year. Travelling via Paris, Avignon, Nice, Genoa and Pisa, the Leweses arrived in Florence in early May and spent nearly five weeks there, with Marian trying to capture as much of the city's atmosphere, topography and historical detail as her colds and headaches and Lewes's generally fragile health permitted. On their return to London, again via Hofwyl to visit Lewes's youngest son, Bertie (Herbert), Marian continued with her studies, reading extensively in medieval and Renaissance Italian history, literature and art. This careful preparation – very much unlike anything she had ever had to do prior to embarking on a new work of fiction before – appears to have had a negative effect on Marian's creative energy: the work on the book, which took several attempts to begin, proceeded slowly, and the situation was helped neither by her – and Lewes's – continued health problems, nor indeed by the confusion into which she was thrown by George Smith's offer to serialise the novel in the *Cornhill Magazine* for the astronomical sum of £10,000. 'The most magnificent offer ever yet made for a novel' (*L*, IV, 17–18), this was of course too good not to be considered very seriously, despite Marian's unease about writing to deadlines and the awkwardness of the position in which she found herself vis-à-vis Blackwood, who was not likely to be able to afford to match Smith's offer. As the work on the novel was not progressing speedily enough to tie in with Smith's original publication plans, the deal had to be renegotiated; ultimately, Marian accepted, for six years' copyright, the sum of £7,000, and the first installment of *Romola* (see Works, **pp. 56–61**) was eventually published in the *Cornhill Magazine* in July 1862.

Much as she expected, the work on the novel proved painful and exhausting for Marian: with continuous health problems affecting her concentration, and with the nature of the material demanding careful attention to matters of sometimes rather obscure detail, she wrote relatively slowly, and she found it difficult to stay sufficiently well ahead of the monthly serial not to worry about deadlines. In addition, unaccustomed as she was to writing to schedule, she was not able to stick to the originally envisaged length of the book, adding two more instalments to the contracted twelve. The manuscript was eventually finished in June 1863, and the whole novel was published in volume form in July, the last instalment appearing in the *Cornhill* in August. Reviewed respectfully, but not without reservations (see Works, **p. 61**), *Romola* did not become a major popular success: it neither significantly boosted the sales of the magazine, nor did it do particularly well when published in book form. Perhaps in an attempt to make a gesture of good will towards Smith, Marian offered him, for free, a short story she had written in the summer of 1860, between *The Mill on the Floss* and *Silas Marner*: 'Brother Jacob' (see Works, **p. 89**) was published in the *Cornhill*, anonymously, in July 1864.

The completion of *Romola* left Marian feeling physically and emotionally exhausted. For nearly a year after she finished the book she did not embark on any new writing projects, occupying herself instead with family and domestic responsibilities: with all the three Lewes boys now back from Switzerland, but by no means independent (Charles, though working, still lived at home; Thornie was unable (or unwilling) to make up his mind about his plans and ambitions for the future and was soon to set out for South Africa to try to build up a career there; Bertie was in Scotland, training to be a farmer), the Leweses certainly had a great deal to think and worry about. The death, in January 1864, of Marian's half-brother Robert, although certainly not as painful as the loss of Christiana a few years earlier (see Life and contexts, **p. 20**), served as another reminder of the problematic nature of her relationship with the Evans family. On the more practical level, things were more positive, but by no means less absorbing; Marian's financial success made it possible for her and Lewes to purchase, in August 1863, the first house of their own. The Priory, a sizeable £2,000 property in the Regent's Park area of north London, to which the Leweses moved in November 1863, was to become, for the following sixteen years, not just their family home but also an increasingly important literary salon, in which Marian, who did not as a rule pay visits herself – she would not risk finding herself embarrassed by people disapproving of her family arrangements – gladly entertained visitors who were prepared to ignore Victorian conventions and meet her socially. The friends who visited the Priory included numerous luminaries of Victorian literature and culture, among them the Leweses' old friend

Herbert Spencer, the naturalist Charles Darwin, the historian and politician Lord Houghton, the poet Robert Browning, the Positivist philosopher Richard Congreve, the political scientist Walter Bagehot, the painter Frederic Leighton, the historian John Morley, as well as Marian's faithful women friends and confidantes – and educationalists and political activists in their own right – Barbara Bodichon and Bessie Parkes.

As things began to calm down on the domestic front, the Leweses, the inveterate travellers that they had become over the previous decade, were back on the tourist trail: in May and June 1864 they went for a extended holiday to Venice, and the following year they spent ten days in Paris in January, followed by an extensive tour of Normandy and Brittany in August and September. More trips were to follow: thus, in June and July 1866, immediately after Marian had completed her next novel, *Felix Holt, the Radical* (see Works, **pp. 61–7**), the Leweses went to Belgium, the Netherlands and Germany. The journey provided Marian with some of the Continental European material she was later to use in *Daniel Deronda*. A few months later, in December 1866, the couple embarked on a visit to France, subsequently extended to include Spain. This trip, which took in all of the country's major sights, from Barcelona and Madrid to the Andalusian cities of Granada, Cordoba and Seville, was undertaken, in part at least, so that Marian could pursue the research on the country that she needed to do for the project she was at the time working on, a verse drama entitled *The Spanish Gypsy* (see Works, **pp. 93–4**).

That particular work, conceived during the Leweses' 1864 visit to Venice, in many ways encapsulated the creative impasse in which Marian found herself in the mid-1860s; although she proceeded with the writing, at first, at a reasonable pace, the project soon began to prove increasingly difficult and frustrating, to the extent that, in February 1865, it was, at Lewes's insistence, put aside as Marian returned to the more congenial material of the England of the 1830s, and to her favourite genre of prose fiction. *Felix Holt* was, in fact, a return to Marian's familiar territory in other ways as well. Not only did it prove, much like the early novels, much easier to write than either *Romola* or *The Spanish Gypsy* – it was completed within little more than a year – but, rejected by Smith, it was published, in June 1866, by her old publisher, Blackwood, who was prepared to pay her the handsome fee of £5,000 for five years' copyright. Although the reception of the novel was not as unanimously enthusiastic as had been the case with her earlier 'English' fictions (see Works, **p. 67**), the re-establishment of the connection with Blackwood, whose friendly support in matters literary as well as commercial could always be counted on, provided the ever-self-doubting Marian with much-needed reassurance as well as a sense of professional stability; always loyal and helpful, Blackwood was prepared to take financial risk with her less successful works – as he did when he accepted *The Spanish Gypsy*, eventually completed after a good deal of rather painful rewriting in April 1868 and published the following month – as well as to devise entirely new publication schemes, as was to be the case with the two novels of the 1870s: *Middlemarch* (see Life and contexts, **pp. 25–6**) and *Daniel Deronda* (see Life and contexts, **p. 27**).

In the meantime, however, the Leweses were getting on with their lives and work; with Charles now married and Bertie joining Thornie in Natal in the autumn of

1866, they were now free from immediate domestic concerns and, despite their health problems – Marian's letters and diaries often sound like a catalogue of more or less serious ailments that she and Lewes regularly complained of – they maintained a punishing schedule of reading, writing, social life and travel. Although the focus of Marian's attention remained, as ever, on literature, history, art and religion, she was becoming increasingly interested in political issues: *Felix Holt*, which had been written during the period of highly charged political debate that led to the passing of Benjamin Disraeli's Second Reform Act of 1867, which extended the franchise to all rate-paying householders, was followed, in 1868, by an 'Address to Working Men, by Felix Holt' (see Works, **p. 65**), the only explicitly political statement in Marian's career. The growing significance of her public voice was also reflected in the changing nature of the Leweses' weekly Sunday afternoon receptions at the Priory: they were gradually turning into increasingly elaborate rituals, involving Lewes marshalling the guests around to ensure that Marian – viewed by some of her visitors not only as a famous writer but also as a spiritual and moral authority, a sage, almost a priestess of some kind of modern secular cult – was spared the conversation of those of her guests who were deemed too boring, too inquisitive or just excessively ardent in their admiration of her work. The Leweses' Continental itineraries remained as busy as ever too, even if, in addition to the usual diet of historical cities, churches, museums and theatres, such as they visited during their two-month trip to Germany from July to September 1867, Marian and Lewes began to frequent spas and holiday resorts, as they did during their journey to Germany and Switzerland between May and July 1868.

The literary triumph (1868–76)

The sense of restlessness and uncertainty about the direction in which her literary career developed, so evident in Marian's life in the mid-1860s, did not leave her until the end of the decade. She continued to experiment with poetry, narrative ('Agatha', see Works, **p. 95**) as well as lyrical (sequence of sonnets 'Brother and Sister', see Works, **p. 95**, based on the personal memories of her childhood which she had earlier used in *The Mill on the Floss*, see Works, **pp. 44–51**), and she developed plans for further works of fiction. Her notes, which would eventually become her 'Quarry' for *Middlemarch* (see Criticism, **p. 105**), indicate that the two plot lines which were eventually to be integrated in what was to become her greatest novel (see Works, **pp. 67–80**) were conceived separately, the story of a young doctor arriving in a provincial town in the Midlands of England, which was to form the basis of the Lydgate–Vincy plot of the ensuing novel, predating the narrative of 'Miss Brooke' by more than a year. Although the 1820s and 1830s, the period in which her new stories were to be set, were for Marian obviously familiar territory, she did, as had by then become her standard practice, embark on a programme of historical research, focusing this time mainly on the history of early nineteenth-century medicine, a subject constituting one of the central thematic concerns of the novel.

Unfortunately, just as Marian was beginning to focus on her new project, the Leweses' established domestic routine was dramatically interrupted. Within a few days of their return to London after a two-month visit to Italy (March–May 1869), they were joined by Thornie, who had written to them a few months earlier complaining of what appeared to be a kidney stone but which was in fact tuberculosis of the spine. The disease was incurable. Marian and Lewes nursed Thornie for more than five months of often agonising pain, until his death on 19 October. That experience cast a painful shadow over the Leweses' lives. Though both still very much middle-aged rather than elderly (Marian turned fifty a few weeks after Thornie's death), they became much more aware of other people's – and their own – mortality, a concern that is clearly evident in George Eliot's last two novels, particularly in *Middlemarch* (see Works, **pp. 67–80**).

The depression caused by Thornie's death took Marian a long time to overcome: rather than returning to her novel, she occupied herself with more experiments in poetry, producing 'The Legend of Jubal' (see Works, **p. 95**) and another verse drama, 'Armgart' (see Works, **pp. 94–5**); poems written during that period were to be collected in *The Legend of Jubal and Other Poems*, published by Blackwood in May 1874. Something of the old routine was re-established with another trip to the Continent, this time to Germany and Austro-Hungary (March–May 1870), followed by more travel within Britain: on what was Marian's first visit to Oxford, the Leweses were staying with their friends Mark Pattison, the educationalist, writer and Rector of Lincoln College, and his wife Emilia – a couple who may have influenced Marian's portrayal of the relationship between Casaubon and Dorothea in *Middlemarch* (see Works, **pp. 67–80**). During that visit, the Leweses met a number of the period's influential thinkers and writers, including the Classical scholar and future Master of Balliol College Benjamin Jowett, the art critic and writer Walter Pater, as well as the young Mary Augusta Arnold, a niece of Matthew Arnold who was to become the popular novelist Mrs Humphry Ward. The kind of social isolation Marian had to endure in the early years of her relationship with Lewes was clearly receding into the past.

When Marian eventually resumed her work on the new novel, it fell to Lewes to negotiate with Blackwood the arrangements for the publication of what was going to be its author's most ambitious – and longest – undertaking to date. Conventional serialisation was out of the question: as the experience of writing *Romola* had demonstrated (see Life and contexts, **pp. 21–2**), Marian did not feel comfortable writing to strict deadlines and, in any case, the dense, concentrated texture of her new book and the measured pace at which she made its complex fictional world unfold resulted in the novel being particularly unsuitable, in structural terms, for any method of publication that would involve dividing it up into short units of two or three chapters. However, as some form of serialisation would make the novel more widely accessible and would maximise the profits, Lewes did manage to come up with a compromise solution: rather than publishing the novel in Dickens-style short monthly parts, Blackwood agreed to issue it in bimonthly volumes (the last two appearing in monthly intervals), each of them constituting a self-contained, structurally autonomous section of the novel, substantial enough to offer the author sufficient space to develop her vision in a manner unconstrained by the structural limitations of the more usual weekly or monthly serials, more often than not constructed out of relatively short episodes rather than broader and leisurely painted canvases (see Criticism, **p. 118**). The method clearly worked: despite interruptions caused by illness and bouts of anxiety, Marian wrote more or less steadily from the spring of 1871 to the autumn of 1872, managing throughout to stay a couple of volumes or so ahead of publication, which took place from December 1871 to December 1872.

The critical as well as popular success of *Middlemarch* (see Works, **pp. 79–80**) – it sold more than 15,000 copies within the first three years on the market and earned Marian, over the years, nearly £9,000 – constituted the ultimate confirmation, if one was needed, of its author's position not only as the greatest living English novelist but also as one of the most influential personalities of the cultural and intellectual life of mid-Victorian London. Marian's social circle continued to expand; during the 1870s, the Leweses became close friends with the Poet Laureate, Alfred Tennyson and his family, while among the more notable of their new acquaintances – and visitors to the Sunday receptions at the Priory – were the Pre-Raphaelite artists Dante Gabriel Rossetti and Edward Burne-Jones, the Russian novelist Ivan Turgenev and the young American writer Henry James. It is a testimony to the power of Marian's personality and the respect she commanded among her contemporaries that the extensive list of people with whom she maintained regular correspondence included, among others, the doyenne of American novelists, Harriet Beecher Stowe, with whom, despite never meeting her in person, she developed an affectionate friendship.

In view of how central to the public debate in the Victorian period was the question of the economic, social, political and cultural position of women in the modern world, it is hardly surprising that Marian's emergence as an influential literary celebrity, widely admired as a figure of moral and intellectual authority despite (or perhaps because of) the unorthodox nature of her domestic arrangements, should have made her an inevitable focus of attention among the more progressive of Victorian women. Although she remained loyal to her old women friends, many of whom, such as Barbara Bodichon and Bessie Parkes (now Belloc), played an important role in the development of the Victorian women's movement, particularly in the area of education, Marian's own position on the woman question was much more ambivalent (see Criticism, **pp. 129–34**): she did not support the idea of female suffrage, and, although she strongly believed in offering women opportunities for education, her practical support for initiatives such as the establishment at Cambridge of a women's college, Girton, was not quite as generous and enthusiastic as one might perhaps have expected. On the other hand, she did in her later years become, in a manner reminiscent of some of her female characters, such as, in particular, the eponymous heroine of *Romola* (see Works, **pp. 56–61**), something of a cult mother figure for a circle of younger women, some of whom, like the philosopher and trade-unionist Edith Simcox, were indeed heavily involved both in intellectual debate and in political activism. Although the emotional intensity with which some of Marian's protégées approached her has given rise to biographical speculation about the nature of their relationships (see Bodenheimer 1994: 249–56; Ashton 1996: 306–9; Hughes 1998: 403–7, 434–6), there is no evidence to suggest that Marian treated women such as Simcox, Elma Stuart – her 'spiritual daughter' – or her long-standing younger friend Maria Congreve as anything other than close friends vis-à-vis whom she could play the maternal role she had evidently enjoyed in her relationship with Lewes's sons and she had been unable to experience otherwise.

The Leweses' lifestyle, in the early 1870s, followed, by and large, the pattern of previous years: immediately after Marian's completion, in September 1872, of the bulk of *Middlemarch* (she was, at that point, still to write the 'Finale'), they set off for a six-week trip to Germany; more Continental holidays were to follow in subsequent years, with a two-month holiday in France and Germany between June and August 1873, and a two-week trip to France and Belgium in October 1874. Keen tourists as they both were, their age and often indifferent health were, however, beginning to show: they were gradually spending more or more time taking waters at spas rather than visiting museums in historical cities – the memories of their visits to places such as Bad Homburg were to inspire Marian's presentation of Continental society in *Daniel Deronda* (see Works, **pp. 80–8**). Even while on home soil they began to appreciate the peace and quiet of the countryside as opposed to the bustle of London – from 1871 onwards, they would tend to leave the capital for a few months over the summer, renting houses in Hampshire, Surrey or Hertfordshire, until they eventually decided to acquire one of their own – the Heights at Witley in Surrey, which they purchased in December 1876.

Marian's long-established reading habits remained, in the early 1870s, as voracious as ever, her attention turning, in particular, to the study of Judaism, an area which she had been exploring, on and off, since her early years in Coventry (see Criticism, **pp. 145–6**). Her interest in all things Jewish, originally deriving from her study of the early history of Christianity, was reinforced by her friendship with the German Talmudic scholar Emanuel Deutsch, who had given her Hebrew lessons and who was to become an important inspiration for the character of Mordecai Cohen in *Daniel Deronda* (see Works, **pp. 80–8**) – the novel which she began to plan in 1873, only a few months after the completion of *Middlemarch*. The work on that new project proceeded at a moderate pace, interrupted by bouts of ill health – the kidney disease which was to mar the last few years of Marian's life began to show itself in 1874 – as well as by family problems, including, in particular, the news of the death, in South Africa, of Lewes's youngest son Bertie in June 1875. The publication of the book, which followed, in terms of its format, the eight-part pattern of *Middlemarch*, with consecutive volumes appearing in monthly rather than bimonthly intervals, began in February 1876. As soon as the final chapters of the novel were completed, in June that year, the Leweses were once again off, on their way to the Continent; the two-month visit to France, Switzerland and Germany took in the usual mixture of historical cities and Alpine resorts.

Widowhood and marriage (1876–80)

Although not as resoundingly successful in critical terms as *Middlemarch, Daniel Deronda* was nonetheless received (see Works, **pp. 87–8**) with all the attention due to a new novel by a writer by then generally recognised as a major modern classic, and it sold very well too, bringing Marian, over the first three years, more than £9,000. It was, therefore, hardly surprising that early in 1877 Lewes, as always indefatigable in his role as Marian's literary manager, suggested to Blackwood the publication of a uniform, standard edition of the collected works (see *L*, VI, 345) – the idea was indeed followed up, and the first volume of the Cabinet Edition, which was to run to twenty volumes, appeared in January 1878. As Marian took an active role in preparing the edition, rereading her works and introducing a number of alterations, she was not in a position to focus on a major new project: she did not write anything for over eighteen months following the completion of *Daniel Deronda*, and when she returned to her desk, in early 1878, it was to write a relatively minor work, the quasi-fictional, essayistic *Impressions of Theophrastus Such* (see Works, pp. 89–90), completed in November that year.

The Leweses' life was in fact beginning to show signs of slowing down in other respects as well: following the purchase of the Heights, they were spending more and more time away from the capital, and there were to be no more Continental holidays. In their intimate, indeed quasi-familial domestic circle, an increasingly prominent place, alongside Marian's female admirers, was occupied by a young banker, John Walter Cross, whom the Leweses first met on a visit to Rome in 1869; now considered a 'nephew', he provided them with help on a variety of matters, performing for them roles ranging from estate agent (he had facilitated their purchase of the Heights) and financial adviser to fitness instructor – in what was a highly unlikely achievement, he introduced the Leweses to the games of tennis and badminton. Although both Marian and Lewes increasingly complained of ill health, their social life nonetheless continued more or less unabated: they were still making new friends, among them the German composer Richard Wagner and his wife Cosima, the daughter of their old acquaintance Ferenc Liszt (see Life and contexts, p. 16), as well as meeting old ones – some of their more frequent companions, in the late 1870s, included the Tennysons and Turgenev. They were also, finally, recognised as a couple by the 'respectable' establishment of Victorian Britain: symbolic moments of that recognition came when they were invited to meet two daughters of Queen Victoria, first, in 1877, the Princess Louise, Marchioness of Lorne, and later, the following year, the Queen's eldest daughter, the Princess Royal, the Crown Princess of Germany.

Although the Leweses were keen to maintain the impression that their life was going on more or less as normal, by the autumn of 1878 it became clear that Lewes's health was taking a major turn for the worse. The diagnosis, in November, of a 'thickening of the mucous membrane' meant, in practical terms, that there was a tumour in his digestive tract, and that the condition was terminal. Within less than a fortnight, on 30 November, he was dead; the funeral took place on 4 December in London's Highgate Cemetery, with his son Charles and John Walter Cross as chief mourners, and a number of old friends, including Spencer, the Harrisons, and the Burne-Joneses, in attendance. The widowed Marian, broken-hearted with grief, remained at home.

For the first few weeks after Lewes's death, Marian was virtually inconsolable: she cut herself off from all contacts with the external world, with Charles Lewes being the only person she was prepared to see. It took her over a month to resume contacts with even the closest of her friends, such as Barbara Bodichon; in course of time, however, Marian began to return to some form of normality, at least in terms of work; she dealt with the final stages of the publication of *Theophrastus Such*, and she edited the last two volumes of Lewes's last major work, *Problems of Life and Mind*, which he had left uncompleted at his death. On a more practical level, although Marian was naturally the main beneficiary of Lewes's will, the status of their partnership – or rather, the lack thereof in the eyes of the law – and the complexity of their financial arrangements resulted in some prolonged legal action, which involved, in a rather ironical twist given that she had thought of herself as Marian Lewes for a quarter of a century, a formal change of name by deed poll; from 1879 on, she was to be known, legally, as Mary Ann Evans Lewes. In a gesture designed to honour her late partner, she made arrangements for the establishment of a Lewes studentship in physiology, the generosity with which she offered £5,000 to create this award contrasting quite dramatically with the relative frugality of the contribution of just £50 she had been prepared to make in support of the establishment of a women's college in Cambridge just ten years earlier. There were also family matters to think about: in April 1879, Bertie Lewes's widow Eliza and her two children arrived in London from South Africa, expecting to be provided for and thus putting a considerable strain on Marian's already fragile state of mind. The situation was not helped, either, by the news about the illness of her old friend John Blackwood, who was to die in October 1879. With headaches, kidney attacks and other complaints continuing to afflict her as well, Marian was clearly at a difficult point in her life.

Rather unexpectedly, given the length and intensity of her relationship with Lewes, but not entirely surprisingly in view of Marian's emotional character, she was lifted from her depression through the help and support of a male guardian/protector. John Walter Cross, himself bereaved around the same time (his mother, through whom he had first met the Leweses, died in December 1878, a fortnight after Lewes), increasingly became for Marian not only a trusted adviser and confidant but also someone on whose admiration and affection she came to rely, particularly after an emotional crisis she went through in the spring of 1879. The precise nature of that crisis remains a matter of biographical speculation – it may have involved a belated discovery of some form of indiscretion on the part of Lewes (see Laski 1973: 112; Ashton 1996: 372) – though it seems clear that whatever happened at that point helped her, in a rather decisive way, to overcome the impasse in which she had found herself after her bereavement and to return to the kind of active life she had enjoyed before. Cross's friendship – which had in previous years amounted to something not unlike celebrity worship – was, during the summer of 1879, becoming more and more intimate, culminating in a proposal of marriage, first made perhaps as early as in August that year.

The nature of the relationship between Marian and Cross remains something of a mystery: a man twenty years younger than her, he may have been an old, faithful and loyal friend, but he was, despite having the kind of practical intelligence that could be expected of a businessman, hardly an intellectual of a calibre remotely comparable to that of the men she had relied on, in a similar way, in the past, such as Spencer and Lewes (see Bodenheimer 1994: 114–15). Although they were becoming evidently closer and closer – when writing to him, Marian would call herself Beatrice, alluding to their reading together, over the summer months, of Dante's *La Divina commedia* – she would undoubtedly have realised the complexity of their relationship: they might have been, on the one hand, a courting couple, happy to share each other's company, in private and in public, much in the way that had characterised Marian's relationship with Lewes, but they were also, on the other hand, at the same time prophetess and disciple, artist and agent, recently widowed late-middle-aged woman and recently orphaned early middle-aged man, and woman with a past and man willing to make her respectable. Aware of all these complexities, as well as of the likelihood that the proposed marriage would create a major sensation of the kind she instinctively abhorred, Marian did not agree to accept Cross's proposal until the spring of 1880. They were eventually married, at the fashionable St George's Church in Hanover Square, on 6 May and embarked on a honeymoon trip to the Continent immediately afterwards.

The two-month tour took the newly wed couple through France to northern Italy then across the Alps to southern Germany and eventually to Luxembourg and back home to England. Much as was the pattern during Marian's travels with Lewes, the Crosses initially embarked on a typical programme of reading, sightseeing and social life; this was, however, interrupted by a rather curious incident involving Cross throwing himself into the Grand Canal in Venice, most likely in a bout of depression. Although the exact circumstances of that incident, and of Cross's subsequent illness, remain a matter of speculation (see Ashton 1996: 376–7; Hughes 1998: 478–80), the very fact that it took place, and that Marian made every effort to conceal the details of what had happened, points to the complex and ambiguous nature of her relationship with Cross and, indeed, to her concern about the perception of her marriage by her friends and acquaintances in England.

That perception was indeed, as Marian had feared, rather mixed: while some of her friends, such as Barbara Bodichon, offered sincere congratulations (see *L*, VII, 272–3), others questioned the motives that had led her not only to marry Cross but also to do so in the conventional fashion, at an ordinary church ceremony. That mixed reaction was, perhaps, to be expected; what might well not have been expected, and what made a major impact, was the fact that among the letters Marian – now Mrs John Walter Cross – received after her wedding, there was a congratulatory note from her estranged brother Isaac, the first communication she had received directly from him in more than twenty-five years (see *L*, VII, 280): for the conventional man that he was, it was not, despite all of Marian's literary fame, until his sister was properly married that she could again be considered a respectable woman. Although, with Marian's immediate response (see *L*, VII, 287), a channel of communication was thus re-established, it did not produce more than a formal reconciliation – the brother and sister were never to see each other again.

On their return to England, Marian and Cross stayed mainly at the Heights, while the house which was to become their new home, situated in Cheyne Walk, a fashionable area in Chelsea, was being prepared for them to be moved into. Although Marian's health problems, particularly her kidney attacks, were becoming increasingly frequent, the couple maintained a reasonably busy lifestyle, travelling around the country to stay with friends, attending concerts and theatre performances and receiving visitors; in her own time, Marian would, as usual, concentrate on her extensive and demanding reading. As she and Cross eventually moved, in early December, into Cheyne Walk, there was little indication that there were likely to be any immediate dangers to her health; a sore throat which Marian developed within less than three weeks of moving in did not initially seem to be a cause for much alarm. As it happened, however, the infection developed to trigger kidney failure; her condition having deteriorated rapidly over a period of twenty-four hours, Marian died on 22 December 1880.

Although Cross and some of Marian's literary friends, led by Spencer, attempted to have her buried in the Poets' Corner of Westminster Abbey, the idea, potentially controversial given the directness with which she had always expressed her agnostic views, did not find enough public support and had to be abandoned, in favour of a burial near Lewes, in the unconsecrated section of Highgate Cemetery. The funeral, which took place on 29 December, became a major public occasion. Apart from the chief mourners, Marian's husband, brother and stepson, it was attended by a great number of her friends and acquaintances, among whom were some of the leading thinkers, writers and artists of the Victorian era, such as Spencer, Browning, Harrison, Huxley and Millais. In paying their final respects to Mary Ann Evans/Marian Evans Lewes/ Mrs John Walter Cross/George Eliot, the daughter of an estate manager who had become one of the greatest intellectuals and artists of Victorian Britain, they were bidding farewell to a woman whose life and work, often difficult, at times highly controversial, but never less than profoundly serious, expressed some of the most fundamental tensions, dilemmas and concerns of her time.

2

Works

Scenes of Clerical Life (1857–8)

> It had always been a vague dream of mine that some time or other I might write a novel, and my shadowy conception of what the novel was to be, varied, of course, from one epoch of my life to another. . . . But one morning as I was lying in bed, thinking what should be the subject of my first story, my thoughts merged themselves into a dreamy doze, and I imagined myself writing a story of which the title was – 'The Sad Fortunes of the Reverend Amos Barton'. I was soon wide awake again, and told G[eorge]. He said, 'O what a capital title!' and from that time I had settled in my mind that this should be my first story.
>
> ('How I Came to Write Fiction', *J*, 289)

Deceptively simplistic as this account of the beginning of George Eliot's career as a writer of fiction might appear to be if we remember that it came from a woman who was already, in 1857, a well-respected translator, editor and literary critic, it does, nonetheless, convey something about the nature of her early works that was to make her, within a few years, one of Britain's most popular and most respected novelists. It is the sense of spontaneity, the feeling of immediacy and directness in the observation and rendering of ordinary, day-to-day events in the lives of 'commonplace people' (p. 81) that first attracts the attention of the reader of the three stories which form George Eliot's first volume of fiction – *Scenes of Clerical Life*. There is, indeed, nothing contrived about the atmosphere of familiarity that the stories generate: almost all of the major characters, as well as the locations in which their stories are played out, are, in fact, drawn either from the author's own recollections of her Warwickshire childhood (see Life and contexts, pp. 2–3), or from the living memory of the community in which she grew up. Thus, to offer but a few examples, the eponymous hero of the first story in the collection, Amos Barton, is a portrait of John Gwyther, the curate of the Evanses' home parish of Chilvers Coton in the 1830s; the Cheverels of Cheverel Manor, in 'Mr Gilfil's Love-Story', are based on the family of Robert Evans's employers, the Newdigates of Arbury; the town of Milby, the setting of the last of the stories, 'Janet's Repentance', is a thinly disguised picture of the market town of Nuneaton, just a few miles north-east of the Evans family home.

The stories George Eliot tells do not strike the reader as unusual either. This is perhaps most evident in 'Amos Barton': set in 1837, it is, in terms of its contents, not much more than a short tale about the life of an impoverished country clergyman. A well-meaning but ultimately rather insensitive and egocentric man, lacking in intellectual sophistication as well as emotional intelligence, he does not appreciate the pressures, social, economic and personal, under which he puts his loving, resourceful but physically fragile wife Milly. It is only through her illness and death that he learns a lesson in moral responsibility and, in consequence, acquires the sympathy and respect of his parishioners. Amos Barton is one of those ordinary people who are 'neither extraordinarily silly, nor extraordinarily wicked, nor extraordinarily wise' (81), whose 'brains are certainly not pregnant with genius, and [whose] passions have not manifested themselves at all after the fashion of a volcano' (81) – but who 'bear a conscience, and have felt the sublime prompting to do the painful right; [who] have their unspoken sorrows, and their sacred joys; [whose] hearts have perhaps gone out towards their first-born, and [who] have mourned over the irreclaimable dead' (81). It is precisely the narrative's focus on those hidden emotions that lies at the heart of George Eliot's achievement in the story: through familiarising the reader with the details of the inner lives of her characters, she manages to create a sense of imaginative sympathy that underlies the story's central theme – the redemption of egoism through the power of human selflessness, devotion and love.

The key to the success of 'Amos Barton' is therefore its narrative technique: the first-person narrator, an anonymous, middle-aged native of Amos Barton's parish of Shepperton, does not take part in the events described in the story but tells the reader about them in a manner which combines omniscience – he not only reports what happens and controls the direction of the narrative but also knows about the characters' past and has access to their thoughts – with a rather relaxed, self-effacing informality of tone which makes it possible for the reader to accept his moralising as simple reflection rather than intrusive sermonising. The fact that the narrator underlines that his 'is not a well-regulated mind' (41) paradoxically enhances his authority. He can, in consequence, switch between the soft, under-stated humour of his presentation of the little ironies of country life and the pathos of the scene of Milly Barton's farewell to her children, and his attention can shift, without any loss of fictional credibility, between a sharp, incisive comment on the character of a rich farmer's widow, Mrs Patten ('she used to adore her husband, and now she adores her money, cherishing a quiet blood-relation's hatred for her niece, Janet Gibbs, who, she knows, expects a large legacy, and whom she is determined to disappoint', 46) and the subtle presentation of the complex dynamics of the relationship between the Bartons and their quasi-aristocratic friend Countess Czerlaski. The discernment of the narrator's psychological insight is matched by his keen observation of the social and eco-nomic reality of the rural world he describes and by his careful attention to physical detail; he knows full well that the Countess's stay at the vicarage costs the Bartons money they can ill afford, and he notices how Milly's clothes and footwear tell the story of her attempts to cope with the family's genteel poverty.

This is not to say that the story is uniformly successful: at times, as for example in the episode of the meeting of local clergymen at Milby Vicarage, the narrator's powers of dramatisation fail to imbue the passage with the kind of dramatic effectiveness achieved, for instance, in the opening scene of Mrs Patten's tea party. Although the style of George Eliot's writing, with the elaborate eloquence and relative formality of its descriptive and analytical passages, tends, on the whole, to sound balanced and consistent in view of the slow, carefully measured pace of the narrative, the prose does sometimes feel excessively ponderous, and some of the narrator's supposedly comic witticisms are clearly less felicitous than intended ('Mr Bridmain had put his neck under the yoke of his handsome sister, and though his soul was a very little one – of the smallest description indeed – he would not have ventured to call it his own. He might be slightly recalcitrant now and then, as is the habit of long-eared pachyderms, under the thong of the fair Countess's tongue; but there seemed little probability that he would ever get his neck loose' (77)). All that said, however, the impression the reader is left with is one of the sheer honesty of the story and of the clarity and insight of its social and psychological observation – a remarkable achievement in what was, after all, the author's first venture into the world of fiction.

The second of the *Scenes of Clerical Life*, 'Mr Gilfil's Love-Story', takes the reader into a rather different world: though the framework narrative returns to the parish of Shepperton and to a time only a few years before that described in 'Amos Barton', the central story goes further into the past and into a different social sphere – the year is 1788 and the environment that of the gentry household of Sir Christopher Cheverel's estate of Cheverel Manor. The plot, more complex and more dramatic than in the previous tale, focuses on Caterina Sarti, a ward of Sir Christopher and Lady Cheverel, brought by them, as a young orphaned child, from her native Italy to England. Rejected by the Cheverels' nephew, Captain Wybrow, in favour of a rich heiress, Miss Assher, Caterina loses self-control and, in a fit of jealousy, prepares to kill her unfaithful lover, only to find him, at a critical moment, dead of a heart attack. She blames herself for his death and, although she finds comfort in the love of the Cheverels' chaplain, Maynard Gilfil, their marriage cannot prevent her from descending into a state of physical and mental fragility, which ultimately brings her to an early death.

In comparison with 'Amos Barton', 'Mr Gilfil's Love-Story' is constructed from much more conventional material: not only does it use some of the stock characters of eighteenth- and nineteenth-century romance, such as the orphaned and distressed heroine, the dashing but selfish young lover (not uncharacteristically, a soldier), and the faithful and honourable if somewhat bland hero, but it also manipulates the plot to introduce scenes of high dramatic tension reminiscent of Gothic fiction and Victorian melodrama – such as, in particular, the rather overcontrived scene of Caterina's discovery, dagger in pocket, of Wybrow's dead body. The story is not free from sentimentality either; repeatedly referred to as a 'little singing-bird' (146), Caterina – or 'poor little Tina' (146), or indeed 'Miss Tiny' (182) – resembles a delicate, vulnerable figure from a painting by 'some English Watteau' (133), whose sudden fit of passion, in the story's climactic scene, strikes a rather discordant note, even if it is consistent with her dark Italian looks and deep contralto voice.

However conventional some of its ingredients, 'Mr Gilfil's Love-Story' displays some of the characteristics that would, over the years, become trademarks of George Eliot's art. The narrative's shifting point of view, offering the reader full insight into the thoughts of most of the major characters, produces some interesting psychological observations, while the convincing portrayal of the generosity and altruism of Gilfil carries the story's central moral message in a manner that is unobtrusive and free from conspicuous didacticism. Finally, the protagonists' romantic entanglements are played out against a carefully presented social background which, on closer analysis, turns out to be far more problematic, in its impact on the characters' lives, than a conventional romantic reading might suggest: the story raises, for example, some important questions about the nature and limits of authority and patronage.

Whatever their merits, both as literary achievements in their own right and as early indicators of the directions in which George Eliot's art was to develop, her first two stories are, nonetheless, too narrow in their narrative focus to offer a clear indication of the author's potential as a novelist. It is only in the final 'scene of clerical life', 'Janet's Repentance', that George Eliot demonstrates the full range of her ability. This may seem something of a paradox, given that the narrative material of the story does not, at first sight, appear very promising: 'Janet's Repentance' is a tale of domestic violence and moral regeneration, its main character, the eponymous Janet Dempster, growing, under the influence of a local Evangelical minister, Edgar Tryan, from a battered wife and an alcoholic into a paragon of the Christian – and unmistakably Victorian – virtues of 'purity and helpful labour' (412). This private story of Janet's spiritual journey is played out against the background of a public conflict splitting the community of Milby in a manner by no means untypical of the late 1820s and early 1830s, the period in which the action of the story is set: Janet's husband, a prominent local lawyer, leads a traditionalist opposition against the supposed dangers of Mr Tryan's Evangelical preaching and his social initiatives (see Life and contexts, p. 4).

The power of the artistic vision of 'Janet's Repentance' derives precisely from the way in which the private and the public stories are interwoven: without sacrificing anything of the intimacy of the analysis of her protagonists' emotional and moral dilemmas, George Eliot manages to present them against a broad picture of the life of a provincial English town in the Reform era, complete with its complex network of family structures, social contacts, business links and factional rivalries. The aggressiveness and ignorance Mr Dempster demonstrates in public life translate, in the domestic context, into alcoholism and physical brutality; on the other hand, Mr Tryan's attempt to organise a programme of evening lectures designed to invigorate the town's religious life is a public expression of the same Evangelical approach to his pastoral duties that he adopts, on a personal level, in his support for Janet when she is turned out of her house by her drunken husband. The complexity of Janet's position, as a wife, a daughter and a daughter-in-law, as well as an individual, gives to the moral choices she has to make a social and indeed, at times, a public dimension: motivated largely, though not exclusively, by her loyalty to her husband, she does after all choose, early on in the story, to contribute to his anti-Tryanite campaign, while her decision to return home to nurse him through the last stages of his delirium is as much a consequence of her personal conversion, and of her acceptance of the gospel of forgiveness and charity, as it is a public expression of the sense of moral duty and responsibility arising from that spiritual transformation. The depiction of the minor characters combines, in a rather similar way, representativeness and individualisation: the scenes at the bar of the Red Lion public house and in Mrs Linnet's parlour introduce the reader not only to the central public conflict of the story, but also to the idiosyncrasies of many of the participants in the ensuing drama, from the selfish medical man Mr Pilgrim to the kind-hearted Mrs Pettifer.

The concern with religious controversy makes 'Janet's Repentance' the only one among the three constituent stories of *Scenes of Clerical Life* to put issues of faith and morality at the heart of its thematic structure. Although George Eliot's sympathy lies clearly on the side of the Tryanites, the story is by no means an apology for Evangelicalism: the narrator makes it clear that 'the movement, like all other religious "revivals", had a mixed effect' (319), and there is no suggestion that Mr Tryan's theological doctrines are in themselves superior to those preached by the traditionalist old curate Mr Crewe or the successive Dissenting ministers in charge of the Independent Salem chapel. What matters is that 'Evangelicalism had brought into palpable existence and operation in Milby society that idea of duty, that recognition of something to be lived for beyond the mere satisfaction of self, which is to the moral life what the addition of a great central ganglion is to animal life' (320); in consequence, the Evangelical Anglican Mr Tryan and the Dissenter Mr Jerome are both, in practical terms, followers of the same creed of empathy, compassion, generosity and self-sacrifice which is clearly not shared by the nominally Anglican supporters of Dempster's anti-Tryanite camp. The theological – or philosophical – fundament on which this altruistic impulse is based is of secondary importance; whether symbolised by 'a head bowed beneath a cross, and wearing a crown of thorns' (285) or founded on 'blessed influence of one true loving human soul on another' (364), the gospel of good will that the story preaches is essentially the same as the moral message of the positivist religion of humanity (see Life and contexts, **pp. 14–15**).

The reception of *Scenes of Clerical Life* was favourable, even if the book was not reviewed particularly widely. The early critics praised the stories for 'a sobriety which is shown to be compatible with strength, clear and simple descriptions, and a combination of humour with pathos in depicting ordinary situations' (*CH*, 62), as well as for the liveliness of the presentation of the characters and for the 'freshness, vivacity, and sweetness' (*CH*, 66) of the descriptions of country life. Interestingly, no reviewer suspected that the stories could have been written by a woman; the only reader to have seen through George Eliot's disguise was Dickens, who noticed 'what seemed to [him] such womanly touches in those moving fictions, that the assurance on the title-page [was] insufficient to satisfy [him]' (*L*, II, 424).

Adam Bede (1859)

The same freshness and spontaneity of descriptions of country life and the same directness and honesty of the portrayal of ordinary, unheroic characters that lay at the heart of the success of *Scenes of Clerical Life* (see Works, **pp. 32–6**) are also the key features of George Eliot's first full-length work of fiction, *Adam Bede*.

This is by no means surprising: the novel, begun within weeks of the completion of 'Janet's Repentance', takes as its starting point an anecdote that was originally intended for another 'clerical scene', and it builds on the achievement of the author's previous work not only in its choice of rural setting and atmosphere but also in exploring the imaginative potential of some of the characters and storylines from the earlier volume – the most obvious example of this practice is the transformation of the simple romantic plot of Caterina and Captain Wybrow, in 'Mr Gilfil's Love-Story' (see Works, pp. 34–5), into the psychologically and morally complex story of the relationship between Hetty Sorrel and Arthur Donnithorne. At the same time, following the pattern established in *Scenes of Clerical Life*, George Eliot continues to draw, in her creation of the fictional world of her novel, on her personal memories and on her knowledge of the history of her family: despite her insistence that 'there is not a single *portrait* in *Adam Bede*; only the suggestions of experience wrought up into new combinations' ('History of *Adam Bede*', J, 297), some of the novel's central characters can easily be traced to their real-life originals. Thus, the novel's loving and honourable, if not entirely idealised, eponymous hero, Adam Bede, owes a great deal to the writer's memories of her father, Robert Evans (see Life and contexts, pp. 2–3), while the story of Hetty's infanticide, trial and punishment is based on an account of a similar case related to the author by her 'Aunt Samuel' – Elizabeth Tomlinson Evans, the wife of Robert Evans's younger brother Samuel, herself a Methodist preacher and the source of inspiration for the creation of the character of Dinah Morris (see L, 174–7). At times, the differences between the 'real' world of family history and the fictional world of the novel become blurred or disappear altogether: the character of the village schoolteacher, Bartle Massey, takes his name directly from the real-life teacher who educated Robert Evans in the village of Ellaston, on the border of Staffordshire and Derbyshire – the place which was to be transformed, in the story, into the Loamshire village of Hayslope.

The main plot of the novel, set over a period of two years, from 1799 to 1801, is relatively simple. A young, honest and reliable Hayslope carpenter, Adam Bede, is in love with Hetty Sorrel, the orphaned niece of a local farmer Martin Poyser; Hetty, however, does not reciprocate Adam's feelings and instead falls in love with the young grandson of the local squire and heir to the family estate, Captain Arthur Donnithorne. Arthur, a well-meaning but somewhat irresponsible young man, does not take the affair seriously; following a confrontation with Adam, whom he had known and liked from childhood, he eventually decides to break up with Hetty and departs for Windsor to join his militia regiment. Soon after his departure, Hetty discovers that she is pregnant; she decides to accept Adam's proposal of marriage, but when her pregnancy becomes advanced, she sets off on a journey in search of her former lover. On arrival in Windsor, she discovers that Arthur's regiment had left for Ireland; exhausted and penniless, she returns to the Midlands, gives birth to her child and leaves it in a forest to die; captured, she is imprisoned, tried for infanticide, found guilty and sentenced to death. In the meantime, Adam goes in search of Hetty; when he finds out the whole truth about her as the news about her imprisonment eventually reaches Hayslope, he is heartbroken, but he decides to stand by her. Hetty initially refuses to see him; instead, she is comforted by the Poysers' other niece, the Methodist preacher Dinah

Morris, to whom she eventually confesses her guilt. Meanwhile, Arthur, recalled from Ireland because of the death of his grandfather, manages to secure a reprieve for Hetty, whose sentence is commuted to transportation to the colonies. Chastened, he then decides to do penance by joining the army and going abroad, rather than staying at home to run the estate, which had always been his ambition. Adam and Dinah recognise each other's goodness and honesty, fall in love and marry. The Epilogue, set in 1807, winds up the story, with news of Hetty dying on her journey back to England, Arthur – now Colonel Donnithorne – returning home a wiser and more responsible man, and Adam and Dinah enjoying happy family life together.

The central story of the novel is played out against a rich background of the social, economic and religious life of Hayslope and the neighbouring villages. The scene shifts between a number of locations around the parish, including the workshop of the local master carpenter Jonathan Burge, the large farm of the Poysers, with its thriving dairy business, the smaller houses of the Bede family and of the schoolmaster Bartle Massey, the rectory at Broxton, the home of the popular and respected Revd Alphonsus Irwine, and the Chase, the family seat of the Donnithornes. The village community is presented at work and at play, on weekdays and on Sundays, in happiness and in grief, in private and in public; it consists of people of all generations, from the nonagenarian Jacob Taft to the toddler Totty Poyser, and of all social classes, from the families of the gentry and the clergy to small tenant farmers and village artisans. Despite its diversity, the community does nonetheless retain a strong sense of unity and cohesion; although social roles and distinctions are clearly defined and the consequent social proprieties are carefully observed, occasions such as Sunday services or the celebration of Arthur's birthday feast produce in the people of Hayslope a sense of common identity and demonstrate their acceptance of, and loyalty to, the model of social organisation that their world represents – that of an established, traditional, essentially conservative structure, evolving in an organic way through the natural processes of life, individual as well as communal.

At the same time, largely self-contained socially and broadly self-sufficient in economic terms as it may be, the idealised pastoral world of Hayslope is, however, neither as entirely isolated from external influences nor indeed as peaceful and cohesive as it might at first appear to be. Arthur Donnithorne is au fait with recent literature, reading and recommending to his godmother, old Mrs Irwine, the recently published *Lyrical Ballads*. Adam Bede's education with Bartle Massey involves not only the study of the Bible and the reading of *The Pilgrim's Progress* but also finding out about 'the canals, an' th' aqueducs, an' th' coal-pit engines, and Arkwright's mills there at Cromford' (p. 53). Among common folk, memories of the Jacobite rebellion of 1745 are evoked as local farmers discuss the echoes of the ongoing conflict with France. Modern agricultural and manufacturing technologies may not have quite arrived in Loamshire yet, but change is just round the corner: old Mr Donnithorne tries to rationalise the use of land on his estate while Dinah brings from her home town of Snowfield into the rural environment of Hayslope the awareness and personal experience of living and working in the newly industrialised world of the mines and cotton mills of Stonyshire. The prospects of change in the traditional patterns of work have their social implications and expose the underlying tensions in the seemingly smooth fabric of village life: Mr Donnithorne's plans to turn the Hall Farm into a special-ist dairy venture threaten the stability of the Poyser household, embodied in the maternal presence of Mrs Poyser, in a way that is potentially at least as disruptive to their circumstances as that more familiar mechanism of the exercise of landlord power over the tenant, acted out by Arthur on Hetty. The contrast between Loamshire and Stonyshire – and, by extension, between the rural world of the Midlands and the industrial cities further north – is not quite as simple as a straightforward Wordsworthian reading might suggest either: although Mr Irwine, in many ways the personification of Hayslope's traditional values, thinks about Snowfield as 'a dreary, bleak place' (133), Dinah's more informed percep-tion of it is radically different: not only does she recognise the economic potential inherent in the development of industry – 'I work in [the mill] myself, and have reason to be grateful, for thereby I have enough and to spare' (133) – but she also contrasts the profound humanity and spiritual openness of the people living 'up those high-walled streets, where you seem to walk as in a prison-yard, and the ear is deafened with the sounds of worldly toil' (137) with the 'strange deadness to the Word' (137) that characterises 'these villages where the people lead a quiet life among the green pastures and the still waters, tilling the ground and tending the cattle' (137).

It is precisely the spiritual side of Dinah and her commitment to Methodism that constitute the most important challenge to the established order of the life of Hayslope. Although the people of the parish are all, technically, dutiful and law-abiding Christians, their religion is indeed largely conventional and formalistic: the weekly church service is for the majority of them predominantly a social occasion, attended, in part at least, out of a traditional, quasi-pagan, magical 'simple faith in its efficacy to ward off harm and bring blessing' (242). Their pastor is not much of a spiritual leader either; Mr Irwine 'really [has] no very lofty aims, no theological enthusiasm: . . . he [feels] no serious alarms about the souls of his parishioners, and would have thought it a mere loss of time to talk in a doctrinal and awakening manner' (112) to his parishioners. Not surprisingly, then, the villagers' reaction to Dinah's Evangelical zeal is at best lukewarm: even Bess Cranage's response – she throws away her earrings, which, in Dinah's words, are 'poisoning [her] soul . . . dragging [her] down into a dark bottomless pit' (75) – is not much more than an act of naive emotionality, spontaneous but shallow and having little long-term impact: her taste for finery appears by no means diminished when she competes, in the hope of getting a prize, in a sack race on the day of Arthur's birthday feast. It is not until the climactic moment of the novel – the scene of Dinah's prayer over Hetty and Hetty's confession – that the power of Christian belief produces its most dramatic effect, as Dinah's words manage to 'melt the hard hart; unseal the closed lips: make [Hetty] cry with her whole soul, "Father, I have sinned" ' (497).

The presentation of Methodism in *Adam Bede* is indeed one of the most powerful, and favourable, portrayals of Nonconformity in Victorian literature (see Cunningham 1975: 147–71) – and yet, paradoxically, George Eliot's novel cannot be seen as belonging to the popular Victorian sub-genre of religious fiction; on the contrary, despite the prominence of religious motifs in the plot of the novel, and despite the biblical resonance of much of its idiom, *Adam Bede* is emphatically agnostic in its philosophical implications and unashamedly secular and humanist in the moral message that it preaches. Although Dinah's commitment to her faith is absolutely genuine, the impact she makes on other people does not depend quite as much on her effectiveness as a preacher as it does on her ability to empathise with those in need and to offer 'a friendly presence' (154) that is physical and psychological rather than spiritual. To Lisbeth Bede, grieving after the death of her husband, Dinah may at first look like 'an angel' (154), but the illusion does not last long: she is soon recognised for what she really is, 'a workin' woman' (154) whose hand may '[bear] the traces of labour from her childhood upwards' (154), but whose sheer commitment to helping those in need, out of her altruistic, compassionate generosity of spirit, makes people 'unconsciously subject to the soothing influence of [her] face and voice' (157). For Hetty, in the climactic prison scene, Dinah's prayer is of secondary importance; 'it [is] the human contact she [clings] to' (494), and it is Dinah's sheer physical presence in the prison cell that makes it possible for Hetty to retain her sanity and eventually to tell the story of her crime in an act which is not so much a confession in the religious sense but a verbalisation of the moment of her most dramatic emotional crisis and, therefore, the first stage in the process of her moral and psychological recovery. It is not Dinah the Methodist preacher but Dinah the compassionate friend and companion that makes the difference; her actions may be motivated by her Christian belief but they make an impact because they respond to Hetty's sense of remorse and fear of death on the fundamentally human rather than spiritual level.

While Dinah personifies the humanist dimension of the Christian message of forgiveness and compassion, it is, again quite paradoxically, through the character of Mr Irwine that George Eliot makes the most explicit statements expressing the novel's secular moral vision. Whatever his shortcomings as a theologian, Mr Irwine '[has] that charity which has sometimes been lacking to the very illustrious virtue – he [is] tender to other men's failings, and unwilling to impute evil' (113), and he demonstrates that charity in practice when, confronted with the dramatic turn of events in the lives of Hetty and Adam, he organises for them a network of support that proves decisive in helping them through their time of trial. This is entirely consistent with the role he plays, and is highly respected for, in his community throughout the novel – offering his 'thoughtful care for the everyday wants of everyday companions' (113). This is not to say that his concern with practicalities of life makes him shy away from offering his parishioners – among them, most prominently perhaps, Arthur Donnithorne – pastoral support and moral guidance; the point is that the morality he preaches is one that is defined in exclusively non-spiritual terms, without reference to divine authority but with a clear focus on the absolute, unremitting nature of individual responsibility:

> 'But surely you don't think a man who struggles against a temptation into which he falls at last, as bad as the man who never struggles at all?'
> 'No, my boy, I pity him, in proportion to his struggles, for they foreshadow the inward suffering which is the worst form of nemesis. Consequences are unpitying. Our deeds carry their terrible consequences, quite apart from any fluctuations that went before – consequences that are hardly ever confined to ourselves. And it is best to fix our minds on

that certainty, instead of considering what may be the elements of excuse for us.'

(217–18)

It is precisely that kind of interpretation of morality that George Eliot illustrates in her construction of the plot of the novel: the story of Arthur, Hetty and Adam is a study of the consequences of common human failures – Arthur's inability to control his youthful sexual energy and Hetty's naivety, self-centredness and social and economic ambition. Although their liaison lies at the root of the ensuing tragedy, Arthur and Hetty can be blamed for little more than irresponsibility, self-indulgence and lack of proper judgement; Arthur, a well-meaning if somewhat reckless young man, does not so much seduce Hetty as let their relationship take its natural course, without much regard for the potential consequences, while Hetty overinterprets Arthur's intentions in the naive hope that their romance can help her fulfil her social and material aspirations. Everything that happens after-wards – Hetty's pregnancy, the break-up of the relationship, Hetty's deceitful treatment of Adam, her journey in search of Arthur, the birth and death of her child, the trial – follows on in a relentless manner, acquiring, as the story progresses, a sense of tragic inevitability that may on the one hand seem to be almost out of proportion with the original transgressions that triggered all the ensuing complications, but that is at the same time a logically consistent and thoroughly convincing analysis of the likely consequences of the characters' actions.

This internal consistency of the novel's narrative logic is achieved as a result of the careful balancing of the construction of the plot and the presentation of characters – very much in line with the narrator's own insistence that 'our deeds determine us, as much as we determine our deeds; and until we know what has been or will be the peculiar combination of outward with inward facts, which constitutes a man's critical actions, it will be better not to think ourselves wise about his character' (359). To facilitate this kind of profound understanding of the protagonists of the novel, the reader is offered direct insight into their minds, interventions of the omniscient narrator coalescing with passages of free indirect speech to produce an impression of intimate familiarity with the characters' uncertainties, doubts and fears. The range of the moods and emotions analysed is reflected in the stylistic diversity of the relevant sections of the text: the sobriety and level-headedness of Arthur's attempts to rationalise his behaviour towards Hetty stands in direct contrast to the emotional intensity of her own thoughts as she is on the point of committing suicide:

It seemed he couldn't quite depend on his own resolution, as he had thought he could: he almost wished his arm would get painful again, and then he should think of nothing but the comfort it would be to get rid of pain. There was no knowing what impulse might seize him to-morrow, in this confounded place, where there was nothing to occupy him imperiously through the livelong day. What could he do to secure himself from any more of this folly?

(184)

She was frightened at this darkness – frightened at the long night before her. If she *could* but throw herself into the water! No, not yet. She began to walk about that she might get warm again, as if she would have more resolution then. O how long the time was in that darkness! The bright hearts and the warmth and the voices of home, – the secure uprising and lying down, – the familiar fields, the familiar people, the Sundays and holidays with their simple joys of dress and feasting, – all the sweets of her young life rushed before her now, and she seemed to be stretching her arms towards them across a great gulf.

(431–2)

The subtlety of George Eliot's psychological analysis in *Adam Bede* is not limited to the presentation of her protagonists' minds in moments of crisis; just as important is her understanding of the dynamics of the processes of character development. As befits the moralistic message of the novel, each of the major characters goes through some form of learning experience, resulting in a greater or lesser degree of character transformation. With some of the characters, the moral lessons they learn are very fundamental, dramatic and painful: Hetty is punished for her self-centred pursuit of her worldly aspirations – in the opinion of some critics, with undue harshness (see, e.g., Barrett 1989: 43–6) – by the trauma of her experience of pregnancy, motherhood and infanticide, as well as by the horrors of her imprisonment and trial, the expectation of execution and the disgrace of transportation; Arthur, in turn, demonstrates his newly acquired sense of moral responsibility when he decides to pay the price of his self-indulgent recklessness and his lack of moral fibre as he accepts his responsibility for Hetty's downfall and leaves Hayslope to seek redemption on the battlefields of Europe. The moral pattern of the novel is, however, very far from black and white. Thus, for example, Adam, the solid, reliable and trustworthy man that he is, has to learn to temper his tendency towards excessive moral rectitude and adopt a more empathetic, compassionate, forgiving approach in his relationships with those who are in need of his support – on learning the truth about Hetty's crime, he needs to follow Mr Irwine's advice to 'stay and see what good can be done for *her*, instead of going on a useless errand of vengeance' (456) against Arthur. Even Dinah, the novel's paragon of moral virtue, needs to come to a better understanding of herself and her vocation in life before she can, at the close of the story, accept Adam's love and her future role as a wife and mother.

The question of the fictional credibility of that ending and of its logical consistency within the context of the narrative framework of the whole novel is one of the main points of criticism that have been made over the years (see, e.g., *CH*, 499, and Harvey 1961: 180–1) about the structure of *Adam Bede*. The story unfolds very slowly at first, setting the scene for the dramatic developments that will ensue; the very long exposition, culminating in the detailed presentation of the day of Arthur's birthday feast, which occupies the whole of Book Third, is relatively static, focusing on the presentation and analysis of the social world of Hayslope and on the characterisation of the contrasting pairs of protagonists (Hetty vs. Dinah, Adam vs. Arthur). The turning point of the plot – the consummation of the romance between Arthur and Hetty – is, in line with the Victorian standards of propriety, implied rather than explicitly referred to; from that moment onwards, the action of the story rapidly gathers pace, culminating in the sequence of scenes describing Hetty's trial, confession and impending execution. The last section – Book Sixth – re-establishes the traditional order of village life, the scene of the harvest supper providing a counterpoint to the scene of the birthday dinner earlier on in the novel; with Arthur and Hetty now away, doing penance for their sins, the marriage between Adam and Dinah becomes a tidy way of rounding off the story and providing it with a conventional happy ending. The problem with that conclusion is, however, that there is relatively little in the earlier sections of the novel to suggest the possibility of that kind of resolution: Adam and Dinah may be the exponents of the key moral values the novel preaches, but they lack credibility as potential lovers (Adam's interest in Hetty is, for all his muscular masculinity, peculiarly restrained, while Dinah, until the last chapter of the novel, sublimates all her sexuality into a quasi-angelic spirituality that emasculates potential suitors, most notably Arthur's own brother Seth), as a result of which their marriage ultimately fails to convince.

The very question of the psychological and logical consistency of the ending of the novel is of course predicated on the basic assumption that the story of *Adam Bede* is meant to be offering a truthful picture of life, a believable account of a reality which, imaginary though it is, remains an accurate reflection of what might have happened in a village in the Midlands of England around the end of the eighteenth century. George Eliot makes that point explicitly in a crucial passage in which she develops the artistic credo she first defined in 'Amos Barton':

> So I am content to tell my simple story, without trying to make things seem better than they were; dreading nothing, indeed, but falsity, which, in spite of one's best efforts, there is reason to dread. Falsehood is so easy, truth so difficult. [. . .]
>
> It is for this rare, precious quality of truthfulness that I delight in many Dutch paintings, which lofty-minded people despise. I find a source a delicious sympathy in these faithful pictures of a monotonous homely existence, which has been the fate of so many more among my fellow-mortals than a life of pomp or of absolute indigence, or tragic suffering or of world-stirring actions.
>
> (222–3)

The careful attention to physical, psychological and social detail that characterises George Eliot's vision of Hayslope in *Adam Bede* ensures that she does indeed 'give the loving pains of a life to the faithful representing of commonplace things' (224), producing a novel which is generally acclaimed as one of the most successful examples of classic realist fiction in English. And yet, paradoxically, it is in the very chapter in which George Eliot puts forward her theory of realism that she also draws the reader's attention to its limitations: not only does she admit that 'the mirror is doubtless defective, the outlines will sometimes be disturbed; the reflection faint or confused' (221), but also she undermines the realistic convention on which the reader's acceptance of the illusion of verisimilitude in the novel depends by introducing a scene in which the narrator meets Adam 'in his old age' (225) and discusses some of the characters in the novel with him. The resulting blurring of the distinction between the 'real' world of the narrator and the 'imaginary' world of the narrative introduces into *Adam Bede* an element of uncertainty and open-endedness; in consequence, rather than providing a model against which to measure the author's later achievements, George Eliot's first novel is better read as the first major step in the development of her complex and often remarkably adventurous approach to the process of the writing of fiction.

The critical reception of *Adam Bede* was almost unanimously enthusiastic. The book was welcomed as 'a first-rate novel, . . . [whose] author takes rank at once among the masters of the art' (*CH*, 77). Early reviewers focused on George Eliot's observation and presentation of character, reserving special praise for the creation of Mrs Poyser, portrayed with a special 'combination of shrewd remark and homely wit with genuine kindliness and racy style' (*CH*, 82); the precision and acuteness of the author's vision of the community of Hayslope left critics wondering 'whether our literature anywhere possesses such a closely true picture of purely rural life as *Adam Bede* presents' (*CH*, 97). The few critical comments tended to focus on what was perceived as the melodramatic quality of the last third of the novel – 'weak, poor, and superficial, compared with the other two' (*CH*, 75). However veiled the modern reader might find the references to Hetty's pregnancy, they were still considered, by some contemporaneous critics, to have been 'indicated with a punctual sequence that makes the account of her misfortunes read like the rough notes of a man-midwife's conversations with a bride' (*CH*, 76) – a comment that foreshadows the accusations of immorality that were to follow, particularly in religious press, once the true identity of the author became known. The quality of that section of the novel was recognised, yet again, by Dickens, who found 'the conception of Hetty's character . . . so extraordinarily subtle and true, . . . so skilful, determined, and uncompromising' (*CH*, 85).

The Mill on the Floss (1860)

George Eliot's second full-length novel, *The Mill on the Floss*, marks an important new stage in the development of her artistic method. While the fictional worlds of *Scenes of Clerical Life* (see Works, **pp. 32–6**) and *Adam Bede* (see Works, **pp. 36–44**) were constructed from a diverse range of motifs derived, in various ways, from the author's direct or indirect familiarity with the public, social aspects of the life of the Midlands of England from the late eighteenth century onwards, *The Mill on the Floss* relies much more on her individual, personal memories and emotions. Although not an autobiographical novel in the strict sense of the word – the tragic story of Maggie Tulliver is quite radically different from that of the young Marian Evans – the book does nonetheless generate, through the blurring of the distance between the present and the past ('I have been pressing my elbows on the arms of my chair and dreaming that I was standing on the bridge in front of Dorlcote Mill at it looked one February afternoon many years ago' (p. 55) and between the narrator and Maggie ('Now I can turn my eyes towards the mill again and watch the unresting wheel sending out its diamond jets of water. That little girl is watching it too: she has been standing on just the same spot at the edge of the water ever since I paused on the bridge', 54–5), an atmosphere of imaginative intensity which conveys to the reader a powerful sense of the author's profound personal identification with her central character. This is true, in particular, of the first volume of the novel, in which the portrayal of the childhood of Maggie and her brother Tom draws heavily on the author's memories of her own, and her brother Isaac's, early years at Griff; the closeness of the relationship between Maggie and Mr Tulliver is evocative of the strength of the bond that existed, for all their conflicts and disagreements, between Marian Evans and her father Robert, while the three Dodson sisters – Aunt Glegg, Aunt Pullet and Aunt Deane – bear close resemblance to the writer's maternal aunts, the Pearsons (see Life and contexts, p. 2). The parallels are not restricted to the initial sections of the novel either: the artistic Philip Wakem shares a number of features with Marian's Geneva friend, François D'Albert Durade (see Life and contexts, p. 10), while the story of Maggie's ostracisation after her ill-fated boat trip with Stephen Guest carries a strong similarity to what her creator herself experienced following her decision to live openly with Lewes (see Life and Contexts, pp. 16–17). In consequence, *The Mill on the Floss* acquires, for all the fictionality of its plot, a quality of quasi-autobiographical truth which places it, in terms of its special role in the author's œuvre, alongside such Victorian classics as Charlotte Brontë's *Jane Eyre* and Dickens's *David Copperfield*.

The action of the novel is set, somewhat vaguely (the exact dates have to be identified on the basis of internal evidence, including references to contemporaneous public events, such as the debate on Catholic Emancipation), between 1829 and 1839, in and around the town of St Ogg's, based on the Lincolnshire town of Gainsborough on the river Trent. The plot is constructed, by comparison with *Adam Bede*, in a relatively loose manner: the narrative, which acquires its rhythm from the natural passage of time rather than as a result of dramatic tension generated by the action, unfolds rather slowly, following the two main characters, Maggie and Tom, from their childhood at Dorlcote Mill on the river Floss through adolescence and into maturity. The happiness of their early years, punctuated by a variety of ordinary events of family life and schooling, comes to an abrupt end when their father, in consequence of a lost lawsuit, goes bankrupt and is reduced to having to accept the post of the manager of the mill, offered to him by his old adversary, the lawyer Wakem, who has now taken control of Mr Tulliver's former property. This has a direct impact on the Tulliver children: Tom leaves school and, motivated by the ambition to earn enough money to pay off his father's debts, finds employment with the St Ogg's industrial firm of Guest and Co., while Maggie is forced, through her loyalty to her father and brother, to keep secret and eventually to give up her friendship with Wakem's disabled son Philip, a former fellow student of Tom's, whom, through their shared intellectual curiosity and literary tastes, over the years she grows to love. Tom's hard work makes it possible for him, after a few years, to pay off his father's debts; the emotional pressure of the day on which the family's financial credentials are re-established proves, however, too much for Mr Tulliver, who, after a violent confrontation with Wakem, suffers a major health crisis and dies. The family home thus gone, Maggie chooses, rather than to join her mother in moving in with one of her Dodson aunts, to go away in order to take up a teaching post, while Tom continues in the business, aiming to buy the mill back, which he eventually succeeds in doing. At that point, Maggie returns to St Ogg's to stay with her cousin Lucy Deane; she renews her friendship with Philip, but she also finds herself attracted, with reciprocity, to Lucy's suitor, the rich Stephen Guest. During a boating trip, Maggie and Stephen lose track of time, miss their destination and, in consequence, fail to return home on the same day, which obviously compromises Maggie's position. She refuses to marry Stephen and returns to St Ogg's to face the opprobrium of the town's public opinion, and, most importantly, to be turned away from Dorlcote Mill by her brother. Shortly afterwards, a flood devastates the area; Maggie rows back to the mill to rescue Tom, but they are both killed when their boat is destroyed by debris carried by the waters of the Floss.

Although the events of the story are played out over a period of little more than ten years, *The Mill on the Floss* has the feel of an extended family saga: rather than attempting, as she did in 'Janet's Repentance' (see Works, pp. 35–6) and in *Adam Bede* (see Works, pp. 36–44), to produce a comprehensive picture of a broader local community at a particular point in time, in her second novel George Eliot focuses in on the lives of the Tullivers and their relatives – some of the novel's most colourful figures are the Tulliver children's aunts and uncles – as they move through life facing not only the natural processes of growing up, ageing and dying, but also the changing circumstances of their personal, social and economic positions. The pace of the narrative varies quite dramatically. Some scenes – such as those depicting family visits – are presented in slow motion, with a great deal of attention paid to the presentation of minute details of setting and action, while elsewhere, months and years are passed over in silence. The reader never gets to know much about Tom's business ventures, or about Maggie's time as a governess. In consequence, the novel's primary concern is not so much with dramatically developed and internally consistent action but with the creation of characters; memorable as many of the incidents in the narrative are, they often function as illustrations of the characters' personalities and attitudes rather than as integral elements of the plot. Thus, the episode of Maggie cutting her hair illustrates her yearning, from an early age, for 'a sense of clearness and freedom' (120), while the scene describing Tom as he tries to impress Maggie with his Latin produces a wonderfully concentrated picture not only of the two siblings' contrasting intellectual temperaments but also of their assumptions regarding their social and gender roles.

This focus on character is of course closely related to George Eliot's interest in psychology, particularly in its dynamic, developmental aspect: *The Mill on the Floss* is one of the classic examples of a Victorian *Bildungsroman* – a novel about the growth of a character, the shaping-up of a personality. In her analysis of the progress of her protagonists from childhood into maturity, George Eliot takes a very broad view of the forces contributing to their development; her novel is, in fact, one of the first major fictions in English not only to include in its investigation of the characters a conventional analysis of their social background, education, etc., but also, very much in the spirit of the mid-Victorian era, to consider the impact, on the development of their temperament, mentality and attitudes, of the forces of heredity. Strongly idiosyncratic as they may be in some aspects of their behaviour – Maggie's thirst for knowledge surpasses the intellectual ambitions of any of her relatives – the Tulliver children are nonetheless clearly the children of their parents, displaying the typical physical characteristics and psychological traits of their respective families. Tom is unmistakably, like his mother, a Dodson, not only 'in his features and complexion, in liking salt, and in eating beans, which a Tulliver never did' (97), but also in his acceptance of the Dodson principles of hard work, perseverance and respectability – in fact, as he grows up he becomes something of an extreme example, almost a parody, of the family type, outdoing his mother, 'a thorough Dodson, though a mild one' (97), in his condemnation of Maggie, but unable to share his aunt Glegg's commitment to the 'fundamental ideas of clanship' (629) because his is 'a nature in which family feeling [has] lost the character of clanship in taking on a doubly deep dye of personal pride' (631). In contrast, Maggie – her father's 'little wench' (59) – is not only physically 'the picture of her aunt Moss, Mr Tulliver's sister' (116), but also temperamentally, in her impulsiveness and disdain for conventionality, a Tulliver like her father, 'descended from one Ralph Tulliver, a wonderfully clever fellow who had ruined himself . . . a high liver, [who] rode spirited horses, and was very decidedly of his own opinion' (365).

A consequence of that particular approach to character is that the protagonists of The Mill on the Floss tend, when confronted with new situations and complex moral choices, not so much to change as to discover in themselves new, hitherto latent, aspects of their personalities. Tom's moral rectitude, which develops, as he grows up, into ruthless inflexibility, has its sources in the attitudes he displayed in his childhood: he 'never disobeyed his father' (90), and 'he was particularly clear and positive on one point, namely that he would punish everybody who deserved it: why, he wouldn't have minded being punished himself if he deserved it, but then, he never *did* deserve it' (91). Similarly, Maggie's moment of realisation, on reading Thomas à Kempis's The Imitation of Christ, 'that all the miseries of her young life [have] come from fixing her heart on her own pleasure, as if that were the central necessity of the universe' (384), and that renunciation could constitute for her 'the entrance into that satisfaction which she [has] so long been craving in vain' (384), has its roots in her readiness, as a child, not only to obey Tom's wishes but also to accept self-denial as a way of earning his approval ('she would have given the world not to have eaten all her puff, and to have saved some of it for Tom[;] . . . she would have gone without it many times over, sooner than Tom should call her greedy and be cross with her', 100). The resulting sense of the stability and consistency of the characters, who come close to becoming personifications of the moral and psychological qualities they represent, gives The Mill on the Floss, despite its resolutely realistic mode of narrative, a quasi-allegorical feel, reinforced by the novel's numerous allusions to the classic work of English allegorical fiction, John Bunyan's The Pilgrim's Progress.

It is precisely the expectation of consistency in the character of Maggie that leaves numerous readers of The Mill on the Floss dissatisfied with the last third of the novel; her romantic involvement with Stephen Guest has often been seen (see, e.g., Stephen 1902: 102–4, and Allen 1965: 114–15) as unconvincing, both in terms of the relative sketchiness of the presentation of Stephen himself, particularly as compared with his rival Philip Wakem and as regards the credibility of Maggie's reaction to his attentions. Admittedly, Stephen is not given quite enough room to develop as a complex character in his own right; on the other hand, however, this may well be not so much a flaw in his characterisation as an indication of the nature of the interest he inspires in Maggie: while her relationship with the disabled Philip develops, over the years, very much as an intellectual and indeed spiritual connection, the attraction between Maggie and Stephen is clearly sexual – and, as such, instinctive and spontaneous rather than demanding justification through a process of gradual development. In any case, what remains certain is that Maggie's romantic dilemma brings into sharp focus the central moral theme of the novel – 'the shifting relation between passion and duty' (627). It is perhaps consistent with the presentation of Maggie's character, combining 'the need of being loved, the strongest need in poor Maggie's nature' (89) with her readiness for self-sacrifice in the name of a greater good, that the novel does not propose a definite solution to that moral dilemma: just as for Maggie there is no clear answer to the moral choices she faces in trying to balance her relationships with Philip and Stephen against the demands of family loyalty and social propriety, so for the narrator and the reader there are no universally valid truths – 'moral judgments must remain false and hollow, unless they are checked and enlightened by a perpetual reference to the special circumstances that mark the individual lot' (628). It is not uncharacteristic of that open-endedness of George Eliot's moral vision in *The Mill on the Floss* that the character who comes closest to being the spokesman for the author's opinions, the Rector of St Ogg's Dr Kenn, is hardly a believer in moral absolutes himself; although, like his counterpart in *Adam Bede*, Mr Irwine (see Works, pp. 36–44), he does believe that 'the Church ought to represent the feeling of the community, so that every parish should be a family knit together by Christian brotherhood under a spiritual father' (624–5), and although he is prepared to extend a helping hand to Maggie when she is rejected by the majority of her family and friends, he does nonetheless succumb to the pressure of public opinion when he is effectively forced to terminate her lessons with his children.

The centrality – and at the same time ambivalence – of Maggie's position in the moral scheme of the novel is paralleled by the key role she plays in George Eliot's analysis of the provincial society of early nineteenth-century England. Although the focus of the narrative is primarily on the domestic sphere of life, the novel makes it clear that the private and the social aspects of existence are inextricably linked; in fact, all the key events in the life of the Tulliver family, from Mr Tulliver's bankruptcy to the ostracisation of Maggie, are primarily public events, determining the subsequent personal choices the characters involved in them have to make. It is by no means insignificant that the impact on the life of the Tullivers – and particularly Maggie – of external social and economic forces is invariably negative: although St Ogg's shares in the early nineteenth-century economic and technological progress, its results on the novel's central protagonists are ultimately destructive. It is worth remembering that the source of Mr Tulliver's financial problems, and of Maggie's subsequent moral dilemmas, is Mr Pivart's plan, supported by Mr Wakem, with regard to the irrigation of his land up the river Ripple, above Dorlcote, with its consequent impact on the operation of Mr Tulliver's mill. Later on in the novel, it is equally significant that Stephen, whose interference in Maggie's life is the direct cause of her downfall, is the son of the local business tycoon and thus the embodiment of the modern industrial success of the community of St Ogg's. Maggie, on the other hand, a true Tulliver like her father, belongs to an earlier, pre-industrial world; she 'love[s] to linger in the great spaces of the mill, ... the unresting motion of the great stones giving her a dim delicious awe as at the presence of an uncontrollable force' (80), in much the same way as her father does, influenced by 'the love of the old premises where he had run about when he was a boy' (351–2), and it is ultimately the modernity of the new, industrial England that quite literally kills her when the boat she and Tom are using to escape from the mill during the flood is hit by fragments of 'some wooden machinery [which have] just given way on one of the wharves' (655).

This conservative, nostalgically Wordsworthian vision of a traditional order of rural life being destroyed by the arrival of the progressive but ruthless forces of modernity is of course in line with the novel's presentation of the world of the Tullivers' Dodson relatives, personifying the very attitudes and values that made the development of the modern, nineteenth-century England possible. George Eliot may be critical of the Dodsons' self-centred materialism, but she cannot help recognising some of the more positive aspects of their approach to life:

> The Dodsons were a very proud race, and their pride lay in the utter frustration of all desire to tax them with a breach of traditional duty or propriety. A wholesome pride in many respects; since it identified honour with perfect integrity, thoroughness of work, and faithfulness to admitted rules; and society owes some worthy qualities in many of her members to mothers of the Dodson class, who made their butter and their fromenty well and would have felt disgraced to make it otherwise. To be honest and poor was never a Dodson motto, still less, to seem rich though being poor; rather, the family badge was to be honest and rich, and not only rich, but richer than was supposed. . . . A conspicuous quality in the Dodson character was its genuineness: its vices and virtues alike were phases of a proud, honest egoism which had a hearty dislike to whatever made against its own credit and interest, and would be frankly hard of speech to inconvenient 'kin' but would never forsake or ignore them – would not let them want bread, but only require them to eat it with bitter herbs.
>
> (364–5)

Although the Dodsons are fundamentally honest and capable of exercising family loyalty in times of crisis, they refuse to accept the validity of worldviews, ideas and even temperaments other than their own – Mrs Tulliver considers the imaginative and high-spirited Maggie 'a wild thing' (60) and 'half a idiot i' some things' (60), while her aunts think 'she's beyond everything for boldness and unthankfulness' (297). Maggie's continued conflict with the world of St Ogg's becomes emblematic of the novel's broader concern with the nature of the relationship between the individual and society, between independence of mind and conformity – a concern which makes *The Mill on the Floss* the most explicitly post-Romantic of George Eliot's major works.

However, Maggie's refusal to conform to the expectations of the society of St Ogg's is not merely a consequence of her fiery temperament and her intellectual curiosity: an important aspect of her rebellion against the world of the Dodsons is that she does not accept the restrictions which her family, community and culture impose on her because of her gender. In cutting her hair, in displaying an interest in learning Latin and in taking up employment in order to avoid having to join her mother to live with the Pullets, Maggie enters territories the nineteenth century associated, essentially, with masculinity; criticised or ridiculed for her supposedly misdirected ambitions ('[Girls] can pick up a little of everything [. . .]. They've a great deal of superficial cleverness: but they couldn't go far into anything. They're quick and shallow', 220–1), she becomes a victim of the kind of social and cultural prejudice which finds its culmination in the public condemnation she suffers following her ill-fated boating trip with Stephen. It is metaphorically appropriate that the decision that eventually causes Maggie's death – to row across the fields to Dorlcote Mill in an attempt to rescue her mother and brother – is also her ultimate act of defiance; it is her refusal to accept the passive role routinely associated with the conventional ideal of womanhood represented by her cousin Lucy Deane that precipitates the final catastrophe.

Thematically consistent with the rest of the novel as the scene of the flood may appear to be when read in the context of Maggie's continued struggle to assert her independence as an individual and as a woman, George Eliot's choice of ending in *The Mill on the Floss* has, nonetheless, often been criticised, on structural grounds, as arbitrary and therefore aesthetically unjustified (see, e.g., Nestor 2002: 71–2); the author herself admitted, shortly after finishing the novel, that 'the third volume has the material of a novel compressed into it' (*L*, III, 285). There is indeed little in the internal logic of the narrative to prepare for the sudden and unexpected twist that the story takes in the last chapter; in consequence, the ending of the novel, in which the shared grave of Tom and Maggie is visited by Lucy and Stephen, and by the 'always solitary' (656) Philip, may well appear to be a forced attempt to impose a semblance of a conventionally neat resolution on the rather complex situation in which the five central characters find themselves after Maggie's disgraced return to St Ogg's. On the other hand, the ending remains consistent with some of the key patterns of imagery recurring throughout the novel: the motif of water is used not only as a conventional symbol of the continuity of life and of the passage of time, but also, in the specific context of the rivers Ripple and Floss, and of Dorlcote Mill, as the symbol of the changeable fortunes of the Tulliver family, the source of their affluence and their downfall alike. The novel opens with the narrator watching the stream at the mill '[lying] high in this little withy plantation, and half drown[ing] the grassy fringe of the croft in front of the house' (54); Mrs Tulliver keeps 'telling [Maggie] to keep away from the water' (61) or else she will 'tumble in and be drownded some day' (61); the town of St Ogg's owes its name to the legend about a boatman who ferried the Virgin Mary across the river Floss and thus secured her blessing – 'from henceforth whoso steps into thy boat shall be in no peril from the storm, and whenever it puts forth to the rescue it shall save the lives both of men and beasts' (182); Mr Tulliver believes that 'when the mill changes hands, the river's angry' (352); finally, Maggie's destiny is compared to 'the course of an unmapped river' (514–15), and it is a trip down the river with Stephen that costs her her reputation and her position in society. In the concluding scene, the rebuilding of Dorlcote Mill marks the return of the local community back to stability, albeit in a new, changed form: though 'to the eyes that have dwelt on the past, there is no thorough repair' (656), five years later 'the desolation wrought by that flood, [has] left little visible trace on the face of the earth' (656), and 'the wharves and warehouses on the Floss [are] busy again, with echoes of eager voices, with hopeful lading and unlading' (656).

The critical reception of *The Mill on the Floss* was generally favourable, though not quite as enthusiastic as in the case of *Adam Bede* (see Works, p. 44) – not least, perhaps, for reasons to do with the ambivalence of the author's personal situation, which may well have coloured the perception of some of the novel's more controversial scenes. The majority of the early commentators noted the mastery of George Eliot's realistic observation of common life, both in its individual and collective aspect. As one of the critics put it, 'there is nothing in which George Eliot succeeds more conspicuously than in this very nice art of making her characters like real people, and yet shading them off into the large group which she is describing' (*CH*, 115–16). There was special praise for the presentation of Tom and Maggie as children – in their portraits, the author demonstrated that she 'possess[ed] in the highest degree the gift of knowing the child-soul in those things which are common to all children' (*CH*, 109) – and for the dynamism of the novel's insight into 'the development of character, from childhood to the spring of life' (*CH*, 127). However, some aspects of the novel were disapproved of; there was a wide agreement that the author's treatment of the story of Maggie's romance with Stephen was unsatisfactory, either because 'it is [not] quite consistent with feminine delicacy to lay so much stress on the bodily feelings of the other sex' (*CH*, 118) or because the very idea of Maggie falling in love with someone like Stephen is inconsistent with her character, 'at variance with all that had before been Heroic [*sic*!] about her' (*CH*, 121). About the ending of the novel, opinions were divided: while one critic compared the flood to the rescue of Hetty in *Adam Bede*, describing the two scenes as 'devices condescended to as external escapes from moral difficulties' (*CH*, 143), another saw it as fully consistent with the overall design of the story, with Tom and Maggie growing from the children into young adults 'even to the hour, when with that sense of the terrible exalted into the sublime, which only genius can make us feel – we see them go down to the deeps of the Floss' (*CH*, 156).

Silas Marner (1861)

George Eliot's third novel, *Silas Marner*, is both a continuation and a new departure. On the one hand, it focuses once again on the author's familiar territory, the Midlands of England as they were in the first quarter of the nineteenth century; 'a story of old-fashioned village life' (*L*, III, 371), it chooses as its subject a seemingly simple and yet powerful domestic tale in which ordinary, unheroic characters find themselves facing dramatic ethical choices, learning to function in new roles and situations and, in consequence, developing into more responsible, more understanding and, therefore, worthier individuals. On the other hand, *Silas Marner* is not just another clerical scene, nor indeed another visit down the author's memory lane: unlike George Eliot's earlier fictions, it is not based on any specific family anecdotes or on her childhood memories beyond a vague 'recollection of having once, in early childhood, seen a linen-weaver with a bag on his back' (*L*, III, 382), and if it does carry any biographical significance, it does so only indirectly, through its investigation of the moral and psychological aspects of problems such as parent–child relationships, childlessness and adoption (see Life and contexts, pp. 20–1). In artistic terms, although it does manage to retain the atmosphere of familiarity and spontaneity that characterised the author's previous works, *Silas Marner* is, nonetheless, a deceptively elaborate exercise in storytelling, in which the fairy-tale-like simplicity of the narrative disguises a structure that foreshadows, in its rejection of conventional patterns of plot construction, in its adoption of mystery as an important structural element of the narrative, and in its use of parallel story lines, the complexity of the author's later works.

The main action of the novel is set in the Midlands village of Raveloe, opening at an unspecified time during the Napoleonic wars, and continuing, after a sudden shift in the narrative, sixteen years later. The eponymous Silas Marner, a self-employed weaver, lives a lonely and embittered existence on the outskirts of the village. He had arrived there fifteen years before the main story takes off, having been excluded from the Calvinist community of Lantern Yard, in his unnamed home town in the north of England, following a false accusation of theft made against him by his best friend, William Dane, who subsequently married Silas's fiancée. One winter night, the weaver's miserly life is shattered when a large sum of money, which he has been obsessively saving over the years, is stolen from his cottage. The reader knows the thief is Dunstan Cass, a dissolute son of a local landowner. A few weeks later, on New Year's Eve, Silas finds in his room a small girl, the daughter of a woman discovered, on the same night, dead in the snow near his cottage. Dunstan's brother Godfrey recognises the dead woman as his own wife Molly, whom he has secretly married some time before and because of whom he has been blackmailed by Dunstan, who has not, however, been seen since the night Silas's money was stolen. Worried about compromising his reputation but at the same time relieved that he will now be free to marry Nancy Lammeter, whom he has been courting for some time, Godfrey does not disclose his connection with the child, or indeed with her mother; Silas, on the contrary, decides to raise the girl – whom he calls Eppie – as his own. Sixteen years later, the skeleton of Dunstan Cass is found after an old pit into which he had fallen on the night of the burglary dries up, following some draining work in the area. The shock of the discovery, and of the memories which it has evoked, brings Godfrey, now married to Nancy but childless, to confess to her the truth about Molly and Eppie. The Casses ask Eppie to take her rightful place in their home as Godfrey's daughter, but she refuses to leave Silas, the only father she has ever known and loved. Rather than contemplating the prospect of moving up in society, she chooses to marry Aaron, the son of her godmother Dolly Winthrop, intending, after the marriage, to continue to live with her father in her old community.

In the simplest of terms, the central story of *Silas Marner* is a parable of moral regeneration through parental and filial love – a theme encapsulated in the lines from Wordsworth's 'Michael' which serve as the epigraph to the novel ('A child, more than all other gifts / That earth can offer to declining man, / Brings hope with it, and forward-looking thoughts'). Silas Marner's life, which has over the years been 'narrowing and hardening itself more and more into a mere pulsation of desire and satisfaction that had no relation to any other being' (p. 68) is radically transformed when he adopts Eppie, who becomes for him 'an object compacted of changes and hopes that forced his thoughts onward, and carried them far away from their old eager pacing towards the same blank limit' (184). The circumstances surrounding Eppie's arrival in Silas's cottage imbue the novel with a strong allegorical quality: as he waits to hear the bells of Raveloe ring in the new year, 'the stillness and the wide trackless snow seem[ing] to narrow his solitude, and touch[ing] his yearning with the chill of despair' (167), he falls, without realising it, into a cataleptic trance, which makes it possible for him to experience a moment of discovery which makes him '[fall] on his knees and [bend] his head low to examine the marvel' (167). As he gradually returns to full consciousness, he sees, in front of his hearth, what at first appears to him to be a heap of gold, 'seem[ing] to glow and get larger beneath his agitated gaze' (167), but what in reality proves to be 'a sleeping child – a round, fair thing with soft yellow rings all over its head' (167), exhausted after she has made her way through the snow to the safety and warmth of Silas's room. In a characteristic George Eliot fashion, the moral vision underlying the allegory is purely human and secular and based on ethical rather than metaphysical premises; for all the quasi-miraculous character of the novel's central scene, the appearance of Eppie matters to Silas because it reawakens his long-suppressed ability to interact with other people – 'as the weeks grew to months, the child created fresh and fresh links between his life and the lives from which he had hitherto shrunk continually into narrower isolation' (184).

This humanist dimension of the story of Silas and Eppie becomes even more marked when contrasted with the novel's treatment of religion. Unlike in George Eliot's previous works, in which moral wisdom tends to be associated with characters – whether clergy of the Established Church, Dissenting ministers or Methodist preachers – whose essentially humanist morality coincides with active and honest, though not always particularly spiritual, Christian commitment, in *Silas Marner* ethical authority resides primarily with ordinary lay people whose allegiance to a particular church or creed matters far less than their sense of empathy, compassion and generosity to their neighbours. Dolly Winthrop's Christianity is simple to the point of ignorance as regards doctrine, but her sense of right and wrong never falters; an illiterate peasant, she may not understand the significance of the letters 'IHS' which she puts on her lard cakes or, in consequence, appreciate the theological inappropriateness of that practice, but in her gesture of sharing her cakes with Silas she transcends the limitations of theology and participates in an act of humanist communion that carries much more significance, in the process of Silas's moral regeneration, than any form of sacrament administered in any formal context of church or chapel. It is also through Dolly that George Eliot articulates the novel's fundamental message of human solidarity, in which God, as the supposedly ultimate moral arbiter, exercises no more authority than the ordinary men and women of Raveloe:

> [A]nd if a bit o' trouble comes, I feel as I can put up wi' it, for I've looked
> for help i' the right quarter, and gev myself up to Them as we must all
> give ourselves up to at the last; and if we 'n done our part, it isn't to be
> believed as Them as are above us 'ull be worse nor we are, and come
> short o' Their'n.
>
> (137–8)

By contrast, the religious communities depicted in the novel are clearly deficient in their ability to exercise the spirit of common humanity personified by Dolly Winthrop: the Rector of Raveloe Mr Crackenthorp is little more than a member of the local establishment, attending parties and dispensing moral platitudes – 'he admonished Silas that his money had probably been taken from him because he thought too much of it and never came to church' (130) – but failing to engage with the genuine concerns of the people of his parish. Even more dramatically, it is the failure of Silas's Lantern Yard congregation to recognise his earnestness and truthfulness that nearly destroys his humanity; their dogmatic refusal to apply the common mechanisms of justice – 'any resort to legal measures for ascertaining the culprit was contrary to the principles of the church in Lantern Yard, according to which prosecution was forbidden to Christians, even had the case held less scandal to the community' (60–1) – and their decision, inspired by their belief in Providence and 'immediate divine interference' (61), to resort instead to drawing lots demonstrates not only the emptiness of their superstitious approach to religion but also, and perhaps, in the light of the overall message of the novel, more significantly, their inability to exercise proper judgement of character and powers of compassion. It is by no means insignificant that on his return to the northern town of his childhood Silas is unable to find any traces of his old chapel or its congregation: for all the earnestness of their belief, the community of Lantern Yard cannot survive the replacement of the humanising influence of Silas's 'ardent faith and exemplary life' (56) by the self-serving hypocrisy of William Dane.

The scene of the expulsion of Silas from the Lantern Yard community is only one of the numerous examples of the crucial role played in the plot of *Silas Marner* by the operation of chance and coincidence. Dunstan Cass's riding accident, which triggers his decision to steal Silas's money, his subsequent drowning, Molly Cass's death in the vicinity of Silas's cottage, the discovery of Dunstan's body – all contribute to the impression of the instability and unpredictability of life that makes the world of the novel appear much more fragmented than in George Eliot's earlier works. There is, in *Silas Marner*, no trace of the relentless narrative logic that characterised the development of the plot of *Adam Bede* (see Works, pp. 36–44), nor much sense of the inevitability of the flow of time that organises the movement of *The Mill on the Floss* (see Works, pp. 44–51). On the contrary, the construction of the story of the weaver of Raveloe is based on the careful selection of isolated incidents, linked to each other through thematic connection rather than by the interlinked logic of character and action. This sense of the logical discontinuity of events is paralleled, on the level of character, by the stress on the unpredictability of Silas's fits of catalepsy: those moments of 'mysterious rigidity and suspension of consciousness' (56), which happen to coincide with some of the key moments in Silas's life, put into question the concept of the internal consistency of character and the possibility of objective perception and understanding of reality.

A similar sense of instability and uncertainty transpires through George Eliot's presentation of the social world of the novel. The juxtaposition of Raveloe and Silas's unnamed home town may at first appear to resemble the contrast between *Adam Bede*'s Hayslope and Snowfield (see Works, pp. 36–44), but the similarities are only superficial. The naively honest but narrow-minded and ultimately morally blind congregation of Lantern Yard is no match for the strong Methodist community which has nurtured Dinah Morris. Similarly, Raveloe itself may be 'a village where many the old echoes lingered, undrowned by new voices ... nestled in a snug well-wooded hollow, quite an hour's journey on horseback from any turnpike, where it was never reached by the vibrations of the coach-horn, or of public opinion' (53), but for all the semblances of Wordsworthian pastoralism it still lacks the organic unity of Hayslope. The recent history of the village has seen outsiders, such as Mr Cliff – 'a Lunnon tailor, some folks said, as had gone mad wi' cheating' (102) – come and go, leaving behind them memories of eccentric behaviour and buildings which are 'out o' all charicter' (103), and even some of the most respectable members of the community, the Lammeter family, are in fact relatively recent arrivals. Most importantly, the social atmosphere of the village has little of the sense of traditional paternalistic inclusiveness that characterises the world of *Adam Bede* – although 'Mr Macey and a few other privileged villagers' (158) attend the New Year's Eve dance at Squire Cass's Red House, they are, significantly, only 'allowed to be spectators ... seated on benches placed for them near the door' (158). The Casses are, in fact, hardly exemplary leaders of the community either – they are dysfunctional as a family, and their ways as individuals are at best disorganised and slovenly and at worst immoral or even plainly criminal. Even the general prosperity of the village has something potentially unstable about it: it is not so much a result of the efficiency of the local economy as a consequence of the favourable market conditions during the period of the Napoleonic wars; the narrator, possessed of the benefit of hindsight, is careful to point out that 'the fall of prices had not yet come to carry the race of small squires and yeomen down that road to ruin for which extravagant habits and bad husbandry were plentifully anointing their wheels' (71).

All the imperfections instabilities, and discontinuities that characterise the moral, social and economic world of Raveloe are personified in Godfrey Cass – the central character in the Cass–Lammeter sub-plot of the novel and the counterpart of Silas Marner in the overall structural pattern of the story. Like Silas, Godfrey undergoes a process of moral transformation, but his is in many ways a more complex case than Silas's: a victim primarily of 'his own ... wavering nature, too averse to facing difficulty to be unvaryingly simple and truthful' (219), rather than of other people's viciousness, he eventually confesses the truth about Eppie to his wife Nancy and receives her forgiveness, but, despite the healing power of his love for his wife – and hers for him – he still has to pay the price for his earlier moral cowardice: his marriage remains childless, and Eppie, alienated by his failure to acknowledge her as his daughter for sixteen years, refuses to choose him over Silas and to come to live with him in the Red House. The contrast between Silas and Godfrey is indeed central to the novel's message: the example of Godfrey qualifies the idealism of the allegorical fable of Silas's moral redemption without undermining its essential humanist vision. Grounded much more firmly than Silas in the realistically presented context of his family background and his social and economic circumstances, Godfrey is not only the novel's most profound psychological study but also its most telling example of George Eliot's sceptical but compassionate understanding of the complexities of human nature.

The critical response to *Silas Marner* was generally very positive, more so than in the case of *The Mill on the Floss* (see Works, p. 51). Most critics saw the novel as a return to the pastoral mode of *Adam Bede* (see Works, pp. 36–44), designed on a smaller scale but executed with an unrivalled artistic assurance – a view best summarised by the opinion that, while '*Adam Bede* still remains perhaps the author's greatest production ... within its limits, *Silas Marner* is quite equal to either of its predecessors, and, in combining the display of the author's characteristic excellences with freedom from blemishes and defects, is perhaps superior' (*CH*, 174). The features of the novel which were singled out for critical praise included, predictably perhaps, its 'truthfulness' (*CH*, 179) and its 'complete correlation between the characters and their circumstances' (*CH*, 186–7), as well as 'the strong intellectual impress which the author contrives to give to a story of which the main elements are altogether unintellectual, without the smallest injury to the verisimilitude of the tale' (*CH*, 176). Although a few of the reviewers were not satisfied with what they saw as the coarseness and dullness of George Eliot's subject matter ('her characters were never remarkable for pleasantness, but here they make themselves more than usually disagreeable', *CH*, 190), *Silas Marner* was soon accepted as representing the author at her most successful and least controversial; the subversive potential of the novel was not properly appreciated until well into the twentieth century.

Romola (1862–3)

In many ways, George Eliot's fourth novel is the least characteristic of her major works. It is the only major prose narrative of hers not to use the familiar setting of provincial England, the only one to be set in a distant rather than recent past, and the only one to incorporate into its fictional world characters and settings taken, in a quasi-documentary manner reminiscent of the writings of Sir Walter Scott, from the actual historical reality in which the action of the novel is supposed to be taking place. By far the most thoroughly researched and meticulously documented of the author's works, *Romola* is indeed, in some respects, both more and less than a novel; in so far as works of fiction can be read as historical studies, it can to this day serve as an authoritative and reliable source of general information on, and as a critical analysis of, the dramatic events that shaped the history of Florence in the years following the death, in 1492, of Lorenzo de' Medici. At the same time, however, it is the one among George Eliot's major fictions in which the author is commonly agreed to have been at her least inspired and spontaneous – though by no means at her least ambitious or competent – as regards her creation of character or her construction of incident and plot. Likened to 'a great Victorian public building ... it shares with them a majesty, a sobriety, a completeness, and a scholarship, but it remains somehow bloodless and unlovable, perhaps, given the nature of its form and function, necessarily unlovable' (Sanders 1978: 196) – *Romola* is one of the most carefully designed of George Eliot's novels, matched in this respect perhaps only by *Middlemarch* (see Works, pp. 67–80), and yet it is the one that is probably the least well-known and the least admired among general readers: 'a book which it is more interesting to analyse than simply to read' (Hardy 1959: 175). It is also, very importantly, the work that constituted a turning point in George Eliot's literary career. Not only did the circumstances of its publication finally confirm its author's arrival as one of the most respected, influential and financially successful prose writers of her day, but also the very process of the creation of the novel changed her as an artist and as a person. As she famously said: '[She] began it a young woman, – [she] finished it an old woman' (Cross, II, 352) (see Life and contexts, **pp. 21–2**).

The plot of *Romola* is very complex, much more so than in any of George Eliot's earlier works. In April 1492, a young Italian-born Greek, Tito Melema, finds himself, in the aftermath of a shipwreck, in the city of Florence; thanks to his affability, intelligence and good education, he quickly makes his way into Florentine society, befriending, among others, the blind scholar Bardo de' Bardi and his daughter Romola, whom he begins to court. Determined to find his feet in his new environment, Tito decides to ignore the fate of his adoptive father, the Classical scholar Baldassarre Calvo, who has gone missing, while on a journey to the Greek island of Delos after the capture of his boat by the Turks; rather than go in search of Baldassarre, Tito stays in Florence and begins to build up a reputation as a scholar and a wit, which quickly brings him into contact with members of the city's intellectual, social and political elite, now facing a time of increased tension following the death of the state's powerful ruler Lorenzo de' Medici and the emergence of a popular anti-aristocratic movement under the spiritual leadership of the influential Dominican preacher, Fra Girolamo Savonarola. As time goes by – the main action of the novel extends over six years – Tito becomes increasingly involved in the public life of the city, manoeuvring his way between the various political groupings and gradually assuming the role of a double agent, using his operations in Florence for material gain and as a stepping stone to a future career in the richer and more powerful environments of Milan or Rome. In the meantime, Tito's personal situation is as complex as his public life. Though now married to Romola, he continues his relationship with the naive peasant-girl Tessa, whom he has deluded into 'marrying' him in a sham wedding ceremony. Their liaison results, in due course, in the birth of two children. Tito's elaborate structure of half-truths, secrets and cover-ups begins to crumble when he is confronted in public by Baldassarre, brought to Florence by a series of coincidences following his release from captivity. Tito denies having ever met his adoptive father, as a result of which the old man, now not only impoverished but also reduced through a form of amnesia to a shadow of his former self, makes it his last goal in life to take his revenge on the young Greek. Tito and Romola's marriage collapses as well, following Tito's sale, after the death of his father-in-law, of his library, originally intended by Bardo for the use of the people of Florence. Romola decides to leave her husband but is persuaded to return when Savonarola, who becomes for her, brought up as a non-believer, a spiritual and moral guide, reminds her of her duty towards her husband and her fellow citizens. However, Savonarola's influence on Romola is not destined to last: she becomes disillusioned by his dogmatic refusal to use his influence to save the life of her godfather, Bernardo del Nero, sentenced to death for alleged treachery, and she decides, once again, to leave Florence. After abandoning herself to destiny as she sets out to sea in a small boat, she eventually lands in a plague-stricken village, where she looks after the sick and the dying in a manner that makes the villagers think of her as the Virgin Mary. In the meantime, in Florence, a complex pattern of circumstances leads up to a dramatic climax. When Tito's duplicitous activities are discovered by the leaders of the aristocratic party of the Compagnacci, he has to make a dramatic escape from the city by jumping into the river Arno and swimming away. Exhausted, he is washed ashore right at the feet of Baldassarre.

In his final, desperate effort, the old man manages to strangle Tito and dies while still clutching the neck of his tunic. The death of Tito coincides with the fall of Savonarola. His execution at the stake, in May 1498, is witnessed by Romola, who, having returned to Florence, finds Tessa and sets up home together with her and her children. The death of Savonarola closes the main action of the novel; the Epilogue, set in May 1509, rounds off the tale with its vision of Romola reflecting, in her conversation with Tessa's son Lillo, on the moral lessons emerging from the stories of Tito and Savonarola.

The fact that the narrative framework within which George Eliot constructs her fictional world is defined in strict reference to historical fact is both the most characteristic feature of the artistic form of *Romola* and, for many readers, its major weakness. On the one hand, the novel's recreation of the world of Renaissance Florence is meticulous not only in its attention to historical and topographical detail – *Romola* can to this day be read as a literary guidebook to the city – but also as a study in social history, with its elaborate descriptions of religious services, processions, public gatherings, popular fairs, as well as details of the social and domestic life of a broad spectrum of Florentines, from the rich Bernardo Rucellai to the simple peasant family of Tessa. However, for all the accuracy and comprehensiveness of her historical vision, George Eliot's pre-occupation with detail may at times appear to take a dynamics of its own, at the expense of the story itself, thus turning the narrative into a sheer exhibition of the author's historical erudition. This is the case with passages such as the description of the historical origin and the contemporaneous context of the celebration, in 1492, of 'the great summer festival of Florence, the day of San Giovanni' (p. 131), which does indeed seem to lack the sense of direct, immediate relevance to the novel's central thematic concerns that characterised, for example, the descriptions of the life of the people of St Ogg's in *The Mill on the Floss* (see Works, pp. 44–51). To a reader unfamiliar with the history and culture of fifteenth-century Florence, the novel may indeed seem rather too densely allusive, both in its presentation of characters based on actual historical figures, such as the writer and political philosopher Niccolò dei Machiavelli and the painter Piero di Cosimo, and in the way it introduces references to the art, architecture and literature, both of Classical antiquity and of Renaissance Italy. Even in purely linguistic terms, George Eliot's pursuit of antiquarian accuracy can sometimes result in a loss of dramatic effectiveness and, indeed, fictional credibility: the speech of a number of the novel's characters is peppered with Italianisms, lexical as well as stylistic, which are clearly meant to convey to the reader something of the col-loquial flavour of the language the people of Renaissance Florence may be assumed to have spoken (' "*Ebbene*", said Bratti, raising his voice to speak across the cart; "I leave you with Nello, young man, for there's no pushing my bag and basket any farther, and I have business at home" ', 72), but which also create an impression of artificiality and obscurity, particularly for readers without a basic knowledge of Italian and, to a lesser extent, Latin.

However important the rendering of the past is in the overall construction of *Romola*, what differentiates it from most other historical fictions of the nineteenth century is its predominantly moral and psychological focus. Unlike, for example, the novels of Sir Walter Scott, whose largely adventure-based plots tended to be constructed using the dynamics of contrasting characters and environments representative of opposing forces involved in the processes of social and political change, *Romola* depends for its narrative thrust not so much on the interactions between its protagonists as on the consequences of the ethical choices that the protagonists have to make. In consequence, the novel becomes a complex, dynamic psychological study; through her presentation of her central characters, George Eliot analyses the mechanisms of the operation of fundamental human desires and instincts, ranging from love and compassion to ambition, hatred and fear. The pride of place belongs, in this respect, to Tito Melema – by far the most complex of the novel's psychological portraits, he is a subtle study of the moral degeneration of a man whose 'unconquerable aversion to anything unpleasant, even when an object very much loved and desired was on the other side of it' (161) gradually transforms him from an ordinary if somewhat self-centred young man, not unlike Captain Wybrow from 'Mr Gilfil's Love-Story' (see Works, pp. 34–5) or *Adam Bede*'s Arthur Donnithorne (see Works, pp. 36–44), into a cold, calculating egoist, prepared to sacrifice the lives and happiness of those closest to him to further his own plans and ambitions. The narrator focuses on those moments in Tito's life when he has to make fundamental moral choices, such as during 'his first real colloquy with himself' (149), when he has to decide whether to stay in Florence or go in search of Baldassarre, or later on, when he faces the choice of whether or not to warn Savonarola of the Compagnacci's plan to kidnap him. Importantly, Tito is not a personification of all evil: not entirely devoid of a sense of right and wrong, he is capable, when making dubious moral choices, of feeling 'the inward shame, the reflex of that outward law which the great heart of mankind makes for every individual man, a reflex which will exist even in the absence of the sympathetic impulses that need no law' (151), and he can recognise and admit his errors, even if his is not 'repentance with a white sheet round it and taper in hand, confessing its hated sin in the eyes of men' (376), but 'a repentance that would make all things pleasant again, and keep all past unpleasant things secret' (376). The sheer ordinariness of Tito's emotions, evident in his exploitative, but nonetheless instinctively natural and sexually fulfilling relationship with Tessa and in his increasingly strong sense of fear of the disclosure of his guilty secrets, makes his moral degradation all the more convincing, and all the more frightening.

The second of the main plots of *Romola* – the story of the fluctuating mentor-pupil relationship that develops between Savonarola and Romola – introduces some of the novel's central philosophical themes, as significant in the context of Renaissance Italy as they were in Victorian Britain: the question of the nature of moral and religious authority, the relationship between morality and religion and the nature of public and private duty. George Eliot's portrayal of Savonarola is, in a way, profoundly respectful of the sincerity of his commitment to his cause, 'the energy of his emotions and beliefs' (434), and his capacity for empathy, encapsulated in 'a gaze in which simple human fellowship expressed itself as a strongly felt bond' (429); at the same time, however, it acknowledges the fundamental dilemma which 'made half the tragedy of his life – the struggle of a mind possessed by a never-silent hunger after purity and simplicity, yet caught in a tangle of egoistic demands, false ideas, and difficult outward conditions, that made simplicity impossible' (576). Savonarola manages to avoid the kind of petty personal egoism that precipitates the downfall of Tito, but he distils his own capacity for selfishness into something more powerful, and potentially – and indeed actually – more dangerous: a prophetic, fundamentalist vision that equates religious conviction with political commitment in a manner that usurps divine authority and disregards the common human sense of individual justice, fairness and compassion:

> 'I have to choose that which will further the work intrusted to me. The end I seek is one to which minor respects must be sacrificed. The death of five men . . . is a light matter weighed against the withstanding of the vicious tyrannies which stifle the life of Italy, and foster the corruption of the Church; a light matter weighed against the furthering of God's kingdom upon earth, the end for which I live and am willing myself to die. . . . The cause of my party *is* the cause of God's kingdom.'
>
> (577–8)

In contrast, Romola represents the pure spirit of humanism; raised by her father in profound scepticism as regards matters of religious belief, she craves spiritual guidance, which she finds, at first, in Savonarola's vision of the kingdom of God and, more importantly, in his message of duty and renunciation. Ultimately, however, as Savonarola's religious intransigence comes into open conflict with her own sense of humanity and compassion, she develops her own metaphysical vision, in which she rejects his theological interpretation of the world in favour of one in which God is effectively replaced by the fellowship of all humans: 'God's kingdom is something wider – else, let me stand outside it with the beings that I love' (578). Romola realises her ideal, which foreshadows the concept of the religion of humanity (see Life and contexts, **pp. 14–15**), first when she carries her newly reinterpreted message of duty – 'so energetic an impulse to share the life around her, to answer the call of need and do the work which cried aloud to be done, that the reasons for living, enduring, labouring, never took the form of argument' (650) – to the unnamed (and thus universalised) valley in which she lands after her departure from Florence, as well as later on, when on her return to the city she takes care of Tessa and her children.

This transformation of Romola into a Madonna-like character and a personification of the fundamental humanistic values of compassion and generosity brings into focus the crucially important symbolic dimension of the novel. Rather paradoxically in view of its insistence on the truthfulness of its representation of the past and the accuracy of its historical references, George Eliot's artistic method in *Romola* goes far beyond conventional realism; all the key elements of the structure of the text – the setting, the characters, the incidents, the pace and focus of the narrative – are carefully patterned to create a web of symbolic meanings contributing to the novel's overall existential and ethical message. A particularly important place belongs, in this respect, to visual images – diverse in form, from the deathbed visions of Dino de' Bardi, through the allusive paintings of Piero di Cosimo, to tableau-like passages in which the action slows down almost to a standstill, as in the scene of Baldassarre's first encounter with Tito on the steps of the Duomo ('it seemed a long while to them – it was but a moment', 283), they acquire an almost allegorical quality, focusing the attention of the reader on the central moral and philosophical problems of the novel. The extent to which the demands of the symbolic structure of the text are convincingly integrated into the narrative logic of the story varies: while Tito's symbolic purchase of a coat of mail – his 'garment of fear' (301) – is fully justified in the light of the danger in which he finds himself following Baldassarre's arrival in Florence, some of the other significant motifs and episodes – such as the story of Tito's ring, or the climactic scene of Baldassarre's murder of Tito and his own subsequent death – rely on coincidence and forced manipulation of the plot in a manner that stretches the fictional credibility of the narrative rather too far.

The critical reception of *Romola* reflected the contrast between the complexity and ambition of its design and its lack of the kind of popular appeal that characterised George Eliot's earlier works. As one of the critics put it: 'It cannot be denied that *Romola* is less popular than its predecessors, but we do not hesitate to say that it is its author's greatest work' (*CH*, 213). The general feeling was that George Eliot did herself little favour when she decided to move her attention from her familiar territory of early nineteenth-century provincial England to the distant world of Renaissance Italy. Although a number of critics saw the relevance, to the contemporaneous world of Victorian Britain, of the book's central purpose – 'to trace out the conflict between liberal culture and the more passionate form of the Christian faith in that strange era, which has so many points of resemblance with the present' (*CH*, 200) – it was generally agreed that, for all the precision of the presentation of the novel's historical detail, 'neither the politics nor the people are really alive, – they are only well dried, preserved and coloured, and the reader feels as though he were ungrateful, in not being better entertained by all that has cost so much time and labour' (*CH*, 197). The author's familiar strengths – such as, in particular, 'the minute analysis of moral growth' (*CH*, 214) – were duly noted, although there was no unanimity about the relative quality of the individual character studies, with some critics praising the presentation of Tito ('nothing can surpass the skill with which he is displayed, gradually entangled in the web of his own subtleties', *CH*, 217), and others preferring Romola or Savonarola. Predictably, there was criticism of the manipulation of the plot in search of 'those extravagantly fortuitous circumstances of which the author makes such free use' (*CH*, 220). On balance, the book was respected rather than liked:

> As a novel *Romola* cannot be called entertaining: it requires sustained attention, and it is by no means light reading; but those who do not seek the mere amusement of an exciting story will find noble things in *Romola* – eloquent and beautiful pages – subtle utterances and lovely thoughts. It has not the powerful interest that is to be found in the author's former novels; but there are indications of much higher powers of mind.
>
> (*CH*, 198)

Felix Holt, the Radical (1866)

George Eliot's fifth novel, *Felix Holt, the Radical*, belongs with its predecessor, *Romola* (see Works, pp. 56–61), to the transitional period of the author's career. While, on the one hand, it returns to the familiar territory of the Midlands of

England and to the period of the writer's childhood – the novel is set in the years 1832–3 – it has, on the other hand, little of the sense of emotional spontaneity and directness that characterised *Adam Bede* (see Works, pp. 36–44) or *The Mill on the Floss* (see Works, pp. 44–51). Although the setting of the novel, the town of Treby Magna and its environs, is vaguely based on Nuneaton, where the young Mary Anne Evans herself witnessed, in December 1832, an election riot which provided her with the inspiration for one the key scenes of her story, there is relatively little else in the text that corresponds directly to the author's personal or family background. Instead, *Felix Holt* shares with *Romola* the attentive approach to the presentation of carefully researched details of the social, political and cultural background against which the main action of the novel is played out. In consequence, the vision of the life of rural England in the period immediately following the passage of the 1832 Reform Bill (see Life and contexts, pp. 2–3) is, in *Felix Holt*, contrived rather than organic, deriving not so much from the author's first-hand experience of the reality she was describing as from her extensive study of the history of the period, particularly in its political aspect.

In addition, *Felix Holt* marks a number of new departures in the development of George Eliot's career as a novelist. In a manner rather similar to *Romola*, the first of George Eliot's novels of public life, *Felix Holt* is the first of her full-length works to attempt an analysis of the mechanisms of power and authority operating across the broad cross-section of modern British society, from country gentry (Sir Maximus Debarry and his family) to the urban and rural proletariat – a topical issue at the time of writing, with the public debate over the question of electoral reform, which was to culminate in the passage of the second Reform Bill of 1867, inevitably evoking the memories of, and inviting comparisons with, the eventful period of the early 1830s. At the same time, *Felix Holt* is also the first of the author's novels to depend, for the structuring of the main events of the story and for the maintenance of its narrative tension, on the kind of mystery plot that was a characteristic feature of the later work of Dickens and that proved particularly influential in the 1860s, with the recent emergence of the popular genre of the sensation novel, practised by writers such as Wilkie Collins, Mrs Henry Wood and Mary Elizabeth Braddon. In both these respects, *Felix Holt* prepares the way for the major works of George Eliot's last period, in particular for her next novel, *Middlemarch* (see Works, pp. 67–80), with which it shares its historical context and some of its themes; it is, in fact, something of an irony that it is largely because of the fact that it constitutes something of a stepping stone towards the author's monumental achievement in the latter work that *Felix Holt* – a novel lesser than *Middlemarch*, but not without its own merits – is often perceived as one of the least interesting of her fictions and one of the least successful artistically.

Part of the reason for the relative unpopularity of *Felix Holt* among literary critics and general readers alike is the immense intricacy of its plot, with its complex interplay of events constituting the main action of the novel on the one hand and the underlying histories involving the majority of its central characters on the other: the emergence of the truth about the parentage of Esther Lyon and Harold Transome, and about the complexity of the legal status of the Transome estate, is crucial to the unfolding of the novel's central moral and psychological drama. The problem is that the nature of the underlying complications, involving a complex will, changed identities, undisclosed illegitimacy, etc., is conveyed to the reader piece by piece, and through different narrative viewpoints: although the story is told, throughout, by a third-person narrator, the shifts of perspective between the various characters playing, at various points, the role of the detective (Rufus Lyon, Matthew Jermyn, Maurice Christian [alias Henry Scaddon], and others) make the piecing together of the details of the plot – in itself complex enough for the author herself to have needed extensive legal advice while constructing it (see L, IV, 216ff.) – a rather difficult and confusing task.

The main story of *Felix Holt* focuses on events surrounding the general election of December 1832 in and around Treby, a polling place in the Tory-dominated constituency of North Loamshire. The election is contested, among others, by sons of two local gentry families: Philip Debarry, the son of Sir Maximus Debarry of Treby Manor, standing on the Tory ticket; and Harold Transome, the only surviving son of the Transomes of Transome Court, standing as a Radical. Harold, returned to England, following the death of his imbecile elder brother Durfey, in September 1832, after fifteen years spent as a successful businessman in the Ottoman Empire, appoints as his electoral agent the family lawyer, Matthew Jermyn. However, their relationship deteriorates rapidly as a result of Harold's disapproval of the canvassing methods adopted by Jermyn's campaigners, as well as in consequence of his discovery of Jermyn's unduly powerful – and dishonest – influence over the financial management of the Transome estate. Jermyn's position vis-à-vis the Transomes, though, is too strong for Harold to fight. Not only does he appear to have the ear of Harold's mother, but also he has at his disposal information which he can use to keep Harold in check: his accidental discovery of the true parentage of Esther Lyon, the stepdaughter of the Treby Dissenting minister, Rufus Lyon, gives Jermyn a vital piece of information relevant to the legal implications of the will of John Justus Transome, an early eighteenth-century ancestor of Harold's, which undermines the Transome family's title to the ownership of the estate of Transome Court and which Jermyn can therefore exploit to blackmail Harold. In the meantime, Harold's vaguely progressive political programme ('we've got Reform, gentlemen, but now the thing is to make reform work', 225–6) is challenged by Felix Holt, the son of the widow of a Treby apothecary; Felix's radicalism, developed during his apprenticeship in Glasgow, involves a powerful element of religious and moral idealism, which he refines in his discussions with Mr Lyon and Esther. On the day of the election, a riot breaks out at Treby. Felix's attempts to control the mob do not succeed, and the disturbances end with the deaths of two people – one of whom is Tommy Trounsem, an impoverished descendant of the Transome family, whose demise makes it possible for Esther to claim ownership of Transome Court. Found guilty of manslaughter, despite a last-minute testimony from Esther, whom he visited on the day of the riot, Felix is sentenced to four years' imprisonment. The Transomes are prepared to surrender the estate to Esther, but she eventually decides to resign all her claims to it. She rejects Harold's offer of marriage and instead chooses to marry Felix, released from prison after obtaining a reprieve through the influence of his Treby friends and supporters, led by Sir Maximus Debarry. Jermyn loses his fight against the Transomes after his last weapon against Harold – his disclosure that he is in fact Harold's natural father – badly misfires. With his reputation now in ruins, he is forced to leave the town, while the Transomes, after spending some time away, eventually return home to reclaim their place in the Treby establishment.

With all of its major characters involved, to a greater or lesser extent, in the political life of Treby Magna, the plot of the novel reflects the narrator's observation that 'there is no private life which has not been determined by a wider public life, from the time when the primeval milkmaid had to wander with the wanderings of her clan, because the cow she milked was one of a herd which had made the pastures bare' (p. 129). The novel's vision of that public life is indeed, in many respects, one of a dynamic process of profound transformation, with the development of new mining and manufacturing industries, the resulting changes in social structure, the increasing diversity of religious belief, and the emergence of new modes of political thinking, culminating in the movement towards political reform, with all its practical consequences:

> If the mixed political conditions of Treby Magna had not been acted on by the passing of the Reform Bill, Mr Harold Transome would not have presented himself as a candidate for North Loamshire, Treby would not have been a polling-place, Mr Matthew Jermyn would not have been on affable terms with a Dissenting preacher and his flock, and the venerable town would not have been placarded with handbills, more or less complimentary and retrospective.
>
> (129–30)

And yet, for all the modernity of the world of *Felix Holt*, the reference to the 'primeval milkmaid' is not a mere rhetorical flourish – paradoxically, despite all the impact of progress and change, the social and political reality of North Loamshire is still deeply rooted in the traditional beliefs and patterns of behaviour developed in the past. The advent of reform has not, for example, changed the basic modes of the operation of party politics: although the Reform Bill has supposedly removed some of the worst abuses of the British electoral system (see Life and contexts, pp. 2–3), it has not succeeded in eradicating paternalism (the Tory nominations remain, effectively, a family affair of the Debarrys), bribery (as practised by Harold's cynical agent John Johnson), or voter intimidation ('Mr Chubb, who wished it to be noticed that he voted for Garstin solely, was one of the first to get rather more notice than he wished, and . . . he had his hat knocked off and crushed in the interest of Debarry by Tories opposed to coalition', 412). Even Radicalism, the new force aiming to shake up the existing political system, dominated as it has traditionally been by 'a stupid set of old Whigs and Tories' (96), is amorphous, directionless and divided, unable to formulate a coherent and meaningful political programme. Its self-proclaimed champion, the rich and privileged Harold Transome, proves unable, for all his education, intelligence and practical business acumen, to define his political ideas in terms that would go beyond vague statements such as 'I am a Radical only in rooting out abuses' (121) or 'I remove the rotten timbers . . . and substitute fresh oak, that's all' (121), while one of the strongest – though, one might suspect, rather awkward – endorsements he receives comes from a working-class leader postulating revolutionary changes foreshadowing the demands of the Chartist movement:

'And to pinch them enough, we must get the suffrage, we must get votes, that we may send the men to parliament who will do our work for us; and we must have parliament dissolved every year, that we may change our man if he doesn't do what we want him to do; and we must have the country divided so that the little kings of the counties can't do as they like, but must be shaken up in one bag with us. I say, if we working men are ever to get a man's share, we must have universal suffrage, and annual parliaments, and the vote by ballot, and electoral districts.'

(397)

The political message of *Felix Holt* is, however, not only to expose the ambivalence of the idea of Radicalism but also to convey a more positive socio-political vision. The novel's eponymous hero, who wants 'to go to some roots a good lower down than the franchise' (368) and 'to give every man a man's share in life' (399), proposes an alternative model of social and political progress – one that underlines, as a necessary condition of the successful functioning of a democratic system, the importance of the political and moral education of common people, growing out of the organic process of social development:

'Now, all the schemes about voting, and districts, and annual parliaments, and the rest, are engines, and the water or steam – the force that is to work them – must come out of human nature – out of men's passions, feelings, desires. . . . I'll tell you what's the greatest power under heaven, . . . and that is public opinion – the ruling belief in society about what is right and what is wrong, what is honourable and what is shameful. That's the steam that is to work the engines. . . . And while public opinion is what it is – while men have no better beliefs about public duty – while corruption is not felt to be a damning disgrace – while men are not ashamed in parliament and out of it to make public questions which concern the welfare of millions a mere screen for their own petty private ends, – I say, no fresh scheme of voting will much mend our condition.'

(400–1)

The extent to which Felix's declaration can be seen as reflecting the author's own views is of course a matter of speculation – Felix's credibility is after all, it may be argued, undermined by his tendency towards dogmatism, evident in some of his conversations with his mother and with Esther. At the same time, however, the fact that George Eliot returned to the discussion of the central ideas of Felix's political ideology in her 'Address to Working Men, by Felix Holt', published, at the suggestion of John Blackwood, in 1868, soon after the passage of the second Reform Bill, seems to indicate that she had come to perceive Felix not so much as a mere character in one of her novels, but as a masque which had acquired some form of autonomous life and which she was prepared to use as a mouthpiece for her own political opinions.

However effective *Felix Holt* may be in focusing the attention of the reader on some of the central concerns of the political debate in Britain in the nineteenth century, the way in which it integrates its political message into the fictional fabric of its story remains relatively less convincing. Harold Transome and Felix Holt may be juxtaposed both as aspiring political leaders and as Esther's suitors, but the way in which they are presented does not generate enough dramatic tension to carry the story along. This is, primarily, a consequence of the rather schematic presentation of the character of Felix: at first 'outrageously ill-bred' (211), speaking 'bluntly' (142) and in 'loud abrupt tones' (140), he has to discover, through love, a softer, more understanding side of himself – 'some subtle, mysterious conjuncture of impressions and circumstances' (419) – that can transform him from an aspiring community leader on a mission into a romantic lover. Because he has relatively little room to develop – not nearly as much as some of George Eliot's other central characters – he remains, for all his idealism and for all his noble ambitions and intentions, a rather unconvincing figure, particularly when contrasted with Harold, whose complex attitude to his family, to his social and cultural heritage and to the problems he faces in his political activity offers far more opportunities for psychological analysis and for the investigation of moral dilemmas, such as those following his discovery of Jermyn's duplicity. Even in the case of Harold, though, George Eliot does not seem to make full use of the narrative potential of her plot: the disclosure, by Jermyn, of the fact that he is Harold's natural father may retrospectively explain a number of earlier developments in the plot, but it fails to generate sufficient dramatic and psychological tension to move the story along, functioning instead as a somewhat anticlimactic quasi-resolution of the novel's central conflict.

This is, however, not to say that *Felix Holt* lacks convincing analysis of character and motivation altogether: in her delineation of Harold's mother, Mrs Transome, George Eliot creates not only by far the most memorable of her portraits of mature women but also one of the few characters in her œuvre who, while remaining thoroughly convincing in the context of the novel's overall realistic vision, at the same time manage to achieve the kind of dramatic power and psychological intensity that makes their predicament comparable to those of the protagonists of classical tragedy. Mrs Transome's fate is determined by the inexorable consequences of an error she committed in her youth, one for which 'she [is] not penitent' (595) as 'she [has] borne too hard a punishment' (595) for it: her love for Harold, which sustains her throughout the years ('she had clung to the belief that somehow the possession of this son was the best thing she lived for; to believe otherwise would have made her memory too ghastly a companion', 98) is at the same time bound, sooner or later, to cause her ultimate suffering as 'all the pride of [Harold's] nature rebel[s] against his sonship' (584). Mrs Transome is no saint, and no reformed sinner: she does not love her eldest son, and she does not fight in herself 'a hungry desire, like a black poisonous plant feeding in the sunlight, – the desire that her first, rickety, ugly, imbecile child should die, and leave room for her darling, of whom she could be proud' (97–8), but she maintains, throughout her life, a sense of dignity that accepts the tragic inevitability of the loss of the kind of love that gives meaning to her life:

> The mother's love is at first an absorbing delight, blunting all other sensibilities; it is an expansion of the animal existence; it enlarges the imagined range for self to move in: but in after years it can only continue to be joy on the same terms as other long-lived love – that is, by much

suppression of self, and power of living in the experience of another. Mrs Transome had darkly felt the pressure of that unchangeable fact.

(98)

The critical reception of *Felix Holt* was initially quite positive: it was described as a 'rich and fascinating story' (*CH*, 258) and 'a work of rare genius' (*CH*, 264). Much of the praise focused, predictably perhaps, on George Eliot's presentation of the familiar world of provincial England:

> The talk of miners over their ale; of the respectable farmers and shop-keepers over their three-and-sixpenny ordinary in the country market-town; of the upper servants in the butler's pantry of an old manor-house, is as witty and as truthful, and in its own way as artistically admirable, as anything that the writer has ever done.
>
> (*CH*, 253)

There was ample praise of the 'intellectual insight and humour which sparkle over the whole surface of the story' (*CH*, 262) and of the way George Eliot 'enlists our sympathies in the lives of her characters – good and bad – with a heartiness which few other . . . writers can even rival' (*CH*, 265). At the same time, there was a sense that George Eliot's handling of her material was less assured than in her earlier works: Felix Holt was called 'a grand *stump* of a character in an impressive but fixed attitude' (*CH*, 259), while the structure of the narrative was seen as flawed because 'in some part of [the] work there is not sufficient movement, and . . . in others where the movement is quite sufficient it lacks continuity' (*CH*, 265). Perhaps the harshest criticism came from the man who was to become the greatest writer among George Eliot's critics: Henry James, while stressing that 'the critic finds it no easy task to disengage himself from the spell of so much power, so much brilliancy, and so much discretion' (*CH*, 273), criticised the novel for the artificiality of its plot and the lack of clear narrative focus – clearly a reflection of the new, pre-modernist aesthetic tastes, stressing the importance, in the construction of works of fiction, of the kind of formal unity which the novels of James himself were over the following decades to exemplify.

Middlemarch (1871–2)

Generally acclaimed as its author's finest achievement, *Middlemarch* is in many ways the culmination of the fifteen-year-long process of George Eliot's development as a literary artist. It brings together the familiarity of the provincial settings of her early fictions (see Works, pp. 32–56) and the elaborate structural complexity of *Romola* (see Works, pp. 56–61), and it successfully integrates the trademarks of her narrative method, such as detailed observation of the psychology of her characters and comprehensive analysis of their moral dilemmas, with the kind of near-documentary reconstruction and analysis of the social, economic and political reality of her settings – in this case, provincial England of the late 1820s and early 1830s – that she first attempted in *Romola* and subsequently translated into the context of modern Britain in *Felix Holt* (see Works, pp. 61–7). In its presentation of a broad, comprehensive and essentially realistic picture of society, and in creating the impression that its plot emerges, in an organic fashion, out of a series of interactions between a well-defined group of distinctively drawn central characters, *Middlemarch* follows the model of some of the most successful of George Eliot's earlier works, such as *Adam Bede* (see Works, **pp. 36–44**). At the same time, it displays the kind of careful patterning of plot and character that characterises the author's more overtly symbolic works, such as *Silas Marner* (see Works, **pp. 51–6**) and *Romola*, while managing to avoid, despite its use of elements of the mystery convention, the excesses of the overcomplicated design of *Felix Holt*. Considered in the broader context of the development of nineteenth-century fiction, *Middlemarch* combines the subtlety of psychological insight and the acuteness of the observation of the mores of modern society that characterise the works of Jane Austen with the understanding of the processes of history that underlies the novels of Sir Walter Scott, and it brings together the scope and power of vision typical of the works of Dickens, the domestic realism of Elizabeth Gaskell, the easy, relaxed storytelling manner of Anthony Trollope and the symbolic intensity of the novels of the Brontës. One of the most ambitious and the most complex of the novels of its time, *Middlemarch* has often been seen as the quintessential expression of the literary spirit of the mid-Victorian era and as the most comprehensive illustration of the artistic possibilities afforded by its genre; frequently described as the most powerful achievement of Victorian fiction, it is a work which, in the words of Henry James, 'sets a limit . . . to the development of the old-fashioned English novel' (*CH*, 359), while at the same time providing something of an aesthetic standard, an encapsulation of the intellectual, moral and artistic values of the mid- to late nineteenth century, admired, neglected or rebelled against as generations of readers have been making their changing responses to the world of Victorian Britain.

The composition of *Middlemarch*, which took George Eliot more than three years in all, was a rather complex process, particularly in its early stages; this was to do both with the author's difficult domestic circumstances at the time (see Life and contexts, **pp. 24–6**) and with a certain lack of clarity about the direction in which the story was developing – the novel began, in fact, as two separate narratives, one focusing on the life of the provincial town of Middlemarch and the other on the story of Dorothea Brooke. As soon as the two stories were merged, the work on the project began to gather momentum. George Eliot had by then completed most of the research she needed for the novel (much of it had in fact been done in preparation for *Felix Holt*, set in the same historical period and dealing, in part at least, with rather similar material), and she felt comfortable in the familiar territory of the provincial England of her childhood. Although *Middlemarch* is not based on the author's personal memories in the same way as some of her earlier novels are, some of its characters and scenes are, to a considerable extent, an evocation of the people and places she knew from her youth. The town of Middlemarch itself shares a number of characteristics with Coventry, while Caleb Garth, the novel's most consistent source of moral authority and generosity of spirit, is a thinly disguised portrait of the writer's own father, Robert Evans (see Life and contexts, **pp. 2–3**). Some of the other possible connections are more tenuous: the novel's focus on matters medical may have been influenced by the writer's memories of her brother-in-law, the ambitious but ultimately unsuccessful surgeon Edward Clarke, while her portrayal of Casaubon may derive some of its features from Robert Brabant, the father of Charles Hennell's wife Rufa, or perhaps from an Oxford friend of the Leweses', the scholar Mark Pattison.

The plot of *Middlemarch*, though rich in character and incident, and combining at least four major semi-independent story lines (Dorothea–Casaubon–Ladislaw, Lydgate–Rosamond, Fred–Mary, Bulstrode), is in some respects less complex, in terms of its use of highly charged episodes, unexpected coincidences, sudden reversals of fortune and dramatic disclosures of fateful secrets from the past, than the plots of some of the author's earlier works, such as *Romola* (see Works, **pp. 56–61**) or *Felix Holt* (see Works, **pp. 61–7**). The action of the novel is set in the three-year period – 1829–32 – immediately preceding the passage of the Reform Bill (see Life and contexts, **pp. 2–3**). The setting is the provincial town of Middlemarch and its environs – the neighbouring estates of Tipton, Freshitt and Lowick. The narrative focuses, at first, on Dorothea Brooke, the nineteen-year-old orphaned niece of Mr Brooke of Tipton Grange; an ambitious and earnest, but somewhat naive young woman, she lives her life trying to 'help to make things a little better' (p. 477) through charity work and pious reading. She rejects the advances of Sir James Chettam of Freshitt Hall – 'the blooming Englishman of the red-whiskered type' (38), who in due course marries Dorothea's younger and more practically minded sister Celia – and chooses instead to marry Edward Casaubon, the middle-aged Rector of Lowick and a Classical scholar, working on the compilation of an all-inclusive 'Key to all Mythologies', a project to which Dorothea hopes to contribute as her husband's assistant and secretary. However, her expectations are disappointed; during the honeymoon, which the Casaubons spend in Rome, she is left on her own as her husband visits the Vatican library, and the emotional emptiness of her marriage becomes clear to her when she finds a friend in her husband's cousin, Will Ladislaw, a young man of varied intellectual interests but no fixed ambitions and relying on Casaubon for financial support.

In the meantime, the reader is introduced to another group of characters – the leading burghers of Middlemarch, among them the mayor, Walter Vincy, his wife Lucy and their two eldest children, Fred and Rosamond; their extended family includes Vincy's sister Harriet and her husband, the affluent banker Nicholas Bulstrode, as well as Mrs Vincy's brother-in-law, the rich and miserly Peter Featherstone and Featherstone's own brother-in-law, the surveyor and land agent Caleb Garth, his wife Susan and his daughter Mary and her younger siblings. At the time the focus of the narrative shifts to Middlemarch, the attention of much of the town's public opinion is occupied by the recent arrival of a new doctor, Tertius Lydgate, an ambitious and well-educated young surgeon and a keen believer both in new scientific methods of diagnosis and treatment and in the need to promote a more progressive approach to issues of public health, including the rationalisation and extension of the existing system of health care for the poor. Lydgate's drive to put his ideas into practice soon involves him in local politics, in which he forges a somewhat uneasy alliance with Bulstrode, on whose financial support he counts in relation to his plans to open a new hospital. In private life, his friendship with Rosamond Vincy, who finds him a promising marriage prospect, develops, through his inertia rather than active courtship, into an engagement and eventually a marriage.

As the novel unfolds, the connections between the town of Middlemarch and the world of the local gentry become increasingly closer. Casaubon seeks medical advice from Lydgate as, following his return from Italy, his health begins to deteriorate; when he eventually dies, Dorothea inherits his fortune, which puts her in a position to support Lydgate in his charitable projects – however, a codicil to Casaubon's will stipulates that she will forfeit the inheritance if she marries Will Ladislaw. In the meantime, a separate chain of events surrounding the protracted illness and death of Peter Featherstone and the execution of his will results in the disclosure, at first only to the reader, of a guilty secret from the past of Nicholas Bulstrode: before coming to Middlemarch, he had made money through cheating the mother of Will Ladislaw out of her inheritance, and he is now blackmailed by a John Raffles, the only man who knows the truth about his past. Lydgate finds himself in trouble too: his marriage to the selfish and materialistic Rosamond proves unhappy, and he falls into debt, which he attempts to pay off by borrowing money from Bulstrode. In complex and suspicious circumstances, Raffles dies. Both Bulstrode, known to the reader to carry the moral responsibility for his death, and Lydgate are implicated in the ensuing scandal. As a result, they are forced to leave Middlemarch in disgrace, Bulstrode to live out his remaining years in obscurity, and Lydgate to start again elsewhere. He gives up his ambitious projects and establishes himself in London, where, in order to cater for the financial demands of his wife and family, he builds a fashionable medical practice. He dies early, leaving Rosamond well off and free to remarry, which she duly does. Dorothea eventually decides to forsake Casaubon's inheritance and to marry Ladislaw, who embarks on a career in politics. In a parallel rounding-off of another sub-plot, Rosamond's brother, Fred Vincy, a kind-hearted if somewhat irresponsible young man, for a long time unable to make a firm decision about his choice of career, eventually settles for a quiet future as a farmer and marries his childhood sweetheart Mary Garth.

The stories of the main protagonists of *Middlemarch* are played out against a meticulously depicted background of the social, economic and political history of Britain in the late 1820s and the early 1830s, a time of profound change in virtually all aspects of the country's life. The novel is full of examples of that dynamic process, both in the broad public sphere (the debate on political reform, the building of a railway) and in small details of the background, such as for instance in Lydgate's use of the stethoscope, 'which had not become a matter of course in practice at that time' (320). The focus on the theme of change and progress is underlined also by the fact that the time scheme of the story is signalled by discreet but unambiguous references to the public events and controversies of the day, from 'Mr Peel's late conduct on the Catholic Question' (31) during the debate on Catholic Emancipation in March 1829 to 'the Lords [throwing] out the Reform Bill' (871) in May 1832. As a result, *Middlemarch* becomes, in a sense, a historical novel, an analysis of a society at a particular point in time – but in focusing on the nature of the process of change, it raises questions relevant to the time of its writing as well: the social, economic and cultural mechanisms that shaped the society of *Middlemarch* were also influencing the Britain of the early 1870s.

George Eliot's treatment of the theme of change and progress is by no means unambiguous. On the one hand, *Middlemarch* is, in the broadest of terms, a story about the struggle between the forces of modernity – represented by Dorothea's charity work, Lydgate's medical and social projects or Will Ladislaw's involvement in reformist politics – and the forces of conservatism, sometimes taking the form of 'the hampering threadlike pressure of small social conditions, and their frustrating complexity' (210) and elsewhere manifesting themselves in the intellectual aridity of Casaubon, the political ineptitude of Mr Brooke, the incompetence of the surgeon-apothecary Mr Wrench or the manipulativeness and hypocrisy of Bulstrode. The results of that confrontation are at best mixed: although some of the representatives of the old order fail the test of modernity and leave the stage to their successors, they can often still try to maintain their influence through 'the rigid clutch of [their] dead hand' (358), as Casaubon does by attempting to prevent Dorothea from marrying Ladislaw. The agents of change are not entirely free from blame either: they can be naive and short-sighted, like Dorothea, or they can be, like Lydgate, people 'who [are] a little too self-confident and disdainful; whose distinguished mind[s are] a little spotted with commonness; who [are] a little pinched here and protuberant there with native prejudices; or whose better energies are liable to lapse down the wrong channel under the influence of transient solicitations' (178–9) – as a result of which they may be forced, like Lydgate, to accept compromises or, like Dorothea, to sacrifice their ambitions and desires in the interest of a greater good. This is not to say that George Eliot refuses to acknowledge the possibility of progress. Will Ladislaw does, after all, manage to become 'an ardent public man, working well in those times when reforms were begun with a young hopefulness of immediate good which has been much checked in our days, and getting at last returned to Parliament by a constituency who paid his expenses' (894). It is, however, quite characteristic that his success is qualified, and that it comes at a price. It is also quite telling that if the novel does suggest some form of an ideal response to the challenges of modernity, it conveys it through the figure of Caleb Garth, a man 'ready to accept any number of systems, like any number of firmaments, if they did not obviously interfere with the best land-drainage, solid building, correct measuring, and judicious boring (for coal)' (284) – in other words, a man prepared to live with change as long as it does not transform those aspects of life that are, on balance, better the way they have always been. His – and George Eliot's – attitude to life, best characterised as progressive conservative, is encapsulated in his perception of that great Victorian symbol of change and development, the railway: 'It may do a bit of harm here and there, to this and to that; and so does the sun in heaven. But the railway's a good thing' (604).

Directly related to the theme of progress is the theme of vocation: through its contrasting presentation of a number of characters facing the problem of defining their aspirations and trying to realise them in the actual context of the social, economic and cultural environment of nineteenth-century Britain, *Middlemarch* explores a broad variety of issues concerning the nature of the relationship between individual and society. The central role that this theme plays in George Eliot's overall conception of her story is signalled in the very first pages of the novel, when the vision of the young St Theresa of Avila – 'the little girl walking forth one morning hand-in-hand with her still smaller brother, to go and seek martyrdom in the country of the Moors' (25), who eventually 'found her epos in the reform of a religious order' (25) – is contrasted with the fate of those who 'found themselves no epic life wherein there was a constant unfolding of far-resonant action; perhaps only a life of mistakes, the offspring of a certain spiritual grandeur ill-matched with the meanness of opportunity; perhaps a tragic failure which found no sacred poet and sank unwept into oblivion' (25). The specific focus of the Prelude is, of course, on the lack of opportunities for the personal and social development of women, both as regards the lack of a 'coherent social faith and order which could perform the function of knowledge for the ardently willing soul' (25) and in view of the implications of their biology ('their ardour alternated between a vague ideal and the common yearning of womanhood', 25). In broader terms, however, the Prelude relates to a much more diverse spectrum of problems, such as the importance of a proper understanding of one's own predispositions and aspirations, the choice between idealistic ambitions and the practicalities of life, the balancing of the involvement in public and private roles, the nature of cultural, social and family expectations, the role and nature of education, and so on. With virtually all its major characters, from Lydgate the ambitious doctor and Celia Brooke the conventional bride, wife and mother, to Casaubon the failed scholar and Mr Brooke the aspiring parliamentarian, having at various points to reflect on their roles in life and to make crucial decisions about their future, *Middlemarch* acquires some of the characteristics of a multistrand *Bildungsroman* – a novel about the moral and social development of a character – in that it analyses the ways in which people construct and reconstruct their professional, social and personal identities.

In some cases, the message of *Middlemarch* is straightforward: the story of Fred Vincy is, ultimately, a simple tale about a young man finding himself at a cross-roads and trying to decide what path to follow in his choice of career. Fred's dilemma about whether or not to go into the Church involves a choice between, on the one hand, pursuing, against his own inclination, a course of action he feels obliged to pursue out of a sense of duty towards his family, who have invested heavily in the kind of academic education that was not suitable for him, and, on the other hand, trusting in his own understanding of himself. It is, in fact, a choice between submission to social expectation and commitment to one's own judge-ment and hierarchy of values. Fred's ability to learn how to stand up to external pressures and keep his own counsel, which eventually earns him the reward of securing both personal happiness and professional respectability – 'he became rather distinguished in his side of the county as a theoretic and practical farmer' (890) – makes him something of a moral exemplar: an ordinary man, fallible but kind, generous and considerate, he follows in the footsteps of his eventual father-in-law, Caleb Garth, thus turning, by the end of the novel, into the guardian of the traditional values that the novel preaches.

For the majority of the characters in the novel, decisions about what they do in their lives involve some form of compromise. The Revd Camden Farebrother, whom Fred, significantly, chooses as his confidant as he considers his future, is clearly 'not altogether in the right vocation' (202): he may be dutiful and competent in carrying out his clerical duties ('his preaching was ingenious and pithy, like the preaching of the English Church in its robust age, and his sermons were delivered without book', 207–8), but he treats his office, in the first place, as a form of employment ('as to the chaplaincy, he did not pretend that he cared for it, except for the sake of the forty pounds', 209) which he needs in order to maintain his family and to 'feed a weakness or two lest they should get clamorous' (202) – it is as an amateur natural historian that he finds genuine intellectual fulfilment and satisfaction. Compromise, too, and often of a rather unhappy kind, is what has to be accepted by the novel's central characters: both Lydgate and Dorothea have, at various points in their lives, to give up, or at least to restrict, their plans and ambitions when they are faced by the demands made upon them by the realities of life, both public and personal. Lydgate begins his career determined that

> he would settle in some provincial town as a general practitioner, and resist the irrational severance between medical and surgical knowledge in the interest of his own scientific pursuits, as well as of the general advance: he would keep away from the range of London intrigues, jealousies, and social truckling, and win celebrity, however slowly, as Jenner had done, by the independent value of his work.
>
> (174)

His idealism is underlined by the fact that he has 'no power of imagining the part which the want of money plays in determining the actions of men' (209). Ironically, it is precisely the power of money that destroys Lydgate's aspirations: his reliance on Bulstrode's support for the funding of a new hospital entangles him in a network of financial dependencies – resulting as much from his public activities as from his inability to satisfy his wife's growing financial demands – which eventually bring about his downfall and departure from Middlemarch. The scale of his disappointment is evident in that he is eventually forced to accept a compromise: 'his skill was relied on by many paying patients, but he always regarded himself as a failure: he had not done what he once meant to do' (893). In an ironic twist, his contribution to medical research is 'a treatise on Gout, a disease which has a good deal of wealth on its side' (892–3). Dorothea too has to learn to live with compromise: her naive but earnest intellectual ambitions ('I should learn everything then. . . . I should learn to see the truth by the same light as great men have seen it by. And then I should know what to do, when I got older: I should see how it was possible to lead a grand life here – now – in England' (51)), which make her hope for a marriage that 'would deliver her from her girlish subjection to her own ignorance, and give her the freedom of voluntary submission to a guide who would take her along the grandest path' (51), are bitterly disappointed as she begins to see through the veil of her idealisation of Casaubon to discover that 'such capacity of thought and feeling as [has] ever been stimulated in him by the general life of mankind [has] long shrunk to a sort of dried preparation, a lifeless embalmment of knowledge' (228–9) and that his work consists in little more than 'sorting what might be called shattered mummies, and fragments of a tradition which was itself a mosaic wrought from crushed ruins – sorting them as food for a theory which was already withered in the birth like an elfin child' (519). And it is not just marriages that are unhappy that involve compromise: while Dorothea 'never repent[s] that she [has] given up position and fortune to marry Ladislaw' (893), she remains aware that 'there was always something better which she might have done, if she had only been better and known better' (893). Dorothea's failure to carry out her aspirations is of course in part also a question of gender and social rank. Her charitable interest in improving the living conditions of the poor tends to be regarded, in her social circle, as little more than a harmless eccentricity, while her intellectual ambitions fall foul of common gender stereotypes and conventional expectations regarding women's social roles: 'I cannot let young ladies meddle with my documents. Young ladies are too flighty' (42), says her uncle Mr Brooke. Dorothea's eventual acceptance of her place in life – '[she] could have liked nothing better, since wrongs existed, than that her husband should be in the thick of a struggle against them, and that she should give him wifely help' (894) – demonstrates her recognition of the fact that human ambitions and possibilities are thus necessarily limited by the circumstances of the surrounding world; as George Eliot puts it in the Finale, 'there is no creature whose inward being is so strong that it is not greatly determined by what lies outside it' (896).

The novel's focus on the problem of defining one's role in public and private life and learning to accept one's own limitations is an aspect of George Eliot's broader interest in the processes of moral and psychological development. As in her previous works, one of the main areas of interest in *Middlemarch* is the study of different forms and sources of egoism, ranging from the innocent self-centredness of Celia Brooke, through the greed and sycophantic hypocrisy of the relatives of old Peter Featherstone, to the complex obsessiveness of Nicholas Bulstrode. But the most prominent analysis of an egoist in *Middlemarch* is Rosamond Vincy – indeed, the contrast between her egoism and the altruism of Dorothea is one of the central compositional elements of the novel. 'The flower of Mrs Lemon's school, the chief school in the county, where the teaching included all that was demanded in the accomplished female – even to extras, such as the getting in and out of a carriage' (123), Rosamond is a perfect product of early nineteenth-century middle-class women's education and of middle-class materialism: intelligent but shallow, adept socially but unable to understand or empathise with others, full of expectations but indifferent to the needs or wishes of those around her, demanding but oblivious to the realities of life ('she never thought of money except as something necessary which other people would always provide', 301), she increasingly behaves like a snobbish, greedy, manipulative social climber, using her charms to ensure that she enters into what she expects to be a socially and economically advantageous marriage. Her selfishness does not end once she becomes Mrs Lydgate: described by her husband as 'his basil plant; ... a plant which [has] flourished wonderfully on a murdered man's brains' (893), she successfully pressurises him into sacrificing his ideals in order to fund what she considers a lifestyle appropriate for their social rank. Paradoxically, however, Rosamond's egoism does not express itself through duplicity and malicious scheming but through moral ignorance and abdication of responsibility; though she lives in a 'dream-world in which she [has] been easily confident of herself and critical of others' (854), she is not incapable, at critical moments in her life, of transcending her selfishness and reaching out to others in a moment of need: 'Rosamond had delivered her soul under impulses which she had not known before. She had begun her confession under the subduing influence of Dorothea's emotion; and as she went on she gathered the sense that she was repelling Will's reproaches, which were still like a knife-wound within her' (856).

Rosamond's crucial meeting with Dorothea is not a moment of moral conversion – her attitude to her marriage in her later life, remains, it is safe to assume, much as it was before – but it demonstrates the complexity of her personality and problematises the evaluation of her character. Interestingly, although Rosamond does, on various occasions, have to pay a price for her egoism, she is ultimately not only a survivor, but, in her own terms, a success – her second marriage, after Lydgate's death, to 'an elderly and wealthy physician, who [takes] kindly to her four children' (893), demonstrates, in an ironic reversal of Dorothea's marriage to Casaubon, that she is capable of achieving her objectives with resilience and determination. A complex and ambiguous character, Rosamond thus becomes much more than a mere exposition of human egoism – a counterpoint to Dorothea, she becomes central not only to the novel's moral vision but also to its investigation of the social, economic and cultural situation of women in the nineteenth century and of its moral and psychological ramifications.

While Rosamond's selfishness may be destructive of her relationships with others, it never leads her to acts of conscious and premeditated wrongdoing. This is clearly not the case with another of the egoists of *Middlemarch*, Nicholas Bulstrode; the only one among the novel's major characters to be directly responsible for active deception, fraud and, in moral if not strictly technical terms, murder, he is duly exposed and punished – and yet, as George Eliot analyses the process of moral degeneration that turns him from a pious and sincere lay preacher into a hypocrite and a criminal, he is treated with the same subtle and, in a way, compassionate insight as the other characters in the novel. As in the case of Tito Melema in *Romola* (see Works, **pp. 56–61**), Bulstrode's descent into moral opportunism is a protracted process of the gradual erosion of moral judgement; it begins in a seemingly innocent way, with the questioning, in a religious context, of the morality of his business ventures:

> He remembered his first moments of shrinking. They were private, and were filled with arguments; some of these taking the form of prayer. The business was established and had old roots; is it not one thing to set up a new gin-palace and another to accept an investment in an old one? The profits made out of lost souls – where can the line be drawn at which they begin in human transactions? Was it not even God's way of saving His chosen?
>
> (664)

In course of time, Bulstrode 'gradually explain[s] the gratification of his desires into satisfactory agreement with [his theoretic] beliefs' (667) and eventually achieves a level of acquiescence in what he considers his moral rectitude that permits him to command a considerable degree of authority in the public life of Middlemarch. When the arrival of Raffles destroys his sense of security, he reverts to the same pattern of self-questioning in a desperate attempt to justify his inclination to accelerate his death:

Should he send for Lydgate? If Raffles were really getting worse, and slowly dying, Bulstrode felt that he could go to bed and sleep in gratitude to Providence. But was he worse? Lydgate might come and simply say that he was going on as he expected, and predict that he would by-and-by fall into a good sleep, and get well. What was the use of sending for him? Bulstrode shrank from that result.

(762)

Characteristically, however, despite all his dishonesty and his ability to deceive himself into believing in his own righteousness, Bulstrode never descends to the point of losing his sense of moral judgement. He may have learnt to stifle the voice of his conscience, but he can still hear it at one of the most critical points in his life, when, confronted by Harriet's questioning look, he cannot bring himself to deny the truthfulness of the accusations that have been levelled against him.

The subtlety of the author's psychological insight is, in fact, clearly evident throughout *Middlemarch*; one of the most characteristic features of the novel is the versatility with which George Eliot's analysis of character and motivation is integrated into every aspect of the fabric of the text, from direct narratorial description and analysis to dialogue, and from passages written in a tone which is bitingly ironical to profound and moving tragedy. As the novel unfolds, characters are seen at various stages of their psychological development: the narrative focuses, at first, on the young, naive Dorothea contemplating the prospect of marrying Casaubon 'with a sort of reverential gratitude . . . almost as if a winged messenger had suddenly stood beside her path and held out his hand towards her' (50) and then continues to trace her growth into maturity through 'the midst of her confused thought and passion' (224) as she realises the mistake she has made, through the experience of finding herself 'in a state of convulsive change' (532) as, on learning of the contents of her husband's will, she first becomes aware of the sexual tension between herself and Ladislaw, to the climactic meeting with Rosamond, when she experiences a 'revulsion of feeling . . . too strong to be called joy' (856) as she learns of his love for her. At the same time, the narrative's shifting point of view makes it possible for the reader to identify, at various points in the novel and in various contexts, with virtually all the other major characters as well: George Eliot's imaginative sympathy is extended to the young Mary Garth as she finds herself in dramatic conflict with old Peter Featherstone, as well as to the old Casaubon when he contemplates the potential impact that Ladislaw's arrival in Middlemarch may have on the stability of his marriage. There is an impressive depth and diversity even to those of the characters who function on the periphery of the main plot: the common-sense if at times insensitive practical-mindedness of Celia Brooke loses nothing of its intensity for being presented through a series of often comic sketches ('And, of course men know best about everything, except what women know better. . . . Well, I mean about babies and those things', 792), while the novel's most dramatic vision of suffering, in its power reminiscent of classical tragedy, comes as Harriet Bulstrode is about to learn the truth about her husband's past:

That moment was perhaps worse than any which came after. It contained that concentrated experience which in great crises of emotion reveals the bias of a nature, and is prophetic of the ultimate act which will end an intermediate struggle. Without that memory of Raffles she might still have thought only of monetary ruin, but now along with her brother's look and words there darted into her mind the idea of some guilt in her husband – then, under the working of terror came the image of her husband exposed to disgrace – and then, after an instant of scorching shame in which she felt only the eyes of the world, with one leap of her heart she was at his side in mournful but unreproaching fellowship with shame and isolation.

(805–6)

The immense diversity of themes and motifs that constitute the world of *Middlemarch* is held together by elaborate patterns of imagery integrating all elements of the novel and functioning on a number of levels, from individual, localised metaphors and similes embedded in the texture of George Eliot's prose to broader symbolic structures of the plot and characterisation. The most prominent among them, indeed directly reflecting the organisation of the novel as a whole, is the image of the web – the leisurely narrative of *Middlemarch* is all about creating a network of connections between characters, incidents and motifs that produces a sense of integration of a great diversity of fictional elements which acquire significance precisely because they are all interlinked to constitute 'this particular web' (170) of events, in which the stories of the various characters are 'woven and interwoven' (170) in a manner that not only brings them together, through various forms of connection and interaction, as threads in the elaborate narrative structure of the novel, but also makes them illuminate, through the extensive use of juxtaposition, parallel, and contrast, the complexity of the characters' experiences and the nature of the moral dilemmas they face and the choices they in consequence have to make. The narrator's insistence that the story of *Middlemarch* is not 'the sample of an even web' (890), but a mere 'fragment of a life' (890), in which 'every limit is a beginning as well as an ending' (890) accounts for the fact that the novel does not follow many of the conventional patterns of plot construction, particularly in the central story lines of Dorothea and Lydgate. The image recurs several times throughout the novel, stressing the increasing interdependence of all dimensions of modern life, not just within the world of the novel but also outside it. In consequence, precisely because 'municipal town and rural parish gradually [make] fresh threads of connection' (122) as the dynamics of social life 'are constantly shifting the boundaries of social intercourse and begetting new consciousness of interdependence' (122), the story of *Middlemarch* becomes much more than an investigation of 'this particular web', acquiring, as its subtitle promises, a more universal significance as 'A Study of Provincial Life'.

Complex patterns of symbols are also an important element of George Eliot's characterisation of her protagonists and of her analysis of their temperaments, states of mind and systems of values. Thus, for example, Casaubon is continuously associated with motifs of enclosure, dryness, darkness and death: his work makes him 'live too much with the dead' (40), his mind is compared to 'ante-rooms and winding passages which [seem] to lead nowhither' (228), and as he walks through the libraries of Rome 'with his taper stuck before him, he [forgets] the absence of windows, and in bitter manuscript remarks on other men's notions about the solar deities, he [has] become indifferent to the sunlight' (230). In much the same way, Casaubon's house at Lowick Manor is 'of greenish stone, ... not ugly, but small-windowed and melancholy-looking' (88), and it has about it 'an air of autumnal decline' (89) which foreshadows its owner's slow decline into death – in his last days, 'even the spring flowers and the grass [have] a dull shiver in them under the afternoon clouds that [hide] the sun fitfully' (516). By contrast, and significantly given the role he plays in Dorothea's life, Will Ladislaw is associated, throughout the novel, with images of light and warmth: when he sees her, unaware as she is of his presence, in the Vatican, the role he will eventually play in her life is symbolised by the appearance of 'a streak of sunlight which [falls] across the floor' (220), which Dorothea '[does] not really see ... more than she [sees] the statues' (235); later, back at home at Lowick, 'the mere chance of seeing Will occasionally [is] like a lunette opened in the wall of her prison, giving her a glimpse of the sunny air' (396). Similarly symbolic are the recurrent references to windows, which often represent a yearning to escape from the constraints and difficulties of life or a feeling of hope for a new future: Dorothea 'look[s] out of the window at the great cedar silvered with the damp' (71) as she contemplates her engagement to Casaubon, Mary Garth '[goes] to the window and gently prop[s] aside the curtain and the blind' (354) as soon as the death of Peter Featherstone puts an end to her dramatic vigil at his bedside, and Rosamond 'look[s] out of the window wearily[,] ... oppressed by ennui' (647) when she realises the extent to which her marriage lacks the passion and commitment that Ladislaw feels for Dorothea. There is also a symbolic quality to George Eliot's choice of the names of some of her characters and locations: their significance can be relatively transparent (though never quite allegorical), as in the surname of Camden Farebrother, or complex and ambiguous – the name of the town of Middlemarch itself can be seen as conveying a sense of the advance of the middle classes, or of the pressures of mediocrity, or indeed of the provincial ordinariness of the world the novel depicts.

Presiding over the stories of Dorothea, Lydgate, Fred and Mary, Bulstrode and their numerous relatives, friends and associates, is George Eliot's narrator – on the one hand omniscient in his or her ultra-realistic description of the provincial life of England around 1830, equally familiar with the characters' innermost thoughts and desires and with minutest details of their actions and the environment in which they live and shifting effortlessly between detached dramatic presentation of events and moralising commentary but on the other hand often bitingly ironical and therefore never to be taken for granted as regards his or her comments on the characters and indeed prepared to question the nature of his or her own narrative stance:

> One morning, some weeks after her arrival at Lowick, Dorothea – but why always Dorothea? Was her point of view the only possible one with regard to this marriage? I protest against all our interest, all our effort at understanding being given to the young skins that look blooming in spite of trouble; for these too will get faded, and will know the older and more eating griefs which we are helping to neglect.
>
> (312)

The dynamic and multidimensional nature of the narrative voice in *Middlemarch* is all about trying to come as closely as possible to finding the objective truth – and yet the very fact that the novel keeps undermining the reader's assumptions and expectations and refuses, for the most part, to pass final, definitive judgements on its central characters (Is Dorothea always invariably noble or is she, more often than not, naive and deluded? Is Rosamond just a plain egoist or a powerful woman who manages to get her own way in a world dominated by men?), may well imply that there may be no objective truth and that whatever passes as truth can only ever be but an approximation and an interpretation, unavoidably undermined by being mediated through the opaque, distorting lens of language. As a result, the very possibility of realism – and *Middlemarch* is, in conventional terms, one of the most quintessentially realistic novels in English, commonly quoted (though at the same time increasingly often interrogated) by critics of the form as an example of 'the classic realist text' (MacCabe 1979: 15) – may itself be subject to questioning. In any case, however, the very fact that the novel problematises concepts as fundamental as those while at the same time engaging as profoundly as it does with an immense diversity of issues – moral, psychological, philosophical, social, political, scientific – is a testimony to its significance not only as its author's most powerful work but also a milestone in the development of the English literary tradition and, perhaps, the most important single achievement of nineteenth-century literature in English.

The critical reception of *Middlemarch*, both during its serialisation and following the publication of the full text, was highly respectful though not quite as unanimously enthusiastic as in the case of some of George Eliot's earlier works, particularly *Adam Bede* (see Works, **p. 44**). It was welcomed, right from the publication of its first installment, as a 'fascinating book' (*CH*, 290), largely on account of the diversity and richness of its delineation of character: in the opinion of one of the critics, it was 'like a portrait gallery . . . voice, eyes, movement, physiognomy, all are photographed from the life' (*CH*, 319). The author was praised for 'the perpetual application of her own intelligence to the broad problems and conclusions of modern thought' (*CH*, 332–3), for 'her own sympathetic insight into the workings of human nature' (*CH*, 333) and for the depth of her 'studies in science and psychology [which] will constantly come in to suggest for the spiritual processes of her personages an explanation here or an illustration there' (*CH*, 333). Generally agreed to be 'extraordinarily full and strong' (*CH*, 331) and 'certainly the most elaborate effort of George Eliot's genius' (*CH*, 346), *Middlemarch* did, nonetheless, leave a number of critics hesitant about the merits of its overall conception, an uncertainty most memorably expressed by Henry James, who described is as 'a treasure-house of details, but . . . an indifferent whole' (*CH*, 353). The criticisms went in different directions: objections were raised against the strength of George Eliot's moralistic bias ('no talent, not genius itself, can quite overcome the inherent defect of a conspicuous, constantly prominent lesson, or bridge over the disparity between the storyteller with an ulterior aim ever before his own eyes and the reader's, and the ideal storyteller whose primary impulse is a story to tell, and human nature to portray', *CH*, 314–15), against the impact of that moralistic bias on the presentation of some of the characters ('what is most apparent is that Will has a great charm for George Eliot, and the only conclusion to which one can in fairness come is that, skilful as she is, she has for once failed to put before the reader a true picture of the man as he appears to her own mind' CH, 349–50), and against the novel's lack of 'an organized, moulded, balanced composition, gratifying the reader with a sense of design and construction' (CH, 353). Despite those reservations, however, virtually all critics recognised the historic importance of *Middlemarch* as a 'contribution of the first importance to the rich imaginative department of [English] literature' (CH, 359).

Daniel Deronda (1876)

The novel that was to turn out to be George Eliot's last major creative effort is in many ways not so much the culmination of her artistic career as a new departure. Begun little more than a year after the completion of *Middlemarch* (see Works, pp. 67–80), it shares with its predecessor the grand scale of its design – its publication followed the same format of eight extended parts, in this case issued in monthly, rather than bimonthly, intervals (see Life and contexts, p. 27) – and the determination and seriousness with which it attempts to combine its focus on the moral and psychological dilemmas faced by the central characters with the presentation of, and profound engagement with, important issues relating to the public life of Victorian Britain. In some respects, *Daniel Deronda* could indeed arguably be considered an even more ambitious enterprise than *Middlemarch*. It is the first of George Eliot's novels to deal with the complexities of the contemporaneous world – its action is set merely a decade before the time of writing and it does not refer to the period's major public events which would have made that small temporal distance significant – and it considerably extends the scope of her analysis of society. It is the first of her major England-based fictions to move its focus away from the provincial and, in the broadest of terms, predominantly lower-to-middle-class world of Shepperton, Hayslope, St Ogg's or Raveloe, or middle-to-upper-middle-class world of Middlemarch, to concentrate, on the one hand, on the life of the largely cosmopolitan Victorian aristocracy and gentry and, on the other hand, on the complex situation of the socially and culturally distinct, and yet internally diverse, community of British, and indeed European, Jews. The adoption of this broader perspective is, in a way, a reflection of the author's own progress: while her earlier novels are deeply rooted in her personal experience of ordinary middle-class life of the Midlands of England in the first half of the nineteenth century, *Daniel Deronda* is clearly the work of an affluent metropolitan intellectual, equally at home in the country houses of the Victorian upper classes, in the bohemian circles of London, and in the fashionable resorts of Continental Europe. A number of the characters in the novel are, in fact, based on the Leweses' London and Continental acquaintances: the portrait of the Jewish scholar Mordecai is likely to have been inspired by the London-based German Jewish intellectual, Emanuel Deutsch (see Life and contexts, p. 27), while the musician Julius Klesmer shares some characteristics with two composers the writer met on her first visit to Germany, the Hungarian Ferenc Liszt and the Russian Anton Rubinstein (see Life and contexts, p. 16). Similarly, too, some of the situations described in *Daniel Deronda* were recreated by George Eliot from personal memories: most notably, the novel's opening scene, describing Gwendolen Harleth gambling at a casino in the German spa of Leubronn, recalls a similar situation the Leweses witnessed during their visit to Bad Homburg in September 1872 (see *L*, V, 314).

The action of the novel takes place over a two-year period, from the autumn of 1864 to the autumn of 1866; the setting moves between London, the country estates around the West English city of Wancester and a number of cities and holiday resorts in Germany and Italy. Unlike in George Eliot's earlier works, the story of *Daniel Deronda* is not narrated in a simple linear fashion; its striking first chapter, in which Gwendolen is being watched by Daniel Deronda as she plays roulette, is followed by a long flashback section, in which the reader becomes acquainted with the background of events leading up to that first encounter between the novel's two main protagonists. Gwendolen is the eldest daughter of the twice-widowed Mrs Fanny Davilow, recently settled in Offendene, a rented house situated close to Pennicote, in the West of England, where Mrs Davilow's brother-in-law, the Revd Henry Gascoigne, is Rector. The family soon become part of the local social scene and before too long, Gwendolen attracts the attention of Henleigh Mallinger Grandcourt, the nephew and prospective heir of Sir Hugo Mallinger of Diplow. However, she refuses to contemplate marrying him when she realises that he has been involved in a long-term relationship with, and has fathered four children by, a married woman, Lydia Glasher, who had abandoned for him her husband and her first child. To escape Grandcourt's attentions, Gwendolen leaves for Germany to stay with friends, and it is there that she and Deronda first become aware of each other. However, before they have an opportunity to meet, Gwendolen is recalled back home when her mother's fortune, inherited from her father, who was a plantation owner in the West Indies, is lost in a failed business venture. Gwendolen's initial hopes for a career as an actress and singer are disappointed when her friend the musician Julius Klesmer declares her insufficiently talented and lacking in professional training. Faced with the prospect of seeking employment as a governess, and with her mother and half-sisters depending on her uncle's charity, she eventually decides to marry Grandcourt. In the meantime, Deronda, a ward of Sir Hugo's, widely presumed to be his natural son, saves from suicide by drowning a young Jewish singer, Mirah Lapidoth, recently arrived in London in the hope of finding her long-lost mother and brother. As he attempts to help her in her search for her relatives, Deronda becomes acquainted with the family of a Jewish pawnbroker, Ezra Cohen, and subsequently befriends their lodger Mordecai, a scholar and thinker who turns out to be Mirah's long-lost brother. It is through him that Deronda is first introduced to the complexities of the spiritual heritage of Judaism and of the contemporary social and political problems of the Jewish people. In due course, Deronda's increasing fascination with the world of Judaism, initially triggered by his acquaintance with Mirah, proves to be an unexpected but thoroughly appropriate preparation for the discovery of his true identity: he learns that he is the son of the Princess Halm-Eberstein, formerly the Jewish singer Alcharisi, and that he was given up, at two years of age, to be brought up by Sir Hugo as an Englishman and a Gentile. Deronda's visit to Genoa, where he meets his terminally ill mother for the first time, coincides with the arrival there of the Grandcourts, who stop over in the city during their yachting tour of the northern Mediterranean; their marriage has not been happy, predominantly because of

Grandcourt's dismissive and arrogant treatment of Gwendolen. Soon after their departure from Genoa, Grandcourt drowns in a boating accident; Gwendolen, who has wished him dead, considers herself responsible for not having done enough to save him and confesses her feeling of guilt to Deronda, who has become for her a friend and a mentor, and with whom she in due course realises she has fallen in love. He cannot, however, reciprocate her feelings. He loves Mirah, and the novel ends with their marriage and their preparations for departure to the East, where they are planning to continue Mordecai's work for the cause of the Jewish people. Mordecai himself dies of consumption before Deronda and Mirah leave England. Gwendolen remains alone, having recognised her mistakes and acknowledged the impact Deronda's friendship has had on the development of her moral judgement and her understanding of herself.

Although the plot of *Daniel Deronda* is not excessively complex, George Eliot's handling of it is rather less assured than in some of her earlier novels. Particularly telling, in this respect, is a comparison with *Middlemarch*: the successful integration, in the earlier novel, of two independently conceived lines of plot into a cohesive multistrand narrative (see Works, **pp. 67–80**) stands in direct contrast to the way in which the tales of Gwendolen Harleth and Daniel Deronda constitute, effectively, two semi-independent half-novels, very different not only in terms of the contents and the internal logic of their respective stories but also as regards their overall atmosphere, the artistic methods adopted in the creation of their two distinctive worlds and the narrator's implied attitude to the characters and events presented. This is not to say that the novel lacks thematic unity: the two plots are linked by their concern with issues such as the social and economic position of women in modern society; the nature of marriage and possible conflicts and compromises it may involve in relation to family and group loyalty, career choices and financial considerations; the problem of parenthood and the mutual responsibilities of parents and children; and the nature of art and its place in the life of modern society. If *Daniel Deronda* does nevertheless fall into two distinct parts, it is because its two sub-plots lack the kind of easy, natural and fictionally credible connection that is found, in *Middlemarch*, in scenes such as those in which Lydgate attends on Casaubon in his illness, or Dorothea offers her support to Lydgate's public-health projects. George Eliot does, admittedly, attempt to link the two stories of *Daniel Deronda* through characters such as Sir Hugo Mallinger, whose role as Deronda's guardian determines his ward's English identity and grants him entrance into the world of academic education and upper-class drawing rooms, and Julius Klesmer, himself 'a felicitous combination of the German, the Sclave, and the Semite' (p. 77), who offers Mirah advice on her singing; this, however, does not change the impression that the development of the relationship between Gwendolen and Deronda, which is evidently intended to constitute the novel's central axis, does not seem to be sufficiently justified within the dramatic structure of the plot, as a result of which their meetings and conversations appear to be artificially engineered rather than naturally emerging from the process of the organic development of the narrative.

The 'English' section of the novel, focusing on the story of Gwendolen and Grandcourt, is primarily a profound, dynamic psychological study of egoism, punishment, suffering and catharsis, perhaps the subtlest in George Eliot's career.

Unlike most of the author's earlier heroines, Gwendolen has none of the moral earnestness and personal integrity that would make the narrator, and in consequence the reader, immediately identify or at least sympathise with her; she is, in fact, right from the very first page of the novel ('Was she beautiful or not beautiful? And what was the secret of form or expression which gave the dynamic quality to her glance? Was the good or the evil genius dominant in those beams?', 35) observed not only from the outside but, indeed, from a certain distance, which allows the narrator the freedom to carry out the analysis of her character from a detached and often ironic standpoint. In consequence, the story acquires a strongly dramatic aspect; although the narrator continues to be able to access the characters' thoughts, they are, more often than not, reported and commented on rather than shared with the reader, generating in the novel an atmosphere of objectivising and indeed quasi-scientific detachment rather than personal intimacy:

'I used to think archery was a great bore,' Grandcourt began. He spoke with a fine accent, but with a certain broken drawl, as of a distinguished personage with a distinguished cold on his chest.
'Are you converted to-day?' said Gwendolen.
(Pause, during which she imagined various degrees and modes of opinion about herself that might be entertained by Grandcourt.)

(146)

This kind of approach, analytical rather than compassionate, characterises George Eliot's investigation of Gwendolen's moral and psychological development. Gwendolen is a quintessential 'spoiled child' (33); brought up as 'the pet and pride of the household, waited on by mother, sisters, governess, and maids, as if she had been a princess in exile' (53) and educated 'at a showy school, where on all occasions of display she had been put foremost' (52), she enters adulthood unaware of her limitations and with a corresponding sense of self-confidence that borders on arrogance: ' "Imagination is often truer than fact," said Gwendolen, decisively, though she could no more have explained these glib words than if they had been Coptic or Etruscan. "I shall be so glad to learn all about Tasso – and his madness especially. I suppose poets are always a little mad." ' (76–7). Although her self-centredness can sometimes take the form of complete disregard for others, indicating her underlying capacity for cruelty – she toys with the feelings of her cousin Rex Gascoigne, and her memory is haunted by 'a disagreeable silent remembrance of . . . having strangled her sister's canary-bird in a final fit of exasperation at its shrill singing which had again and again jarringly interrupted her own' (53) – Gwendolen does, nonetheless, have some redeeming features. She differs from George Eliot's earlier women egoists, such as Hetty Sorrel or Rosamond Vincy, in that she has the intelligence to become increasingly capable not only of self-reflection and of making conscious (though not always right) moral judgements but also of thinking beyond the limitations of her station in life and, indeed, of the social and cultural order within which she operates: she is 'inwardly rebellious against the restraints of family conditions' (83), and 'her ideal [is] to be daring in speech and reckless in braving dangers' (94), an ambitious and yet potentially dangerous attitude, symbolised throughout the novel by two recurrent sets of images, associated with horse-riding on the one hand and with gambling on the other. Gwendolen's drama consists in the fact that this desire for freedom is continually being curtailed, either by the circumstances of the outside world, such as her mother's loss of her fortune or by the consequences of her own moral choices; it is the suffering that she has to accept as a punishment for the wrong choices that she makes that eventually brings her to a fuller understanding of herself.

The most significant restrictions on her freedom that Gwendolen has to face in her life are imposed on her by her husband: while, in first imagining her marriage, she 'wished to mount the chariot and drive the plunging horses herself, with a spouse by her side who would fold his arms and give her his countenance without looking ridiculous' (173), as the story unfolds she gradually realises the error she has made; her relationship with Grandcourt, even before they are married, makes her feel 'as if she had consented to mount a chariot where another held the reins' (373). Grandcourt himself is consistently presented as a personification of ruthless, animalistic authority and dominance: he hunts, he keeps dogs – 'so many . . . that he was reputed to love them' (161) – and his idea of marriage is 'to be completely master of this creature [Gwendolen] – this piquant combination of maidenliness and mischief' (346). After their marriage, Gwendolen increasingly recognises that her 'continued liability to Grandcourt's presence and surveillance' (648) leaves her feeling 'like an imprisoned dumb creature, . . . not noting any object around her in the painted gilded prison' (651); the sense of resentment that her husband's despotism generates in her brings her to the ultimate moral and emotional crisis in the climactic scene of the boating accident. Her account of that experience, which she gives in the quasi-confession she makes to Deronda, offers a powerful example of George Eliot's psychological insight:

'I saw him sink, and my heart gave a leap as if it were going out of me. I think I did not move. I kept my hands tight. It was long enough for me to be glad, and yet to think it was no use – he would come up again. And he *was* come – farther off – the boat had moved. It was all like lightning. "The rope!" he called out in a voice – not his own – I hear it now – and I stooped for the rope – I felt I must – I felt sure he could swim, and he would come back whether or not, and I dreaded him. That was in my mind – he would come back. But he was gone down again, and I had the rope in my hand – no, there he was again – his face above the water – and he cried again – and I held my hand, and my heart said, "Die!" – and he sank; and I felt "It is done – I am wicked, I am lost!" – and I had the rope in my hand – I don't know what I thought – I was leaping away from myself – I would have saved him then. I was leaping from my crime, and there it was – close to me as I fell – there was the dead face – dead, dead. It can never be altered. That was what happened. That was what I did. You know it all. It can never be altered.'

(761)

In George Eliot's analysis, the story of Gwendolen – a subtle, insightful study of genuine suffering in an intelligent but surprisingly unlikeable character – comes close to achieving tragic poignancy. The reason for that is that, for all her selfishness, Gwendolen is at the same time a victim of the social, economic and cultural environment which has produced her. The vision of the world of the British upper classes in *Daniel Deronda* is indeed highly critical; although George Eliot avoids adopting the explicitly satirical approach of Dickens, Thackeray or Trollope, her presentation of such aspects of the life of the establishment of mid-Victorian Britain as the crucial role of money as the most important single factor defining an individual's place in the existing social order, the disadvantageous social and economic position of women, xenophobia and the patronising treatment of artists and intellectuals turns the novel into an indirect but nonetheless powerful interrogation and critique of the fundamental social and cultural values governing the life of the British people in the third quarter of the nineteenth century. This sharpening of the critical focus of George Eliot's presentation of the social reality she describes in the novel is related partly to her use of a near-contemporary setting, with its qualities of immediate familiarity and at least potential topicality, partly to her consistent and extensive use of suggestive imagery, such as the recurring motifs of gambling and hunting, and partly to her presentation of her characters as lacking a firm sense of connection with the social fabric of their respective environments. Unlike in the author's earlier fictions, notably absent from the 'English' section of *Daniel Deronda* are characters and scenes whose primary function is to contribute to the presentation of the social, economic or cultural background to the main narrative: in the world of the Mallingers, the Arrowpoints and the Gascoignes there is no trace of an organically developed network of social and personal links that would resemble the village community of Hayslope in *Adam Bede* (see Works, **pp. 36–44**), the chorus of the patrons of the Rainbow Inn in *Silas Marner*, or the customers of Nello's barber's shop in *Romola*.

The theme of the significance of the community and of the search for one's family, social and cultural roots lies at the heart of the second major sub-plot of *Daniel Deronda* – the section of the novel centred on the eponymous hero's journey of cultural and personal discovery, which eventually brings him back into the Jewish community into which he was originally born. The process of Deronda's intellectual progress, which begins with his wish 'to understand other points of view' (224) and his intention 'to get rid of a merely English attitude in studies' (224) and finally takes him to a point where he not only embraces his Jewish identity but also decides to follow in the footsteps of his grandfather, the Jewish scholar and physician Daniel Charisi, and declare: 'I hold that my first duty is to my own people, and if there is anything to be done towards restoring or perfecting their common life, I shall make that my vocation' (792), provides a counterpoint to the story of Gwendolen's moral education. The main difference between the two systems of values the novel depicts, and thus the key point of the novel's moral message, is that the culture of Judaism that Deronda accepts as his own is, unlike the self-centred and largely materialistic world of the Gentile West, underwritten by an idealistic vision of human progress, even if its focus is restricted to the Jewish nation only:

> 'Revive the organic centre: let the unity of Israel which has made the growth and form of its religion be an outward reality. Looking towards a land and a polity, our dispersed people in all the ends of the earth may

share the dignity of a national life which has a voice among the peoples of the East and the West – which will plant the wisdom and skill of our race so that it may be, as of old, a medium of transmission and understanding. Let that come to pass, and the living warmth will spread to the weak extremities of Israel, and superstition will vanish, not in the lawlessness of the renegade, but in the illumination of great facts which widen feeling, and make all knowledge alive as the young offspring of beloved memories.'

(592)

Very importantly, the focus of Mordecai's engagement with the cause of his nation, and of Deronda's subsequent work, is moral and social rather than spiritual: George Eliot is careful to ensure that her presentation of Judaism does not imply any form of proselytism or idealisation of Jewishness as such. The novel does not engage in any significant way with the strictly religious aspect of Judaism. It also demonstrates that individual Jewish people are subject to the same passions and the same weaknesses and failings as Gentiles (Mirah's father's obsession with gambling easily exceeds Gwendolen's), and that they face the same difficulties and pressures in personal, family and professional life – thus, for example, the history of the life of Deronda's mother, although summarised rather than dramatised and therefore perhaps less prominent than the stories of Gwendolen and Mirah, does nonetheless produce a number of important insights contributing to the novel's analysis of the broad spectrum of problems relating to issues of gender and family relations. George Eliot's portrayal of the Jewish people, based on extensive historical and cultural research, does indeed manage to avoid oversimplification or reduction to easy racial or religious stereotypes. She draws a picture of a community that is very diverse in terms of social class and cultural affiliation, and she introduces the reader, directly or indirectly, to affluent intellectuals as well as ordinary, lower-middle-class London tradesmen and to proto-Zionist ideologists as well as apostates determined not only to assimilate into the Gentile world but also to remove all traces of their own Jewish ancestry and connections. This comprehensiveness and, at the same time, subtle discrimination in the presentation of the world of British and indeed European Jews make *Daniel Deronda* by far the most ambitious attempt in mainstream Victorian fiction to deal with the question of the nature of modern Judaism and its place in and contribution to the life of modern Western society, overshadowing not only the largely one-sided and clichéd portrayals of Jews in the novels of Dickens and Trollope but also the highly romanticised Jewish components of the novels of Benjamin Disraeli.

However successful George Eliot may be, in *Daniel Deronda*, in conveying her sense of respect for Judaism and the Jewish people, her handling of this section of the novel appears to be less than fully satisfying artistically, particularly when contrasted with the subtlety of her treatment of the Gwendolen–Grandcourt plot. The process of Deronda's discovery of his true identity and heritage is more about acquisition of knowledge than about any form of genuine transformation or awakening: right from his young age, Deronda is idealised as a boy whose 'disposition was one in which everyday scenes and habits beget not *ennui* or rebellion, but delight, affection, aptitudes' (208), and who then grows into a man of 'early-wakened sensibility and reflectiveness' (412) and 'plenteous, flexible sympathy' (412), 'fervidly democratic in his feeling for the multitude, and yet, through his affections and imagination, intensely conservative; voracious of speculations on government and religion, yet loath to part with long-sanctioned forms which, for him, were quick with memories and sentiments that no argument could lay dead' (412–13). In consequence, he comes across as a rather schematic element of the novel's narrative design rather than as a convincing character in his own right. Much the same could be said about the portraits of Mirah, whose 'sweet purity . . . clothe[s] her as with a consecrating garment' (247) and 'in whom bodily loveliness seems . . . properly one with the entire being' (421), and of her brother Mordecai, radiating 'a sense of solemnity . . . as utterly nullifying his outward poverty and lifting him into authority as if he had been that preter-natural guide seen in the universal legend, who suddenly drops his mean disguise and stands a manifest Power' (551). The development of the story of Deronda and Mirah depends rather too much on chance and coincidence, while the fact that the plot relies on such conventional narrative devices as changed identities and discoveries of long-lost relatives results in the need for lengthy passages of explanatory narrative. In consequence, the section of the novel focusing on Deronda acquires something of the quality of an allegory – not inappropriate perhaps in view of its thematic focus, but sitting somewhat uneasily vis-à-vis the radically different, sharper, at times almost acerbic tone of the narrative of Gwendolen and Grandcourt. Thus, the fictional experiment that is *Daniel Deronda* proves to be only a partial success: immensely ambitious on the thematic level, carefully researched and conceived in powerfully symbolic terms, it does not quite manage to negotiate the problem of reconciling the structural difficulties arising from its adoption of the complex pattern of a double plot and from its attempt to fuse together two stories which, for all their thematic and symbolic connections, remain very firmly – perhaps rather too firmly – anchored in their two separate social contexts and two distinct imaginative modes.

The disjunction between the 'English' and Jewish sections of *Daniel Deronda* was noted by the majority of the novel's early critics. The predominant perception was that in creating Gwendolen, George Eliot achieved 'an overwhelming success: and the minutest and least friendly examination [would] hardly discover a false note or a dropped stitch' (*CH*, 372); Henry James, in what has become the best-known of the novel's early analyses, called her history 'the most *intelligent* thing in all George Eliot's writing . . . so deep, so true, so complete, it holds such a wealth of psychological detail, it is more than masterly' (*CH*, 430). The presentation of the Jewish plot, on the other hand, met with a much more mixed reception: while some critics expressed their satisfaction that the author has gone 'a considerable way towards filling an intellectual void – faithful pictures of modern Anglo-Jewish domestic life' (*CH*, 408) and has produced 'the vindication of a long maligned race against ignorant misrepresentation or wilful aspersion, the defence of Jews and Judaism against fanaticism and prejudice' (*CH*, 416), others criticised the Jewish aspect of the novel as at best irrelevant and at worst unwelcome: '[N]ot only are these [Jewish] personages outside our interests, but the author seems to go out with them into a world completely foreign to us. What can be the design of this ostentatious separation from the universal instinct of Christendom, this sub-sidence into Jewish hopes and aims?' (*CH*, 377). Similarly divided were critical opinions about the presentation of the novel's Jewish characters: Deronda himself was called, by various critics, 'a type which, though scarcely likely to appeal to the masses, ought to teach more than one lesson to serious thinkers' (*CH*, 411) as well as 'a brilliant failure' (*CH*, 424) or 'a pallid shadow rather than a man' (*CH*, 442). There was relatively little recognition of the richness and ambition of the novel's thematic concerns and symbolic structure: numerous critics took exception to the way in which the scientific detachment of George Eliot's analyses expressed itself through her use of formal or technical vocabulary ('we cannot away (in a novel) with "emotive memory" and "dynamic quality" ', *CH*, 374), and only a few recognised the experimental quality of the book, with its rejection of the certainties of conventional realism in favour of the imaginative freedom offered by the tradition of the romance:

> *Daniel Deronda* is a probably unique example of the application of the forms of romance to a rare and difficult problem in human nature, by first stating the problem – (the transformation of Gwendolen) – in its extremest form, and then, with something like scientific precision as well as philosophic insight, arranging circumstance so as to throw upon it the fullest light possible.
>
> (*CH*, 398)

Other prose

'The Lifted Veil' (1859)

George Eliot's first short story, conceived and executed while the author was in mourning after the death of her sister Christiana, is by far the least characteristic of her fictional writings: described by the writer herself as a 'slight story of an outré kind – not a *jeu d'esprit*, but a *jeu de melancolie*' (*L*, III, 41), it is the only work in the George Eliot canon to depart from conventional realism and to include elements of the supernatural, which give the tale a strong Gothic flavour, and it is the only one of her prose fictions to focus almost exclusively on the analysis of a hypersensitive, and possibly diseased, mind, and to do so through the medium of first-person narrative coming from within, rather that outside, the imagined world of the story. The main protagonist, Latimer, is a man possessed of powers of envisioning the future; as he awaits his death, he tells, in a flashback, the story of his youth. Born into affluence, but lacking a sense of emotional security after the early death of his mother, he marries Bertha Grant, the former fiancée of his elder brother Alfred, killed in a riding accident. He does that despite having had a premonition of the unhappiness of their marriage and of Bertha's hatred of him. The secret – Latimer has no insight into Bertha's mind – is disclosed when a servant of the Latimers', Mrs Archer, on her deathbed following a sudden illness, manages, during an attempt at resuscitation by Latimer's medical friend Charles Meunier, who gives her a blood transfusion, to accuse her mistress of attempting to poison her husband. The couple separate, and Latimer's remaining years are lived out under 'the curse of insight' (42).

On the simplest level, the story's preoccupation with death reflects the author's personal concerns at the time of writing (see Life and contexts, **p. 20**); at the same time, its concentration on what is, effectively, a psychological case study and its strong grounding in contemporaneous scientific and para-scientific debate link it to George Eliot's and, primarily, George Henry Lewes's sustained interest in physiology, psychology and medicine. The story may be seen as something of an experiment, prefiguring the complex psychological studies in the author's later fictions; it is also an interesting exercise in fictional form, with its use of retrospect narrative and the prominence of visual imagery foreshadowing the techniques adopted in most of George Eliot's later works, most prominently perhaps in *Daniel Deronda* (see Works, **pp. 80–8**).

'Brother Jacob' (1860, published 1864)

The second of George Eliot's stories is, in comparison with 'The Lifted Veil' (see Works, **pp. 88–9**), much lighter and much more conventional: it is a simple comic tale with a predictable moral message, set against a satirically presented background of contemporary lower-middle-class life. The protagonist of the story, the confectioner David Faux, steals money from his mother and runs away to seek his fortune in Jamaica. Having failed to establish himself there, he returns to England, where he builds up a business in the town of Grimworth, under the assumed name of Edward Freely. He does not contact his family until after the death of his father, when he comes forward to claim his share of the inheritance. The family disown him, and he is subsequently punished when, as he is about to marry Penny Palfrey, a daughter of a well-off local farmer, his mentally handicapped brother Jacob, who had witnessed his theft of his mother's money, arrives at Grimworth and thus triggers a series of events leading to the disclosure of the confectioner's secret and his forced departure from the town.

Written only weeks before George Eliot embarked on the work on *Silas Marner* (see Works, **pp. 51–6**), 'Brother Jacob' is a comic sketch constructed around the same basic anecdote that was soon to be developed into the story of the weaver of Raveloe: the two works share the central incident of the theft of a substantial sum of money, they exploit the motif of money for symbolic purposes, and they display similarities in their cast of characters – Jonathan and David Faux are an early version of the Cass brothers, while Jacob's innocence foreshadows that of Eppie as a toddler. 'Brother Jacob' is, of course, a much slighter work than *Silas Marner*; it remains firmly within the genre of a comic moral *exemplum* – it is, in fact, George Eliot's only work of fiction to adopt a consistently comic tone – and the message it conveys does not go far beyond the conventional truths about guilt and punishment. Perhaps the most memorable aspect of the story is its comic portrayal of the burghers of Grimworth. Its mixture of satire and insightful observation of contemporary social mores makes for an amusing and at times quite incisive picture of the domestic life of a small English town in the middle of the nineteenth century.

Impressions of Theophrastus Such (1879)

George Eliot's last work, *Impressions of Theophrastus Such*, is by far the most unusual among her writings. It occupies the middle ground between narrative fiction and cultural criticism in that it is a series of character sketches and more general reflective essays about the intellectual and literary culture of mid-Victorian Britain, delivered by Theophrastus Such, a somewhat mysterious, semi-realistic and semi-allegorical London intellectual. The work, very appropriately in view of its central concern with the state of modern literary culture, abounds in diverse literary allusions and associations: the very name of the supposed author (rather than narrator – the book is not a narrative in the strict sense of the word) of *Impressions of Theophrastus Such* is a direct allusion to the ancient Greek creator of the tradition of 'character writing'; the use of the convention of the character sketch sets the book in the context of seventeenth-century prose; finally, its use of a quasi-fictional framework (however sketchy) and the concern with the contemporaneous literary and cultural scene are reminiscent of the tradition of early eighteenth-century periodicals.

The structural fluidity of *Impressions of Theophrastus Such* means that one of the key questions about it is whether, and, if so, to what extent, the opinions expressed in the text are meant to be read at face value, as an expression of its author's own views. The fictional dimension of the book involves, in the first instance, the creation of the character of Theophrastus himself, a middle-aged bachelor son of a liberal-minded clergyman from the Midlands of England; however, his role as a character/narrator fades away as the text unfolds, blurring the lines between the dramatic and the discursive modes of presentation and, in consequence, adding to the sense of ambivalence and instability that the book generates. The majority of the sketches introduce more characters, who illustrate specific points Theophrastus (or George Eliot?) makes about the intellectual world of the Victorian era; with their names deriving, in an allegorical manner, from the Classical tradition, they illustrate various types of ignorance, pretentiousness and intellectual snobbery. At times, as in the essay on Merman the aspiring scholar ('How We Encourage Research'), the characters are placed within a broader fictional context; elsewhere, as in the story of Spike the opportunistic voter ('A Political Molecule'), they are little more than personifications of specific attitudes. The last essay, 'The Modern Hep! Hep! Hep!', by far the longest in the book, dispenses with the fictional apparatus altogether, presenting its argument on the nature of nationalism and national traditions, combined with a strong defence of the cause of the social, political and cultural emancipation of Jews, in a direct manner, reminiscent of conventional newspaper journalism.

The question of the aesthetic qualities of *Impressions of Theophrastus Such* is as ambivalent as that of its generic characteristics: it cannot be assessed according to the conventions of traditional literary genres, but at the same time it does not produce a powerful enough sense of its own significance as a literary achievement to set up its own standards of merit. Some of its sections offer potentially interesting and insightful satirical comments about the operation of the mechanisms of the world of Victorian *literati*, and some attempt, with varying degrees of success, to present their case in a humorous vein; all in all, however, the book lacks the immediacy of appeal of a conventional work of fiction and is likely to remain the least popular and the least discussed of George Eliot's works, perceived as it tends to be as a literary curiosity rather than a serious work of art.

Literary criticism and other journalist writings

The breadth of George Eliot's – or rather Marian Evans's – intellectual interests and the extent of her erudition are demonstrated by the range of the journalist work she undertook in the early years of her career, writing at first (1846–9) for Charles Bray's Coventry-based *Herald and Observer* and, subsequently (1851–7), for the two London periodicals she was closely associated with – the *Westminster Review* and the *Leader*, for which George Henry Lewes worked as literary editor; she also produced occasional articles for *Fraser's Magazine* (1855), the *Saturday Review* (1856) and, later, for the *Pall Mall Gazette* (1865) and the *Fortnightly Review* (1865). The range of her contributions, almost invariably published anonymously, was immense: she wrote about English, French and German literature, as well as about history, philosophy, politics, religion, travel and contemporaneous social issues. The majority of the essays originated as reviews of recent publications; however, in line with standard Victorian practice, her critical discussion of the books she was reviewing often constituted a starting point for a broader analysis of the issues in question and for the expression of her own philosophical, political, religious and artistic ideas. Thus, for example, the 1851 review of R.W. Mackay's *The Progress of the Intellect*, a study of the origins of Western religious systems, leads the sceptically minded author to state her own conception of the role of religious belief in the life of modern society:

> It would be wise in our theological teachers, instead of struggling to retain a footing for themselves and their doctrine on the crumbling structure of dogmatic interpretation, to cherish those more liberal views of biblical criticism, which, admitting of a development of the Christian system corresponding to the wants and the culture of the age, would enable it to strike a firm root in man's moral nature, and to entwine itself with the growth of those new forms of social life to which we are tending.
>
> (281)

In a rather similar vein, the essay on 'Evangelical Teaching: Dr Cumming' (1855) criticises the Evangelical approach to Christianity, stressing its failure to promote what the author sees as the fundamental human values of sympathy and solidarity:

> Dr Cumming's God . . . is a God who instead of sharing and aiding our human sympathies, is directly in collision with them; who instead of strengthening the bond between man and man, by encouraging the sense that they are both alike the objects of His love and care, thrusts himself between them and forbids them to feel for each other except as they have relation to Him. He is a God, who, instead of adding his solar force to swell the tide of those impulses that tend to give humanity a common life in which the good of one is the good of all, commands us to check those impulses, lest they should prevent us from thinking of His glory.
>
> (67)

Another essay, 'Woman in France: Madame de Sablé' (1854), uses the discussion of the historical and cultural role of women in seventeenth- and eighteenth-century France to make a strong statement in support of the cause of the social and cultural emancipation of women:

> Let the whole field of reality be laid open to woman as well as to man, and then that which is peculiar in her mental modification, instead of being, as it is now, a source of discord and repulsion between the sexes, will be found to be a necessary complement to the truth and beauty of life. Then we shall have that marriage of minds which alone can blend all the hues of thought and feeling in one lovely rainbow of promise for the harvest of human happiness.
>
> (37)

Among the most important of Marian Evans's journalist writings are the essays in which she expresses her opinions about the contemporary literary scene and about the nature and aims of literary art. The reviews she published in the *Westminster Review* include discussions of some of the leading writers of the Victorian period, including Tennyson, Browning, Carlyle and Ruskin. She was also prepared to take a broader view of the directions in the development of mid-nineteenth-century fiction, criticising, in her essay on 'Silly Novels by Lady Novelists' (1856), the artistic weakness of the majority of novels written by her female contemporaries, as well as the unwillingness of reviewers and critics to engage in frank and constructive discussion of their literary merits. In Marian Evans's opinion, women writers deserve to be treated seriously, which means that their work needs to be judged by the same standards as the work of their male counterparts:

> Every critic who forms a high estimate of the share women may ultimately take in literature, will, on principle, abstain from any exceptional indulgence towards the productions of literary women. For it must be plain to every one who looks impartially and extensively into feminine literature, that its greatest deficiencies are due hardly more to the want of intellectual power than to the want of those moral qualities that contribute to literary excellence – patient diligence, a sense of the responsibility involved in publication, and an appreciation of the sacredness of the writer's art.
>
> (161)

It is precisely a sense of moral responsibility that is, in Marian Evans's view, inevitably linked to any process of artistic creation, and it is that sense of responsibility that she embraced when she adopted the literary persona of George Eliot. It is by no means surprising, therefore, that it is one of her early critical essays, 'The Natural History of German Life' (1856), that offers the most succinct summary of what was to become the central aim of George Eliot's literary art:

> The greatest benefit we owe to the artist, whether painter, poet, or novelist, is the extension of our sympathies. Appeals founded on

generalizations and statistics require a sympathy ready-made, a moral sentiment already in activity; but a picture of human life such as a great artist can give, surprises even the trivial and the selfish into that attention to what is apart from themselves, which may be called the raw material of moral sentiment.

(110)

Poetry

The Spanish Gypsy (1868)

The significance of *The Spanish Gypsy*, by far the longest and the most ambitious of George Eliot's poems, lies not so much in its intrinsic literary merits as in the fact that it encapsulates the sense of uncertainty about the future direction of her literary work that the author of *Adam Bede* and *The Mill on the Floss* faced in the mid–1860s (see Life and contexts, **pp. 22–4**). The gestation of the poem was uncharacteristically long: originally designed as a play in blank verse, *The Spanish Gypsy* was begun in 1864, but it was laid aside as George Eliot embarked on the writing of *Felix Holt, the Radical*; it was not until well over two years later, after the Leweses' visit to Spain, that the work on the project – now redesigned as a combination of an epic narrative and a dramatic poem – was resumed; the writing proved difficult, and it was another year before the text was eventually completed and published.

The action of *The Spanish Gypsy* is set in southern Spain at the end of the fifteenth century, shortly before the final collapse of the last outposts of Moorish rule in the Iberian peninsula. The poem tells the story of love between a young Spanish military commander, Don Silva, Duke of Bedmár, and a beautiful ward of his late mother's, Fedalma, who proves to be the daughter of Zarca, the chieftain of the Gypsy clan of the Zincali and an ally of the Moors. Both Fedalma and Silva face dramatic choices between love, on the one hand, and national, religious and family duty and loyalty on the other. Fedalma decides to reject personal happiness and to remain-faithful to her people, whom after her father's death, at Silva's hands, she has the duty to lead; conversely, Silva's shifting loyalties leave him, at the end of the poem, dishonoured but intent on fighting to win back the respect of the people of Spain – he goes to Rome 'to seek / The right to use [his] knightly sword again; / The right to fill [his] place and live or die / So that all Spaniards shall not curse [his] name' (p. 449). The central themes of the poem: the nature of duty, the relationship between the individual and society, the origin and significance of moral and political authority, are all reminiscent of Classical and neoclassical tragedy and of the heroic epic; at the same time, they recall the concerns and motifs explored in some of George Eliot's earlier novels, in particular *The Mill on the Floss* (see Works, **pp. 44–51**) and *Romola* (see Works, **pp. 56–61**) – Fedalma's choice between love and family loyalty resembles a similar dilemma experienced by Maggie Tulliver, and the story of her discovery that Zarca is her father, including in particular the scene of their first meeting in the Plaça Santiago, is reminiscent of some aspects of the relationship between Tito Melema and Baldassarre Calvo. The poem's thematic focus is not, however, restricted only to the exploration of traditional moral and philosophical problems; in asking, in *The Spanish Gypsy*, questions about the nature of national identity and in focusing on the situation of non-Christian and consequently underprivileged communities of late medieval Spain, among them Jews, George Eliot signals her interest in issues that will be explored more fully in her later works, in particular in *Daniel Deronda* (see Works, **pp. 80–8**).

For all its intellectual ambitions, *The Spanish Gypsy* is not, however, among George Eliot's most successful works in artistic terms: the formality of the convention the poem adopts imposes constraints on the freedom with which the author can explore the emotional potential of the situations she creates, and the construction of the plot, with its lengthy exposition and a rather hurried denouement, is not particularly well balanced. At times, the poem reads like a versified piece of traditional narrative fiction: the interweaving of passages of narrative and of dialogue and the use of conventional fictional devices such as external observers whose role is to introduce and contextualise the main story line clearly demonstrate the impact, on the form of the poem, of George Eliot's experience as a novelist. The resulting impression is one of competent but laboured craftsmanship rather than inspiration. Even the most powerfully dramatic passages, such as the above-mentioned scene of Fedalma's first encounter with Zarca, tend to suffer from verbosity and a certain artificiality of tone:

> But this prisoner –
> This Gypsy, passing, gazing casually –
> Was he her enemy too? She stood all quelled,
> The impetuous joy that hurried in her veins
> Seemed backward rushing turned to chillest awe,
> Uneasy wonder, and a vague self-doubt.
> The minute brief stretched measureless, dream-filled
> By a dilated new-fraught consciousness.
>
> (251)

The Legend of Jubal and Other Poems (1874, 1878)

George Eliot's second volume of poetry, published in 1874 and expanded four years later, may be a rather mixed body of work, but it does include a number of poems that shed some interesting light on the author's ideas and her creative method. Although the poems included in the collection vary quite widely, both in their subject matter and in their generic characteristics, a common thread that runs through the majority of the pieces is the motif of music as a symbol, and indeed a repository, of highest moral and aesthetic values. At the same time, some of the individual poems are worth noting in connection with their association with some of George Eliot's major works of fiction or because they reflect particularly characteristic features of the author's ideas and perceptions.

As befits an author whose major achievements are in narrative prose, some of her most successful writings in verse are of a narrative and dramatic rather than lyrical kind. Perhaps the most ambitious of the poems in the volume, 'Armgart', is in fact a short poetic drama dealing with the question of the nature of art as a vocation, and of the moral choices and psychological dilemmas which are an integral part of the career of an artist. Set in nineteenth-century Germany, the poem dramatises the story of a renowned singer, Armgart, who rejects the possibility of marriage only to find herself deprived of her singing voice in consequence of an illness. In its contemporary setting, in its concentration on the motif of music, and specifically singing, as the purest and yet the most fragile form of artistic expression, and in its psychologically complex portrayal of the central character, a talented but self-centred woman who has to learn to adapt to new realities of life, the poem foreshadows a number of the key concerns of *Daniel Deronda* (see Works, **pp. 80–8**).

Among other poems in the volume, 'Agatha', resembling *The Spanish Gypsy* (see Works, **pp. 93–4**) in its combination of conventional narrative and dramatisation, carries a strong Wordsworthian flavour in its praise of the simplicity and harmony of rural life, which find its fullest impression in the organic unity of the music that the community produces:

> Their song made happy music 'mid the hills.
> For nature tuned their race to harmony,
> And poet Hans, the tailor, wrote them songs
> That grew from out their life, as crocuses
> From out the meadow's moistness.
>
> (60)

Some of the other poems in the collection are to a greater or lesser extent conventional narratives. 'The Legend of Jubal' tells, in a moralistic manner reminiscent of the heroic poems of Matthew Arnold, the story of the biblical creator of the first musical instruments, who thus became the father of music as a form of art, while 'How Lisa Loved the King', on the other hand, is a retelling of a story from Boccaccio's *Decameron*, illustrating the theme of the emotional power of music.

George Eliot's best-known shorter poems collected in *The Legend of Jubal and Other Poems* are, however, of a lyrical nature. The sonnet sequence 'Brother and Sister' is a nostalgic recreation of the world of the author's Warwickshire childhood, as well as a return to the memories of her now estranged brother (see Life and contexts, **p. 3**); in their focus on the significance of childhood memories and perceptions, and in their presentation of an idealised, pastoral vision of the natural world, the sonnets are, like some of the other poems in the volume, strongly reminiscent of the poetry of Wordsworth, while the nature of their largely autobiographical subject matter, including some vividly remembered and lovingly presented details (the children's departure on a fishing expedition), links them directly with the quasi-autobiographical vision of the author's childhood recreated in the early chapters of *The Mill on the Floss* (see Works, **pp. 44–51**). In sharp contrast to the profoundly personal tone of the sonnets ('But were another childhood-world my share, / I would be born a little sister there', 90), George Eliot's most important philosophical poem, 'O May I Join the Choir Invisible' is effectively a Positivist prayer in praise of the creative and moral potential of humanity, symbolised, once again, through the vision of the undying power of music:

        May I reach
That purest heaven, be to other souls
The cup of strength in some great agony,
Enkindle generous ardour, feed pure love,
Beget the smiles that have no cruelty –
Be the sweet presence of a good diffused,
And in diffusion ever more intense.
So shall I join the choir invisible
Whose music is the gladness of the world.
                                    (50)

3

Criticism

Early biographies and criticism

George Eliot's – or rather Marian Evans Cross's – untimely death (see Life and contexts, **p. 30**) came at a time when her literary standing was at its highest. As Leslie Stephen noted in the opening of the anonymous obituary he published in the *Cornhill Magazine*, '[H]ad we been asked, a few weeks ago, to name the greatest living writer of English fiction, the answer would have been unanimous. No one – whatever might be his special personal predilections – would have refused that title to George Eliot' (*CH*, 464). Although her career as a novelist had lasted for little more than twenty years, she had managed to build up a reputation not only as an outstanding literary artist but also as an intellectual and a moralist; in fact, as early as in the early 1870s she had already become something of a cultural icon, not only highly respected both by the reading public and by the intellectual elites of mid-Victorian Britain but also positively venerated by a faithful circle of devoted admirers, some of whom entertained literary ambitions of their own (see Life and contexts, **p. 26**). In consequence, it does not come as a surprise that the first book devoted exclusively to George Eliot's writings was not a critical study *sensu stricto*, but a collection of *Wise, Witty, and Tender Sayings in Prose and Verse, Selected from the Works of George Eliot* (1872), compiled by Alexander Main; republished several times over the following two decades, it may have been a token of its editor's appreciation of George Eliot's work, but it did little to stimulate critical discussion of her achievement – if anything, it presented the writer in a rather solemn light, and it created, through its selective use of quotations, an impression that her work was excessively sententious and moralistic.

This perception was not entirely out of line with the critical consensus that began to emerge in the immediate aftermath of George Eliot's death, as the authors of obituary notices and commemorative articles attempted the first summative assessments of her literary career. The majority of commentators juxtaposed the early novels – the products of personal memories and of the spontaneous recreation of the familiar world of the past – with the more complex, more reflective, more intellectual later works. The main criterion used to make that distinction was, in the words of Leslie Stephen, 'the growing tendency to substitute elaborate analysis for direct presentation' (*CH*, 478). To illustrate the point that George Eliot's 'reflective faculties have been growing at the expense of the imagination, and that, instead of simply enriching and extending the field of interest, they are coming into the foreground and usurping functions for which they are unfitted' (*CH*, 479), Stephen points to *Romola* (see Works, **pp. 56–61**) – a novel which, in his view, 'gives unqualified satisfaction only to people who hold that academical correctness of design can supply the place of vivid directness of intuitive vision' (*CH*, 479).

With the tendency towards increasing intellectual seriousness identified as the defining feature of the creative momentum behind George Eliot's literary career, the early discussions of her œuvre inevitably combined critical analysis with literary and intellectual biography. Perhaps inevitably in view of the history of the Leweses' unconventional marital arrangements and their impact on the way Marian's social position changed over the years, the majority of the early comments focused on the person she became in the late 1860s and the 1870s; in consequence, the picture of the writer that emerges from those personal records and memoirs is, again, one of profoundly serious and earnest but at the same rather stern individual, gentle in manner and yet unflinching in her firmly held beliefs and convictions (see Life and contexts, **pp. 21–4**). One of the best illustrations of this kind of comment can be found in the well-known account, by the educationalist and writer F.W.H. Myers, of one of the Leweses' visits to Cambridge, during which Marian made a fundamentally important statement of the essence of her philosophical position:

> She, stirred somewhat beyond her wont, and taking as her text the three words which have been used so often as the inspiring trumpet-calls of men, – the words *God, Immortality, Duty*, – pronounced, with terrible earnestness, how inconceivable was the *first*, how unbelievable the *second*, and yet how peremptory and absolute the *third*. Never, perhaps, have sterner accounts affirmed the sovereignty of impersonal and unrecompensing Law. I listened, and night fell; her grave, majestic countenance turned towards me like a Sibyl's in the gloom; it was as though she withdrew from my grasp, one by one, the two scrolls of promise, and left me the third scroll only, awful with inevitable fates.
>
> (Hutchinson 1996: I, 637)

The culmination of this process of the creation of the public image of George Eliot as the personification of the ideal of moral and intellectual seriousness preached in her novels came in 1885, with the publication, by the writer's widower J.W. Cross, of the three-volume story of *George Eliot's Life as Related in Her Letters and Journals*. A classic example of an official Victorian biography, Cross's book remained, until the 1960s, the standard source of information about the writer's life; it focuses, in particular, on her intellectual development, charting the history of her pursuit of self-education, the changing nature of her religious and philosophical ideas, the diversity and range of her reading, the impact of travel and, last but by no means least, the influences of her family, friends and acquaintances, in particular the personal and intellectual companionship of Lewes. Despite its merits, Cross's biography does not, however, escape the common fault of its genre and its time: in an attempt to create an authorised image of George Eliot for posterity, Cross is not only selective in his choice of primary materials and in the editorial treatment he gives them and rather conservative in toning down the humorous or simply informal passages from the original sources, but he also makes a positive effort to sanitise the picture he paints. Thus, for example, the book remains either silent, or at most highly circumspect, in its discussion of some of the potentially contentious issues in the writer's biography, such as, for example, her friendships with John Chapman (see Life and contexts, pp. 10–11) and Herbert Spencer (see Life and contexts, pp. 12–13). It was no doubt evasive comments such as the description of Marian's turbulent early London years as 'a new period in George Eliot's life, and emphatically the most important period, for now she is . . . thrown in contact with Mr Lewes, who is to exercise so paramount an influence on all her future, with Mr Herbert Spencer, and with a number of writers then representing the most fearless and advanced thought of the day' (Cross, I, 258) that led William Gladstone to refer to Cross's book as 'a Reticence in three volumes' (L, I, xiv). With a great deal of attention paid to matters of purely factual detail in relation to the Leweses' Continental itineraries, their reading lists and their social diaries, Cross's Life was, at the time of its publication and for several decades later, an informative and dependable source of information; for the twenty-first-century reader, however, it is primarily an illustration of a particular methodology of biographical writing and of a particular stage in the development of George Eliot scholarship.

Cross's biography of his wife may have been by far the most substantial of the early studies of her life and career, but it was not the first: within three years of the writer's death, a volume on *George Eliot* (1883) was published, in the *Eminent Women* series, by the German-born writer and critic Mathilde Blind. Written without access to the then still unpublished material in Cross's possession, the book is, for the modern reader, quite interesting in being free from the influence of Cross's editorial and hagiographical efforts; based, to a considerable extent, on primary research, conducted with the help of the writer's brother Isaac and her Coventry friends Charles and Caroline Bray and Sara Hennell, Blind's portrayal of Marian's personality is strikingly human in its stress on her ordinariness and vulnerability:

> Though not above the middle height Marian gave people the impression of being much taller than she really was, her figure, although thin and slight, being well-poised and not without a certain sturdiness of make. She was never robust in health, being delicately strung, and of a highly nervous temperament. In youth the keen excitability of her nature often made her wayward and hysterical. In fact her extraordinary intellectual vigour did not exclude the susceptibilities and weaknesses of a peculiarly feminine organisation. With all her mental activity she yet led an intensely emotional life, a life which must have held hidden trials for her, as in those days she was known by her friends 'to weep bucketfuls of tears'.
>
> (Blind 1883: 41–2)

Although designed to be balanced evenly between biography and criticism, Blind's book approaches George Eliot's creative achievement in a conventional biographical manner: her comments on the individual works tend to concentrate on the relationship between their contents and their author's personal background rather than on a more autonomous critical assessment. Nonetheless, Blind does make a number of interesting points and suggests a few evaluations that reflect the way in which George Eliot's work was perceived in the late Victorian era: she praises the artistic success of the early novels (*Adam Bede* [see Works, **pp. 36–44**]) is, in her view, 'a novel in which the amplest results of knowledge and meditation were so happily blended with instinctive insight into life and character, and the rarest dramatic imagination, as to stamp it immediately as one of the great triumphs and masterpieces in the world of fiction', Blind 1883: 106–7), and she remains respectful of *Romola* (see Works, **pp. 56–61**) – 'a majestic book . . . the most grandly planned of George Eliot's novels' (Blind 1883: 150) – but she thinks that *Middlemarch* (see Works, **pp. 67–80**) is, for all its merits, 'a story without a plot' (181), and she is highly critical of the way in which *Daniel Deronda* (see Works, **pp. 80–8**) embodies the new political ideology of Jewish nationalism in the characters of Mordecai and Daniel himself – 'the two most unsuccessful of George Eliot's vast gallery of characters[,] they are the representatives of an idea, but the idea has never been made flesh' (Blind 1883: 193). Overall, however, Blind's assessment of George Eliot's art is unambiguously enthusiastic:

> She undoubtedly adds to the common fund of crystallised human experience, as literature might be called, something which is specifically feminine. But, on the other hand, her intellect excels precisely in those qualities habitually believed to be masculine, one of its chief characteristics consisting in the grasp of abstract philosophical ideas. This faculty, however, by no means impairs those instinctive processes of the imagination by which true artistic work is produced; George Eliot combining in an unusual degree the subtlest power of analysis with that happy gift of genius which enabled her to create such characters as Amos Barton, Hetty, Mrs. Poyser, Maggie, and Tom Tulliver, Godfrey Cass and Caleb Garth, which seem to come fresh from the mould of Nature itself.
>
> (Blind 1883: 5–6)

Oscar Browning's volume in the *Great Writers* series, *Life of George Eliot* (1890) offers a brief but vivid introduction to the writer's life; Browning draws heavily on material from Cross's biography, but as the book progresses, his account becomes increasingly personal, not surprisingly in view of his fifteen-year-long friendship with the Leweses – he offers, for example, an interesting account of a typical Sunday afternoon reception at the Priory (Browning 1890: 89–90). In critical terms, the book offers only some very general comments; for Browning, the essence of George Eliot's art is 'to paint the lives of those she saw about her, to describe their joys and sorrows, their successes and failures, and, by insisting on the deep importance of this world, to teach us to hinder as little as possible the good which is burgeoning around us' (Browning 1890: 153). At the same time, Browning goes against the received opinion of his time in stressing the continuity of the development of George Eliot's art. Her best achievement is, in his view, *Daniel Deronda* (see Works, **pp. 80–8**): 'an effort to realize the highest purposes of art, to seize the strongest passions, the loftiest heights and the lowest depths of human nature' (Browning 1890: 144).

The most prominent of the early critical studies of George Eliot's work was the 1902 monograph by Leslie Stephen in the *English Men of Letters* series. The book adopts the familiar chronological life-and-works format, but it is clearly weighted towards critical commentary rather than biography, and it covers the author's œuvre quite comprehensively, including a separate chapter on *The Spanish Gypsy* (see Works, **pp. 93–4**) and the rest of the poetry, and a discussion (albeit short) of *Impressions of Theophrastus Such* (see Works, **pp. 89–90**). In line with the epoch's received opinion, Stephen values the achievement of the early novels far above the later works; for him, 'the first part of *The Mill* [*on the Floss*] represents . . . the culmination of George Eliot's power' (Stephen 1902: 88), not least because:

> George Eliot throws herself so frankly into Maggie's position, gives her 'double' such reality by the wayward foibles associated with her nobler impulses, and dwells so lovingly upon all her joys and sorrows, that the character glows with a more tender and poetic charm than any of her other heroines.
>
> (Stephen 1902: 88–9)

In the later novels, on the other hand, 'the imaginative sense is declining, and the characters are becoming emblems or symbols of principle, and composed of more moonshine than solid flesh and blood' (Stephen 1902: 191). The reason for that is that George Eliot's mind was of a theoretical rather than practical bent:

> She had not . . . the experience which could enable her to describe contemporary life, with its social and political ambitions and the rough struggle for existence in which practical lawyers and men of business are mainly occupied. She thinks of the world chiefly as the surrounding element of sordid aims into which her idealists are to go forth with such hope as may be of leavening the mass. She could not, therefore, draw lifelike portraits of such characters as were the staple of the ordinary novelist.
>
> (Stephen 1902: 202–3)

Where she does have the necessary experience, and where she therefore excels, is the moral, intellectual and emotional experience of women: 'one is always conscious that her women are drawn from the inside, and that her most successful men are substantially women in disguise' (Stephen 1902: 204). As a result,

> she is singularly powerful in describing the conflicts of emotions; the ingenious modes of self-deception in which most of us acquire considerable skill; the uncomfortable results of keeping a conscience till we have learnt to come to an understanding with it; the grotesque mixture of motives which results when we have reached a *modus vivendi*; the downright hypocrisy of the lower nature, or the comparatively pardonable and even commendable state of mind of the person who has a thoroughly consistent code of action, though he unconsciously interprets its laws in a non-natural sense to suit his convenience.
>
> (Stephen 1902: 205)

Some of the key points made by Leslie Stephen are developed further by his daughter Virginia Woolf in her influential essay of 1919. Virginia Woolf agrees with her father in her praise of George Eliot's early novels and in noting the imaginative energy with which the majority of the novels focus on the presentation of their female protagonists; in her view, however, the two impulses – George Eliot's attachment to 'the romance of the past' (Woolf 1925: 213) and her self-consciousness as a woman writer are at odds with each other, making the dynamics of her fiction more complex and therefore more interesting than critics accustomed to praising the relative simplicity of the early works would be prepared to allow. Virginia Woolf admits that 'there is no doubt that [George Eliot's heroines] bring out the worst in her, lead her into difficult places, make her self-conscious, didactic, and occasionally vulgar' (Woolf 1925: 213–14); at the same time, however, she notes that 'if you could delete the whole sisterhood you would leave a much smaller and a much inferior world, albeit a world of greater artistic perfection and far superior jollity and comfort' (Woolf 1925: 214). The reason for that is that 'the ancient consciousness of woman, charged with suffering and sensibility, and for so many ages dumb, seems in [George Eliot's heroines] to have brimmed and overflowed and uttered a demand for something – they scarcely know what – for something that is perhaps incompatible with the facts of human existence' (Woolf 1925: 217) – a reflection of the experience of the author herself,

> a memorable figure, inordinately praised and shrinking from her fame, despondent, reserved, shuddering back into the arms of love as if there alone were satisfaction and, it might be, justification, at the same time reaching out with 'a fastidious yet hungry ambition' for all that life could offer the free and inquiring mind and confronting her feminine aspirations with the real world of men.
>
> (Woolf 1925: 218)

It is the seriousness of that ambition that takes George Eliot beyond 'the quiet bucolic scene' of the early novels – not insignificantly, Virginia Woolf singles out for criticism her father's favourite, *The Mill on the Floss* (see Works, **pp. 44–51**, and Criticism, **p. 101**) – to create 'the mature *Middlemarch*, the magnificent book which with all its imperfections is one of the few English novels written for grown-up people' (Woolf 1925: 213).

Despite Virginia Woolf's praise, as the twentieth century progressed, George Eliot's reputation as a major novelist suffered a major downturn: her focus on moral issues appeared, in the inter-war period, too unfashionably Victorian in its didacticism, and her traditional, leisurely mode of storytelling and her focus on provincial life had little to offer, it seemed, to the more adventurous tastes of the increasingly dynamic, inventive, urban literary establishment of the modernist era. It was not of course the case that her achievement was forgotten or that her major works went out of print; rather, she was relegated to the status of a respected but rather unpopular classic, a representative of a bygone era, a writer likely to appeal to a scholar or an antiquarian rather than to a sophisticated modern reader. In that spirit, Anne Fremantle has the following to say in her study of *George Eliot* (1933) in the *Great Lives* series:

But we must grant George Eliot two enduring qualities: she is herself, historically, one of the most important figures in the social life of the mid-Victorian era, and her books are, historically, also invaluable guides to the Victorian attitude of mind. . . . Her attempt to carry ethical purpose and erudition into art nearly destroyed that art: it was as though she had harnessed a racehorse to a plough and wondered that it broke down without moving the cumbersome instrument even a few yards. She subordinated Passion and Faith, Youth and Beauty, to Duty and Destiny, and used the loveliness of nature as illustrative of scientific fact.

(Freemantle 1933: 141)

And yet, Fremantle continues, though

it is true she had no sense of form, and no love of, nor gift for handling, words, nor much dramatic power, . . . she has an almost unparalleled power of description, and her characterisation is unequalled. Her people are all living, warm, vivid and human, her countryside is absolutely alive and real, and in no other novel are everyday things so solidified – one can cuddle her children and eat her apples and smell her flowers as one can no one else's. . . . And, in spite of her faulty emphasis, she was so terribly in earnest that her emotions reach us, in spite of our instinctive suspicion of them.

(Freemantle 1933: 142–3)

This kind of ambivalent approach towards George Eliot's literary art transpires not only through the relatively less favourable accounts of her work but also, somewhat paradoxically, through the views of critics willing to recognise the significance of her achievement. Perhaps the most characteristic example of that kind of criticism is to be found in the relevant chapter of Lord David Cecil's influential study of *Early Victorian Novelists* (1934). Cecil is ready to recognise the fundamental modernity of George Eliot's literary art: he appreciates the intellectual integrity of her vision of the world, the seriousness of her moral purpose, as well as her assured command of the form of the novel; he is, in fact, prepared to admit that

her story is conditioned solely by the logical demands of situation or character; it ends sadly or happily, includes heroes or omits them, deals with the married or the unmarried, according as reason and observation lead her to think likely. . . . Hers are the first examples in English of the novel in its mature form; in them, it structurally comes of age.

(Cecil 1934: 289–90)

There is, in Cecil's account, a good deal of praise for George Eliot's power of description, for the subtlety of the analysis of the social scene of her novels, for the psychological richness and consistency of her depiction of character and for the balance and symmetry of the overall design of the novels. Despite all that, Cecil agrees that 'George Eliot's loss of reputation is not wholly undeserved' (Cecil

1934: 321): he blames the limited nature of her provincial outlook ('*Middlemarch* may be the nearest English equivalent to *War and Peace*, but it is a provincial sort of *War and Peace*', Cecil 1934: 322), the overcontrived tidiness of her plots, evident for instance in the arbitrariness of the marriage of Adam and Dinah at the end of *Adam Bede* (see Works, **pp. 36–44**), and the lack of dynamism and vitality in the presentation of her characters. Ultimately, Cecil says, George Eliot's talent was not equal to her intellect and ambition:

> Indeed – and here we come to the root cause of her failure to attain that supreme rank to which she aspired – there was something second-rate in the essential quality of George Eliot's inspiration. Her genius was built on the same grand scale as that of the greatest novelists; but it was not, as theirs was, compounded of the best material. She had more talents than most writers; but they were none of them of the finest calibre. . . . But her intellect was always forcing her to attempt things that needed supreme talents for their achievement. . . . The intellect was the engine which started the machinery of the imagination working. But the engine was too powerful for the machine: it kept it at a strain at which it could not run smoothly and easily. So that it never produced a wholly satisfactory work of art.
>
> (Cecil 1934: 326–8)

Echoes of a similar sense of unease about the intellectualism of George Eliot's writings and about the atmosphere of moral seriousness that permeates the world of her fictions can be detected even in the comments made on her works by the most fervent admirers of her talent: thus, for example, Blanche Colton Williams, the author of *George Eliot: A Biography* (1936), perhaps the most enthusiastic of the inter-war studies of the writer and her work, characterises her literary style in the following terms:

> Her immediate style is enriched by apt figures that integrally clarify and adorn, not decorative scrollwork obscuring architectural design. From natural phenomena early observed on the farm at Griff, rises the first class; from interest in science, heightened by her association with Lewes, follows the second; in classical literature and in music is her third source. No logician ever wrote sentences more logical, however complex and involved; variety of sentence proves her past-master of rhetoric. Her dominant tone, mood, and atmosphere are deep and sad; she was unable, through her ineradicable seriousness, long to free herself from the rhythm of gloom and melancholy.
>
> (Williams 1936: 322)

Beginnings of modern criticism

The first impulses towards a reassessment of George Eliot's place in the tradition of modern English literature came from biographers rather than critics – somewhat paradoxically, perhaps, given that it was precisely the areas of biography and textual criticism that could well have appeared, in the 1930s and 1940s, to be in little need of significant new research. Cross's *Life* was there as the standard biography, and it is a measure of its influence that it remained the main source of biographical information for George Eliot scholars for over half a century; although the majority of critical works published until the 1950s followed the traditional life-and-works format, their biographical sections tended to rely on Cross for matters of factual detail, quotations from the letters and journals and other information – Elizabeth S. Haldane, the author of *George Eliot and Her Times: A Victorian Study*, was indeed prepared to state, quite unequivocally, that 'it is of course improbable that [Cross's biography] will ever be superseded' (Haldane 1927: vii). Much the same could be said about the relevant bibliographical research and the textual study of George Eliot's works; with the twenty-volume Cabinet Edition of 1878–80, editorially supervised by the author herself, established as the authoritative text, the George Eliot canon appeared to be firmly defined and in little need for further investigation.

One of the first scholars to challenge this state of affairs was Anna Theresa Kitchel, whose *George Eliot and George Lewes: A Review of Records* (1933) was the first major attempt to bring into the study of George Eliot's artistic biography the evidence of independent research; with the focus of her book mainly on the influence on George Eliot's work of Lewes's philosophical knowledge and ideas, Kitchel offers an important contribution to the study of the intellectual background of the novels, particularly with regard to the impact of the Positivist philosophy of August Comte (see Life and contexts, **pp. 14–15**). Kitchel also pioneered the study of the technical aspects of George Eliot's creative method: her 1950 edition of the *Quarry for 'Middlemarch'* – the notebook the writer used during the planning and composition of the novel (see Life and contexts, **pp. 24–6**) – demonstrated, on the one hand, the extent of the research, particularly into medical science and recent social and political history, which George Eliot engaged in before embarking on her project, and, on the other hand, the precision with which she planned the structure of the book, including in particular the compositional balance of its individual parts. In this way, Kitchel paved the way for further textual study of the novel, which culminated in the publication, in 1960, of Jerome Beaty's *'Middlemarch': From Notebook to Novel* – to this day the most authoritative account of the history of the writing of George Eliot's most important work.

Significant as Anna Theresa Kitchel's contribution to George Eliot studies was, the pride of place among the writer's mid-twentieth-century biographers belongs, without doubt, to Gordon S. Haight. His first major publication, *George Eliot and John Chapman* (1940), offers a detailed account, based largely on the evidence of Chapman's diaries, of Marian Evans's life in the crucial period of the early 1850s, the time during which she first established herself as a significant presence in the world of the intellectual elite of Victorian London (see Life and contexts, **pp. 10–15**). Almost entirely suppressed in Cross's biography (see Criticism, **pp. 98–9**), largely, one might well assume, because of the highly unconventional lifestyle of the Chapman household and the ambiguity of Marian Evans's position in it, the story of her friendship with her first publisher and editor offers some fascinating insights into her own personality, much more passionate and spontaneous than Cross would have had his readers believe, into the mechanisms of her editorial work on the *Westminster Review* and into the social mores of the mid-nineteenth-century London *literati*.

Gordon S. Haight's reputation as a leading George Eliot scholar was consolidated with the publication, in 1954, of the first three volumes of his monumental edition of *The George Eliot Letters*; the remaining four volumes followed in 1956 and two additional ones, including some newly discovered letters as well as a significant amount of supplementary material, were added in 1978. The product of more than twenty years of research, the *Letters* are an indispensable source for all serious students of George Eliot's work: the collection includes not only all of the letters available at the time of publication which she wrote to members of her family, her friends, acquaintances, publishers and admirers, as well as a selection of letters she received from her numerous correspondents, but also an extensive selection of other documents, among them excerpts from her own journals, letters to and from Lewes, excerpts from his diaries and a broad variety of other relevant papers; some of the most interesting materials in the collection include extensive correspondence between the Leweses and George Eliot's publishers, particularly John Blackwood, as well as, included in the two supplementary volumes, numerous letters from Lewes's sons, both during their time at school and following Thornie's and Bertie's emigration to South Africa, and substantial excerpts from the autobiography of Edith Simcox (see Life and contexts, **p. 26**). Very importantly, Haight's edition is based, where possible, on original manuscript sources, making it possible for him to restore the full text of numerous letters first published, sometimes in a significantly amended form, by Cross; a comparison of the full text of the letters with the versions published in the 1885 *Life* offers some very interesting perspectives not only on the letters themselves, and the character of the writer as she emerges from them, but also on Cross's editorial practice, reflective both of his own perception of his role as his late wife's biographer and of the social and cultural assumptions and expectations of the late Victorian society for whom the *Life* was compiled (see Criticism, **pp. 98–9**). With its extensive annotations, covering not only detailed background information necessary to contextualise the letters, but also explanations of references to literature, music and the visual arts, sources of literary and biblical allusions, etc., Haight's work remains to this day a standard research resource, unlikely to be superseded in the foreseeable future.

The new developments in biographical research on the author of *Middlemarch* were bound to result, in due course, in a critical reassessment of her place in the literary tradition of the English language. One of the first signs of a change in the critical climate was the publication of Gerald Bullett's study of *George Eliot: Her Life and Books* (1947). The general approach adopted in this work may be quite conventional in its predominantly biographical focus – the section devoted to the critical assessment of the novels occupies less than a third of the volume – but even in his account of the writer's life, the tenor of Bullett's commentary is distinctly modern: thus, for example, he uses the evidence of the earlier studies of Kitchel (see Criticism, **p. 105**) and Haight (see Criticism, **pp. 105–6**) to discuss, at considerable length, the question of the impact that developments in Marian Evans's personal life, in particular her relationships with Chapman, Spencer and Lewes, had on the crystallisation of her moral ideas and her understanding of psychology. The real significance of Bullett's book lies, however, in his reassessment of the literary value of George Eliot's works, both against each other and – perhaps more importantly – in relation to the broader context of Victorian fiction. Although he does agree with his predecessors in perceiving the dynamics of George Eliot's development as an artist to be the function of the dichotomy of 'intention versus inspiration' (Bullett 1947: 195), he is firmly of the view that the tension between the two finds a successful resolution in *Middlemarch* (see Works, pp. 67–80), which has for him 'some claim to be regarded as the greatest English novel of its time' (Bullett 1947: 215); the breadth and depth of the vision she produces in this book, 'the richness and variety of colour, the warm undertones of meaning, the mingling of comedy and tragedy and dramatic irony, the abundance of invention, the densely populated provincial background, the author's imaginative saturation in her theme' (Bullett 1947: 227), all contribute to create 'an amplitude and a delicacy of draught[s]manship which are almost Tolstoyan' (Bullett 1947: 221). The comparison with Tolstoy is not a hyperbole: in Bullett's view, George Eliot surpasses her predecessors and contemporaries, including Jane Austen, the Brontës, Dickens, Thackeray and Trollope, in being 'a first-rate imaginative artist who was also an abstract and analytical thinker' (Bullett 1947: 161), able to 'enter intuitively into the lives of her dramatis personae, feeling their joys and sorrows and imaginatively sharing . . . their intellectual limitations, while at the same time remaining a little aloof, ready to relate all human experience to a general philosophy' (Bullett 1947: 161).

Gerald Bullett's book was followed by Joan Bennett's *George Eliot: Her Mind and Her Art* (1948). Refocusing the conventional all-inclusive biographical approach to concentrate on the influences that shaped George Eliot's creative imagination, Joan Bennett discusses the impact of the future writer's years in Coventry and as a journalist in London before embarking on an extensive analysis of her artistic method and, subsequently, on a critical discussion of each of the seven novels. The book's central argument is that the key element of George Eliot's vision of the world lies in achieving, in her presentation of the social world of the novels, a sense of organic unity: '[W]hen we try, after an interval, to recall any one of them we find ourselves thinking as much about the life of a village or a provincial town or of the interrelation of groups of families as about the central drama' (Bennett 1948: 78). It is the handling of the social world of the novels that determines the degree of their artistic success; 'the relative failure of *Romola, Felix Holt* and *Daniel Deronda* is partly due to the fact that in these three works, for different reasons, the social background is imperfectly focussed' (Bennett 1948: 83). The discussions of the individual novels deal, in some detail, with their themes, the presentation of characters, the construction of the plots, the use of diverse narrative modes and so on: the overall impression is one of sustained comprehensiveness which made the book, at the time of its first publication and for a decade to come, perhaps the best full-length study of the novels and their background. To the twenty-first-century reader, Joan Bennett's work may well appear somewhat bland and pedestrian, but there is not much there to disagree with, and the clarity of the argument ensures that the book has not dated quite as badly as some of the other studies from the 1940s and 1950s.

By far the most important of the critical accounts of George Eliot's work published in the 1940s was, however, F.R. Leavis's seminal study *The Great Tradition* (1948; the George Eliot section originally appeared in *Scrutiny* in 1945 and

1946). Leavis's central thesis is that George Eliot is one of a relatively small number of English novelists – Jane Austen before her, Henry James, Joseph Conrad and D.H. Lawrence after her – whose moral, psychological and aesthetic seriousness justifies their inclusion in what he defines as 'the great tradition of the English novel' (Leavis 1948: 7). In Leavis's view, 'the great novelists in that tradition are all very much concerned with "form"; they are all very original technically, having turned their genius to the working out of their own appropriate methods and procedures' (Leavis 1948: 7); at the same time, 'they are all distinguished by a vital capacity for experience, a kind of reverent openness before life, and a marked moral intensity' (Leavis 1948: 9). This 'capacity for experience' is, however, not to be identified with the kind of quasi-autobiographical spontaneity so familiar to the readers of the early works of George Eliot, particularly *The Mill on the Floss* (see Works, **pp. 44–51**); in fact, Leavis's analysis of that novel goes against the flow of the conventional critical opinion in declaring that in the early parts of the book, 'George Eliot's attitude to her own immaturity as represented by Maggie is the reverse of a mature one' (Leavis 1948: 42), while genuine psychological insight and understanding can be found in the presentation of Maggie's inner conflict as she falls in love with Stephen. The comments on the later novels are equally unconventional: Leavis praises the bold treatment of the Transome–Jermyn plot in *Felix Holt* (see Works, **pp. 61–7**) – 'although [Mrs Transome's] case is conceived in an imagination that is profoundly moral, the presentment of it is a matter of psychological observation – psychological observation so utterly convincing in its significance that the price paid by Mrs Transome for her sin in inevitable consequences doesn't need a moralist's insistence' (Leavis 1948: 56) – but he criticises the presentation of Dorothea, in the otherwise successful *Middlemarch* (see Works, **pp. 67–80**), as characterised by 'day-dream self-indulgence' (Leavis 1948: 77). The pinnacle of George Eliot's art is, in Leavis's opinion, the Gentile part of *Daniel Deronda* (see Works, **pp. 80–8**); the measure of the success of this notional half-novel, which he calls *Gwendolen Harleth*, is that in structural and thematic terms it is a subtler and more profound predecessor of a major late-Victorian classic, James's *The Portrait of a Lady*. In her subtle presentation of Gwendolen's tragedy, George Eliot

> exhibits a traditional moral sensibility expressing itself, not within a frame of 'old articles of faith', but nevertheless with perfect sureness, in judgments that involve confident positive standards, and yet affect us as simply the report of luminous intelligence. She deals in the weakness and ordinariness of human nature, but doesn't find it contemptible, or show either animus or self-deceiving indulgence towards it; and, distinguished and noble as she is, we have in reading her the feeling that she is in and of the humanity she presents with so clear and disinterested a vision.
>
> (Leavis 1948: 123)

An energetic, provocative, highly idiosyncratic book, *The Great Tradition* does not attempt to offer a comprehensive or balanced study of George Eliot's novels, but it proposes a reading that still remains an important point of reference in the critical debate about her work.

The culmination of the early period of the development of George Eliot criticism came with the publication, in 1959, of Barbara Hardy's book *The Novels of George Eliot: A Study in Form*. As the title suggests, the focus of the study is consistently on the design of George Eliot's fiction: Barbara Hardy takes issue with early twentieth-century critics of the genre, such as Henry James and Percy Lubbock, who, in their pursuit of the ideal of the tightly patterned, dramatised, highly symbolic fictional form, tended to ignore the structural intricacies of the multiplot novels of the Victorian period and describe them, as James did in his Preface to *The Tragic Muse*, as 'large loose baggy monsters'. Barbara Hardy argues for a more inclusive understanding of the concept of form in fiction:

> The novel may be described in terms of the outline – the disposition of its trunk and limbs – but it must also be recognized as depending on the presence of pattern in every unit, like the pattern within the pattern of a Chinese puzzle or of any bit of matter. The form of the novel may mean the form of everything which contributes to its six hundred pages of story and scenes and events and characters and words and tone.
>
> (Hardy 1959: 8)

In line with this statement, Barbara Hardy embarks on a detailed analysis of the works of George Eliot in an attempt to demonstrate how the writer's tragic vision is conveyed through the formal organisation of her imagined world. With her focus firmly on George Eliot's artistic method rather than on the interpretation of individual novels as such, Barbara Hardy rejects the conventional chronological novel-by-novel approach and discusses, taking her examples from the full range of George Eliot's works, different aspects of the construction of her fictions, from the presentation of characters through the structure of plots, the diversity of narrative voices and the use of imagery. The analysis identifies a number of recurrent motifs, types of characters and patterns of plot. Thus, for example, George Eliot's conception of a tragic character changes from the unheroic protagonists of her early fictions, such as Amos Barton or Hetty Sorrel, to the more complex presentation of tragic heroines in the later fictions, from Maggie Tulliver to Gwendolen Harleth. The significance of ethical considerations in George Eliot's fiction is underlined by the careful patterning of characters: egoists and altruists – Arthur Donnithorne and Adam Bede, Tito Melema and Romola Bardi, Rosamond Vincy and Dorothea Brooke – are paired off against each other to bring out their contrasting moral perceptions and attitudes. Similarly fruitful is the use of the motifs of coincidence, contrast and repetition in the construction of the plots of the novels. Barbara Hardy singles out, in particular, the use of parallel sub-plots to underline the significance of the characters' moral choices and their implications. George Eliot's narrators modulate between different tones and levels of distancing from the story they tell: the shifting point of view of the novels is delivered through a narrative voice that moves between the soft, domestic tone of personal intimacy, the omniscient mode of prophecy and the virtual self-effacement of dramatic presentation; this multiplicity of narratorial stances is paralleled by the diversity of symbolic modes, ranging from pathos (images of wounded animals, flowers and children) to irony (complex images of mirrors and labyrinths in *Middlemarch* [see Works, **pp. 67–80**] and of horses in *Daniel*

Deronda [see Works, **pp. 80–8**]). It is indeed this complexity of the formal organisation of the novels that makes George Eliot such a profound analyst of the moral and psychological problems of humankind:

> She shows all the human variables: the successes as well as the failures, the mixed cases, even the unacted possible lives that haunt all our commitments. The result is moral definiteness, maybe, but it is also human movement. We are left with the impression, after reading one of her novels, that this is as close as the novelist can get to human multiplicity – that here form has been given to fluidity and expansiveness. We can trace the form as we can trace a diagram but the form is always there in the interest of the human picture.
>
> (Hardy 1959: 237–8)

A rather similar formal approach to the analysis of George Eliot's novels is adopted by Reva Stump in her monograph on *Movement and Vision in George Eliot's Novels* (1959). The fundamental premise of her study is that the key element of the metaphorical structure of George Eliot's fiction is the motif of vision: the characters' changing perceptions of the world and the dynamic perspective from which the reader observes the characters create a sense of movement which generates the novels' central moral message:

> In each of the seven novels of George Eliot . . . a rhythm is established and perpetuated by a complex pattern of vision imagery, by a group of themes united through the concept of vision, and by the dramatic action which for the most part derives its tension from the contradictory urges to see and to avoid seeing. This rhythm, a movement produced by the recurrence of remembered and expected elements connected with vision, is the structure of all George Eliot's novels. [. . .]
>
> The rhythm works both in terms of the reader who perceives it as structure and the character with whose vision the novel is concerned. For the character who moves toward vision is in the process of learning to expect his future, consider his present, and remember his past, all in realistic terms and in relation to a broader referent than self. The character who moves away from vision has destructive daydreams about his future, fails to consider his present in terms of the larger pattern of existence, and is frequently cut off from his own and the larger past. In each case the life pattern of the character is worked out through the expected recurrence of elements, a series of progressively clearer or progressively duller visions, depending on the direction of the movement.
>
> (Stump 1959: 3–4)

To demonstrate the operation of this mechanism, Stump analyses the imagery of three novels – *Adam Bede, The Mill on the Floss* and *Middlemarch* – identifying, in each case, the specific pattern the story follows. Thus, in *Adam Bede* (see Works, **pp. 36–44**), Arthur and Hetty's movement towards moral blindness is contrasted with, and eventually rectified by, Adam and Dinah's movement towards a more complete understanding of themselves and of the world; in *The Mill on the Floss* (see Works, **pp. 44–51**), the pattern is one of Maggie's painful and ultimately tragic progress towards clarity of moral vision and self-understanding against the pressures she encounters in the world which cannot accommodate her uncompromising distinctiveness; finally, *Middlemarch* (see Works, **pp. 67–80**) is described in terms of its central metaphor of a web of dynamic interconnections which together produce a complex structure in which individual elements continuously illuminate one another, generating the novel's multifaceted moral vision. The exercise is carried out convincingly if somewhat mechanically: even if her overall argument feels, at times, somewhat schematic, Stump does manage to incorporate into her analysis, and relate to her central topic, a broad range of motifs, such as the images of animals in *The Mill on the Floss*, or of windows and labyrinths in *Middlemarch*. Overall, the book is a perceptive account of the way George Eliot organises the metaphorical structures of her works. Ironically, it would have made more of an impact if its publication had not coincided with that of Barbara Hardy's seminal study.

Biographical studies and related works

It was in many ways a natural consequence of the publication of *The George Eliot Letters* (see Criticism, **p. 106**) that Gordon S. Haight's next major project was a new full-length biography based on the material he had collected; published in 1968, *George Eliot: A Biography* was indeed the first major study of the life of the author of *Middlemarch* to adopt a critical rather than hagiographical approach to its subject, and the success with which it achieved its goal ensured that it became, for the next quarter of a century, the standard account of Marian Evans's life. With its roots firmly in Haight's research towards his earlier publications, the book makes extensive use of the documentary evidence from both *George Eliot and John Chapman* (see Criticism, **pp. 105–6**) and the *Letters*; Haight is, in consequence, the first of the biographers to write extensively about Marian's time with the Chapmans and to offer a detailed account of her own and, perhaps even more importantly, Lewes's dealings with publishers and of the financial side of her literary career. The book also offers some interesting insights into the future novelist's early literary attempts: Haight prints, for the first time, two pieces of her juvenilia, an incomplete essay on 'Affectation and Conceit' and, more importantly, a few scenes from her first-ever venture in the world of fiction – a historical tale of the English Civil War, 'Edward Neville'. The biography acknowledges research carried out by other scholars as well: Haight pays a good deal of attention to the role played, in the last decade or so of Marian's life, by her female friends and admirers, in particular by Edith Simcox, whose unusually intense attachment to Marian was first studied in a monograph by K.A. McKenzie (1961). Although not without its weaknesses – Haight glosses over a number of questions relating to the relationship between Marian and Cross and the circumstances surrounding their marriage (see Life and contexts, **pp. 29–30**), while his relatively heavy reliance on quotations from original sources may sometimes get in the way of the smooth flow of the narrative – *George Eliot: A Biography* remains one of the most reliable, unbiased, and level-headed sources of information about its subject.

Haight's biography easily eclipsed other biographies written since the Second World War, such as Lawrence and Elizabeth Hanson's *Marian Evans and George Eliot: A Biography* (1952), Margaret Crompton's *George Eliot: The Woman* (1960), or Rosemary Sprague's *George Eliot: A Biography* (1968) – all of them rather traditionalist in approach and lacking the kind of immersion in primary sources that permeates Haight's study. The authority his book imposed on the world of George Eliot scholarship resulted, understandably if somewhat paradoxically, in a considerable slow-down in serious biographical research: instead, the early 1970s saw, for example, the publication of Marghanita Laski's *George Eliot and Her World* (1973), full of very interesting illustrations but otherwise clearly a popular rather than scholarly work. For over twenty years there appeared, in fact, no new full-length general biographies; the only study published during that period and devoted specifically to the writer's life, Ruby Redinger's *George Eliot: The Emergent Self* (1976), is not so much a straightforward biographical narrative as an extremely detailed analysis of the development of the complex network of personal relationships and psychological interdependencies that over the years shaped Marian Evans's personality, social and intellectual as well as private and emotional. As the title of her book indicates, Ruby Redinger concentrates her attention on the process of the emergence, after a long period of gestation, of the creative impulse that was to turn Marian Evans the translator, essayist and editor into George Eliot the creative writer; her book seeks to explain how it happened that 'although George Eliot was unable to write even when youth, talent, and opportunity were present, creativity did not wither within her, but stayed alive and mysteriously protected, so that when it finally burst forth, it did so with as much vigor and freshness as if she had been in the spring of her life' (Redinger 1976: 4). In Ruby Redinger's view, a genuine insight into the process of the development of George Eliot's creative self can be gained only through a sustained effort to probe the personal experience that lies at the heart of her artistic impulse. It is the joys, dilemmas, and fears of the writer's past that provide the key to the understanding of the sources of her inspiration and of the nature of the creative process that transformed them into works of literary art:

> An exploration of the causes of her long period of frustration and her release from it provides considerable insight into her career as a writer; it also illumines, as individuated in her, the unfolding self – its power and uncanny strategy, whether or not it leads, as in her instance, to the tangible production of genius. . . . [T]he more one is aware of the depth and power of her frustration, the more remarkable does it seem that she triumphed over it. That triumph was not achieved by one leap into fiction writing: rather, hers was a gradual and tenuous history, which might well have been fatally interrupted at any time during the period of her writing. For hers was not the self to come forward in an instant, like Athena, full-armed. There were latent powers to be awakened, and their awakening came as a result of the subtly continuing, modulating force of her writing present upon her buried past.
>
> (Redinger 1976: 4–5)

In her account of the development of George Eliot's artistic personality, Ruby Redinger focuses on the early and middle years of the writer's life (see Life and contexts, pp. 2–15), including her family and religious background, her formative years in Coventry, her experiences after her arrival in London and the influence of George Henry Lewes. The subsequent years of her career as a writer of fiction are treated in less detail, with the novels and stories discussed as illustrative of specific aspects of their author's psychological development rather than as works of art in their own right. Although quite lengthy and somewhat difficult to navigate for readers wishing to consult it rather than read it through (its long chapters are divided into untitled sections, and the method of annotation adopted throughout the volume is very inconvenient for readers to use), *George Eliot: The Emergent Self* remains a complex and engaging study, probably the subtlest psycho-biography of the novelist available to date.

The title of Valerie A. Dodd's 1990 book, *George Eliot: An Intellectual Life*, does not reflect the contents of the volume quite precisely enough: it is not, as one might perhaps expect, a comprehensive study of the way in which the diverse intellectual interests of the author of *Middlemarch* are reflected in her novels but rather a study of the impact on the young Marian Evans (the book ends at the point when she is about to embark on her new career as a novelist and hardly mentions any of her works other than the periodical essays and the translations) of the ideas of some of the leading late eighteenth- and, predominantly, nineteenth-century philosophers. The exploration of the breadth of Marian Evans's interest in recent German (Georg Wilhelm Hegel, Ludwig Feuerbach, David Friedrich Strauss), French (Jean-Jacques Rousseau, Claude-Henri de Saint-Simon, Auguste Comte) and British (Thomas Carlyle, John Stuart Mill, John Ruskin, Herbert Spencer) thinking is certainly an important aspect of the investigation into the intellectual background of the writings she was in due course to produce as George Eliot; at the same time, however, the comments that 'Marian Evans's quest to express the truth in fictions partook of the strenuousness of philosophical inquiry, but her novels were to contemplate the complexity of reality from a flexible viewpoint, and the reality she described was to reflect her sense of wonder and beauty' (Dodd 1990: 314), and that 'her varied modes of perception, and her representational wisdom derived from the sceptical eclecticism of much of the philosophy of her age, and were literary counterparts of it' (Dodd 1990: 314) are really invitations for a further discussion of her works rather than satisfactory conclusions to a book-length study. The reader is not helped by the structure of the book either. It opens with a discussion of the state of the philosophical debate in Britain in the first half of the nineteenth century, with particular focus on Carlyle and Mill, and it subsequently moves on to an account of Marian Evans's life, interspersed with sections devoted to the discussion of the work of the thinkers whose writings she read at various stages of her life, and the impact that their ideas had on her own intellectual development. With this uncertainty of focus and with its consistent refusal to indicate the relevance of its investigations to the study of George Eliot's writings, Valerie Dodd's study, though well researched and potentially quite valuable in terms of the importance of its subject area, is, as a result, rather less useful than it might at first sight appear to promise to be.

George Eliot: Godless Woman (1993) by Brian Spittles, in the Writers in their Time series, is a very successful attempt to contextualise the life and work of the author of *Middlemarch* against the background of the social, economic, cultural and political life of Victorian Britain. Using a broad range of contemporaneous sources, both documentary and literary, Spittles draws a vivid picture of the dynamic world of socio-economic and intellectual interdependencies that defined the environment in which George Eliot's works were written and published: he focuses, in particular, on issues which had a major significance in the context of her specific interests and concerns, for example on the changes in Victorian attitudes towards religion and the emergence of agnosticism, or on the educational and professional prospects of Victorian women. Spittles is particularly enlightening in his account of the economic factors which shaped the world of George Eliot's novels: he offers some very interesting material on the mechanisms of the Victorian publishing industry and book trade and on the functioning of the Victorian marriage market; he is acutely aware of the financial circumstances of Victorian women and of the subtle distinctions of class and status that defined their roles in the society of the day. Although his book makes frequent reference to the works of George Eliot, it does not do so in the spirit of literary analysis: characters and situations from her novels and poems are brought into his argument in the same way as evidence from historical documents, the works of other writers, or her own critical writings and correspondence – to illustrate particular points about the structure and functioning of Victorian society and in this way to prepare the reader for a more informed reading of the novels and poems. Undoubtedly influenced by the intellectual atmosphere of new historicism, Spittles' book belongs more in the field of cultural history and literary biography than in literary criticism; vividly written and very easy to follow, it is an important source of information for all readers wishing to acquire a more profound understanding of the world which shaped George Eliot as a thinker and artist.

The most unusual and, from the literary-critical point of view, the most interesting of the biographical (or, in this instance, semi-biographical) works published in the 1990s is a study by Rosemarie Bodenheimer, *The Real Life of Mary Ann Evans: George Eliot, Her Letters and Fiction* (1994). Not a biography in the strict sense of the word, Rosemarie Bodenheimer's book investigates selected aspects of the writer's life as illuminated by her letters and her works of fiction; it pays a good deal of attention to the period of Marian Evans's adolescence and youth, as well as to her early years as a novelist; there are individual sections on her relationships with George Henry Lewes and John Walter Cross, with her Lewes stepsons, and with Alexander Main, Elma Stuart, Edith Simcox and her other young protegées. The purpose of the project is 'to suggest some ways in which George Eliot's works may be read autobiographically, as meditations on and transformations of the most intimate paradoxes of her very paradoxical experience' (Bodenheimer 1994: xv); Rosemarie Bodenheimer's interest lies, importantly, not so much in using fictional material for purposes of biographical inference and speculation but in exploring George Eliot's 'great and flexible capacity for self-understanding, for transforming painful preoccupations into distanced fictional structures' (Bodenheimer 1994: xvi). Thus, for example, the analysis of the future novelist's early letters to her friends and confidantes offers some interesting insights into the origins of the tone of quiet but assured and determined self-control that characterises the narrative voice of her fictions; the correspondence from the period in which she began her relationship with Lewes is shown to illuminate the moral dilemmas of Maggie in *The Mill on the Floss* (see Works, **pp. 44–51**); the developing quasi-maternal relationship with Lewes's sons, particularly Charles, serves as the background for the discussion of the theme of surrogate parenthood in *Silas Marner* (see Works, **pp. 51–6**); finally, the role of spiritual guide Marian Evans Lewes adopted, in the last decade of her life, towards her circle of young admirers is discussed as offering a background for the analysis, in *Daniel Deronda* (see Works, **pp. 80–8**), of the relationship between Daniel and Gwendolen in the broader context of the theme of mentorship. Through her analyses, Rosemarie Bodenheimer demonstrates how

> George Eliot's teaching and ideology . . . emerge from dynamic reactions and counterreactions within her emotional economy[:] . . . her special valuation of memory and her doctrine of sympathy were born of reactions to what she imagined as her own transgressions and can be initially understood as the instincts of remorse and repair, rather than as the adopted beliefs of an agnostic humanist or the self-establishing ideologies of a Victorian liberal intellectual.
>
> (Bodenheimer 1994: 266)

A sophisticated psychological study, *The Real Life of Mary Ann Evans* manages to combine thorough and authoritative biographical investigation (it offers, for example, a detailed, exhaustive discussion of the Liggins affair, see Life and contexts, **p. 19**) with insightful literary criticism, and it demonstrates the nature of the interdependence between the writer's life and her creations:

> Her reluctance to confront any direct form of autobiographical writing was of a piece with the fundamental instinct to perform her self-understanding through outward projections. George Eliot must have known – as she knew so much about herself – that her only real opportunity for evoking the many-sided truths of her inward experience lay in the imaginative activity of fiction-making.
>
> (Bodenheimer 1994: 267)

Frederick Karl's extensive study, *George Eliot: A Biography* (1995), appears to have been intended to supersede Gordon S. Haight's 1968 book (see Criticism, **p. 111**) as the standard biography for the 1990s: it is conceived on a grand scale, it incorporates the findings of recent scholarship, for example in its discussion of Marian Evans's friendship with Herbert Spencer (see Life and contexts, **pp. 12–13**), and it aims to portray her, against the background of her time, as the 'voice of the century[:] . . . more than anyone else in the period . . . most representative, most emblematic of the ambiguities, the anguish, and divisiveness of the Victorian era' (Karl 1995: xi). Accordingly, Karl sets out to present a vision of the writer's life as a process of continuous struggle in which Marian Evans – 'a deeply divided woman, a deeply divided thinker, and, as part of this, an artist desperately trying to hold together many disparate and even contradictory forces' (Karl 1995: xi) – attempted to define her place in the world in the face of numerous challenges she faced in her personal, intellectual and professional life, as a daughter, an aspiring provincial intellectual, an agnostic, a journalist, a rebel against conventions, a creative writer but, most importantly, a woman attempting to assert her place in the largely patriarchal world of mid-nineteenth-century Britain. It is the dynamics of those different and often ambiguous or contradictory roles which Marian Evans played in her life that lies, in Karl's opinion, at the heart of her personal, social, intellectual and artistic development, as an individual, a thinker and a writer:

> To an extent, Eliot deconstructed her life at each decisive point, since she moved the center of it to uncertain and ambiguous places: renouncing the religion of her father, moving up to London to carve out a career, going off with Lewes, then attempting fiction. She was opening herself up to potentialities without any assurance that what she was doing would turn out correctly for her. This very cautious young woman had become a less than cautious mature person. She chose courses she could not rationally defend, and yet rational defense became the cornerstone of her humanistic impulses, the basis of her secularism. In effect, she split herself as a further means of renewal.
>
> (Karl 1995: xv)

Extensively researched and full of information as it is, Karl's biography does not, unfortunately, fully live up to what it promises. The difficulty lies, it seems, in the way in which the author's insistence on the comprehensiveness and inclusiveness of his treatment of the minutiae of factual detail begins, at times, to create the impression that the central narrative loses its edge: as a result, the impression created on the reader is that the portrait of Marian Evans that Karl paints may well be complex and rich but that it is also rather confusing and that it lacks the precision, the structural clarity and the kind of directness of storytelling method that are needed in a book which is meant not only to be read in its entirety but also to be used for reference purposes. The style of Karl's discourse and the presentation of the volume do not help either: in a manner that would be disappointing in any biography, Karl's book does not immediately engage the reader with its central story, and the vagueness of the titles of the individual sections of the work, the lack of a clear indication of its chronological structure and the adoption of a rather inconvenient method of annotation make it less reader-friendly and ultimately less useful than it clearly had the potential to be.

Perhaps the best of the general biographies published in the 1990s is the 1996 book by Rosemary Ashton, *George Eliot: A Life*. Meticulously documented but at the same time vividly written and therefore thoroughly engaging both for a serious student of Victorian literature and for the general reader alike, it offers a clear, straightforward and yet impressively detailed account of the life of a woman who, Rosemary Ashton believes, came to symbolise the complexity and the dynamism of the social and cultural reality of mid-nineteenth-century Britain:

> If any writer of the age captures sympathetically the discontinuities, contradictions, and bewilderments of the Victorian age and its immediate predecessor, it is George Eliot, born, as it happens, in the same year as Queen Victoria herself. More than any other novelist – even Dickens – she gives imaginative expression to the excitement and the pain of

being caught up in a society in flux. Her career as a novelist began relatively late, when she was in her late thirties. By that time she had lived an already rich and extraordinary life, moving from provincial piety to metropolitan scepticism, from scholarly spinsterhood to stimulating partnership, from sexual frustration to sexual fulfilment, from Church-and-State Toryism to liberalism of a conservative kind.

(Ashton 1996: 9)

Although the focus of Rosemary Ashton's book is firmly biographical, her book does weave into its account of the story of Marian Evans's life a number of short but perceptive critical essays on her writings; those passages do not in themselves constitute a sustained analysis of George Eliot's œuvre, but they offer a fair amount of useful background information and are therefore a good starting point for more advanced critical discussion. With its carefully maintained balance between solid documentary accuracy and non-speculative and yet insightful critical assessment, and between the concentration on the central narrative and the presentation of its broader social, economic and intellectual background (an aspect of the book in dealing with which Rosemary Ashton excels), this is a reliable source of factual information about Marian Evans's life and a stimulating introduction to the study of her works – perhaps, indeed, the closest that recent George Eliot scholarship has come to superseding Gordon S. Haight's 1968 book (see Criticism, **p. 111**) as the standard biography of the author of *Middlemarch*.

Rosemary Ashton's biography was followed, in 1998, by Kathryn Hughes's *George Eliot: The Last Victorian*. Similar in its scope and its consistently biographical rather than critical focus, the latter book is, in its way, as successful as its predecessor, the difference between them being one of approach rather than merit: while the earlier study is an extremely readable scholarly biography which may well appeal to readers outside academia, Kathryn Hughes's book is written primarily for the educated general reader and, in consequence, adopts a more popular, though by no means less rigorous, approach to its subject. In comparison with Rosemary Ashton's biography, *George Eliot: The Last Victorian* devotes less attention to the social and cultural background of the Victorian era and more attention to the individual people among whom Marian Evans lived her life; the book is full of memorable character sketches, including those of some of the most prominent members of the mid-nineteenth-century literary establishment, such as, for example, Harriet Martineau and Herbert Spencer. With more than half an eye, the academic reader might suspect, on the effect of her approach on the sales of her book, Kathryn Hughes is happy to discuss, in some detail, areas of biographical controversy and uncertainty (to do, inevitably, mainly with Marian Evans's personal life) and, indeed, to engage in some gossipmongering; while her conclusions are not necessarily more radical than those of the more discreet academic biographers, she is prepared to engage in speculation rather than restrict herself to the discussion of documented biographical facts. The difference in approach is clear in the short comments on George Eliot's works as well – rather than offering an attempt at brief critical commentary, they tend to provide summaries of the texts in question and to trace the real-life models for the characters and situations presented in them. Those quasi-critical passages are, in fact, not always fully precise in their account of the works; Kathryn Hughes clearly feels much more assured in the general narrative of Marian Evans's life, which she describes, rather refreshingly, with the kind of humour and eloquence not normally associated with formal academic writing:

> There followed a tricky nine months during which events conspired to push Mary Ann and the officially unengaged Charles Hennell together. [. . .] In July [1843] things came to a painful head when the same party [Mary Ann, Hennell and the Brays], this time supplemented by Rufa [Brabant], took a longer trip to Wales. [. . .] The news that [Rufa] had resumed her engagement with Charles Hennell, this time with her father's approval, only pointed up the differences between the two young women. Both were clever and serious. But one was pretty and well connected and the other was not. And it was Rufa, with her magnificent hair and a pedigree rooted in the intellectual middle classes, who had bagged Charles Hennell.
>
> (Hughes 1998: 91)

Somewhere, halfway between biographical, bibliographical and literary critical studies belongs Carol A. Martin's monograph *George Eliot's Serial Fiction* (1994). Principally a study of the four works of George Eliot originally published as serials – *Scenes of Clerical Life* (see Works, **pp. 32–6**), *Romola* (see Works, **pp. 56–61**), *Middlemarch* (see Works, **pp. 67–80**) and *Daniel Deronda* (see Works, **pp. 80–8**) – Martin's meticulously documented book is, in fact, more than a work of literary criticism: it is, in fact, as much a study of the development of George Eliot's artistic method, from her earliest to her last work of fiction, as it is a comprehensive account of the impact of serialisation on the Victorian literary market and on the complex relationship between Victorian novelists, publishers, editors of periodicals, reviewers and the reading public. Martin devotes a great deal of attention, for example, to the negotiations of the conditions of the publica-tion of George Eliot's serials, both from the point of view of their suitability for and effect on the artistic shape of the works in question and, in more practical terms, as regards their earning potential; she also offers extensive discussions of the dynamics of the relationship between George Eliot and her reviewers, correct-ing the frequent perception that she proceeded with the writing of her serial fictions unaware of, and uninfluenced by, the early responses of her readers. Although George Eliot was by no means typical among Victorian novelists in publishing only half of her major works in serial form and in attempting to reduce the impact of that mode of publication on the artistic shape of the novels, for example through the negotiation of the unusual half-volume format for the serial-isation of *Middlemarch* and *Daniel Deronda* (see Life and contexts, **pp. 25–6**), she was nonetheless subject to the same pressures of writing to deadlines, con-forming to requirements regarding the length of individual installments and manipulating the contents of the installments to maximise their dramatic effect. Martin's study deals with all those aspects of George Eliot's creative practice in a well-informed, lucid and thoroughly readable manner.

Purely bibliographical research into the history of the writing and publication of George Eliot's works has, over the years, produced a number of important studies and editions, not only of her fiction and her poetry, but also of her essays and personal writings. With the publication of the Clarendon Edition of the Novels of George Eliot, scholars have now at their disposal definitive textual editions of all of her major fictions except *Silas Marner*; in addition to Gordon S. Haight's edition of the letters (see Criticism, **p. 106**), there is now also an edition of *The Journals of George Eliot* (ed. Margaret Harris and Judith Johnston, 1998), as well as editions of a number of her notebooks, including those used specifically in preparation for the writing of her two most complex novels, *Middlemarch* (ed. John Clark Pratt and Victor A. Neufeldt, 1979) and *Daniel Deronda* (ed. Jane Irwin, 1996). A summary of the findings of George Eliot bibliographers is provided by William Baker and John C. Ross in *George Eliot: A Bibliographical History* (2002), a comprehensive source of information on all aspects of the history of the publication of the writer's works, likely to remain the definitive source of information for George Eliot scholars for the foreseeable future.

General critical studies

The new seriousness that began to mark the criticism of George Eliot's work following the publication of Barbara Hardy's 1959 study (see Criticism, **pp. 109–10**) found its first major expression in W. J. Harvey's monograph *The Art of George Eliot* (1961). Harvey's book, substantially completed before Hardy's study appeared in print, takes a similar formal approach to George Eliot's writings and organises the material in a similar way: it discusses the broad structural features of the novels, such as the construction of the narratorial voice, the manipulation of fictional chronology and narrative time, the presentation of character and the patterns of imagery in the whole of the author's œuvre, illustrating its points with relevant examples from different novels rather than developing its argument around detailed readings of individual works. A clear mark of the modernity of Harvey's approach is his clear awareness of the need to establish a theoretical framework for the study of George Eliot's works (or rather, in broader terms, Victorian and indeed pre-Victorian fiction) as he recognises the insufficiency of the critical paradigm deriving from the critical comments and the literary practice of Henry James. Paradoxically, however, this particular aspects of the book is what makes it appear, to an early twenty-first-century reader, rather antiquarian in spirit: Harvey's engaged, argumentative tone places his discussion of George Eliot very much in the context of his own time, and the general theoretical points he makes, however valid many of them may be, are now of historical rather than current critical value. In consequence, Harvey's study has aged rather less well than some of the other works from its period: structured to be read in its entirety rather than to be consulted in a more selective manner, it hides some of its more useful sections, such as its analysis of different aspects of narratorial omniscience or its typology of George Eliot's characters, behind its rather old-fashioned conceptual façade and away from readers seeking focused discussions of specific texts rather than broad and therefore relatively more abstract generalisations about George Eliot's work as a whole.

By comparison, Bernard J. Paris's study of *Experiments in Life: George Eliot's Quest for Values* (1965) remains an important contribution to George Eliot studies. It is still one of the fullest analyses of the way in which the moral vision of the novels is underpinned by their author's early experience of Christianity and by her subsequent rejection of the theological worldview in favour of the positivist philosophy of Comte. Building his argument on the evidence of Marian Evans's letters and other non-fictional writings, considered against the background of some of the central developments in mid-nineteenth-century philosophy, sociology and science, Paris defines the moral universe of George Eliot's novels in dynamic, developmental terms:

> Moral development, for George Eliot, consists in a movement from the subjective to the objective approach to reality. The three stages of moral development take place within the indifferent but orderly cosmos of positive science; a discovery of the true nature of the cosmos is part of the science; a discovery of the true nature of the cosmos is part of the process of maturation. In the course of moral evolution, experience of suffering (the second stage) leads to vision and vision intensifies sympathy. In the third stage of moral development, George Eliot's characters arrive at some version of Feuerbach's religion of humanity.
>
> (Paris 1965: 128–9)

This contention is subsequently tested as Paris analyses characters from across the George Eliot canon, focusing in particular on Adam Bede, Maggie Tulliver and the main characters of *Middlemarch*; he demonstrates how the novels gradually build up a system of values in which subjective feelings of other men and women become a composite measure of the moral value of an individual's actions and, therefore, an objective rationale for morality. This is, of course, in the advanced critical climate of the twenty-first century, a rather traditionalist interpretation of George Eliot's moral philosophy, but it is traditionalist in the best sense of the word – the sheer comprehensiveness of Paris's treatment of his subject and the precision with which he develops his argument continue to impress, even if the book's structure, reflective of its primary concern with the history of ideas rather than literary criticism *sensu stricto*, may make it appear, particularly to the inexperienced reader, rather more abstract and therefore difficult to follow than it actually is.

In contrast to Paris's rewarding study, Walter Allen's monograph on George Eliot (1965) in the Masters of World Literature series comes as something of a disappointment: over a third of it is devoted to a rather unbalanced account of Marian Evans's life, focusing on her childhood and youth at the expense of the years of her career as a novelist, while the remaining part of the book offers a rather cursory and superficial account of the novels. Impressionistic rather than analytical, Allen's comments do little more than restate some rather old-fashioned views of George Eliot as a thinker and an artist: he complains about her prose style and her narratorial intrusions, praises *Adam Bede* (see Works, pp. 36–44), *Silas Marner* (see Works, pp. 51–6) and *Middlemarch* (see Works, pp. 67–80), and criticises the final scene of the flood in *The Mill on the Floss* (see Works, pp. 44–51), the lack of imaginative insight in *Romola* (see Works, pp. 56–61) and the character of Will Ladislaw. Perhaps the only significant critical point in the book relates to the assessment of George Eliot's place in the tradition of nineteenth-century fiction, not only in Britain but also in the broader context of Europe:

> If we set her . . . side by side with her European contemporaries, . . . it is the last novels, *Felix Holt* – if only for the tragic figure of Mrs. Transome – *Middlemarch* and the Gwendolen Harleth parts of *Daniel Deronda*, that become of most value. These novels are distinguished by a psychological realism unknown before in English fiction except, perhaps, in Fielding's *Amelia* and Jane Austen's *Emma*. Character has become destiny, and character is subjected to intense critical scrutiny. At the same time, the effects of environment on character are studied with such minuteness that she can almost be seen as a fore-runner of naturalism, abhorrent though naturalism would have been to her as an aesthetic doctrine.
>
> (Allen 1965: 180)

It is this focus on psychology that prompts Allen to compare George Eliot to such Continental masters of mid-nineteenth-century fiction as Gustave Flaubert and Ivan Turgenev; it is also that aspect of her work that makes her a major influence not only on the work of her immediate successors, Henry James, Thomas Hardy and D.H. Lawrence, but also on the complex psychological fiction of the French novelist Marcel Proust.

R.T. Jones's 1970 volume on George Eliot in the British Authors series is precisely what the subtitle of the series promises: a thoroughly engaging and useful 'introductory critical study'. The book's critical approach is unashamedly traditionalist: it aims, among other things, 'to show how the art of George Eliot the novelist can reach further in understanding, in sympathetic imagination, and in the exploration of moral values, than can the expository and speculative prose of an essay – even when the essayist is George Eliot herself' (Jones 1970: 3). The analytical chapters that follow, on the writer's six 'English' novels, recapitulate established critical points in a lucid and unpretentious manner; it does, however, come as something of a surprise that the book offers no account of *Romola* (see Works, pp. 56–61) – or rather, that what is says about it serves as an explanation of the rationale for leaving it out:

> *Romola*, on the other hand, is unquestionably a novel as far as its form is concerned, and George Eliot certainly regarded it as one. [. . .] Perhaps it is because her sense of what is permanent in human nature was not free to direct her imagination, that it appears instead in the form of generalizing paragraphs and abstract accounts of motives and consequences. In *Romola*, the author's finest insights are expressed in the mode of the essayist, not the novelist. Thus it is in *Romola* that we find some of the most precise descriptions of processes that, in the other novels, we experience with the people involved in them. [. . .] It contains [. . .] a good deal of George Eliot's wisdom, which is worth having in any form, and some of the most concise and lucid formulations of those 'general laws' that she persistently sought in human behaviour and its consequences. But to discuss it at length beside such novels as, say,

Silas Marner and *Middlemarch* would be, inevitably, to demonstrate more fully that it is something less than a novel.

(Jones 1970: 4–5)

Neil Roberts's monograph *George Eliot: Her Beliefs and Her Art* (1975), in the Novelists and Their World series, is another general study; its analysis of the novels is predicated on the initial premise that, while George Eliot presents in her works 'an infinitely complex reality whose highest complexity is the human world of values and moral action' (Roberts 1975: 16), and while 'her novelist's art might be described as a kind of sympathetic immersion in this reality, which checks and qualifies the preconceptions that she brings to it' (Roberts 1975: 16), she

> by no means always succeeds in reconciling reality with her preconcep-
> tions, or in qualifying her beliefs in accordance with reality; [. . .] in
> several of her books (though in markedly different degrees) she *does*
> distort, both locally and more generally; [. . .] these distortions can be
> identified in her language, construction and (in Henry James's sense)
> selection.
>
> (Roberts 1975: 16)

Although Roberts's critical method is straightforward and systematic – he opens his study with an account of the key features of George Eliot's moral and social philosophy, focusing in particular on her conservatism, her moral determinism and her meliorist belief in evolution, and he continues with an analysis of the individual novels – and his comments are at times genuinely illuminating (as in the discussion of the open-ended, experimental structure of *Daniel Deronda* [see Works, **pp. 80–8**]), the book as a whole, however, strikes the twenty-first-century reader as curiously old-fashioned; it covers famil-iar territory, and its peculiar brand of liberal-humanist approach lacks the kind of vigour and dynamism that would have helped it to stand the test of time.

George Eliot's debt to the philosophical thought of the Romantic period is investigated by K.M. Newton in his book on *George Eliot: Romantic Humanist* (1981). Stressing her philosophical closeness not to the Positivists Comte and Spencer, but rather to Feuerbach and Lewes, whose work he sees as deriving from the Romantic concept of the centrality of the human mind as a key element shaping our perception of the world, Newton describes George Eliot as 'an advanced Romantic who developed the anti-metaphysical implications of Romantic thinking to an extreme' (Newton 1981: 3), and he associates her with the 'organicist' dimension of Romanticism, which 'attempted to move beyond the nihilism and assertive egotism associated with egotistic Romantics such as Byron and searched for a positive philosophy or belief which could pro-vide the ego with definition' (Newton 1981: 11). In consequence, the book sets out

> to show that George Eliot has two main aims as a philosophical novelist:
> first, to attack the nihilistic and egotistic philosophies that could be derived
> from the set of ideas that she herself accepted, and, second, to support

a humanist philosophy similar in many respects to the moral and social thought of the organicist Romantics without denying that set of ideas.

(Newton 1981: 12)

The structure of the book reflects these objectives: Newton first discusses George Eliot's criticism of nihilism and egotism in *Romola* (see Works, **pp. 56–61**), *Felix Holt* (see Works, **pp. 61–7**) and in her poetry (see Works, **pp. 93–6**), then proceeds to analyse her early fictions as an expression of her belief in the concept of society as an organic unity held together by a shared sense of culture and shared memories of the past. The book's final chapters focus on the writer's last two works, *Middlemarch* (see Works, **pp. 67–80**) and *Daniel Deronda* (see Works, **pp. 80–8**), which Newton sees as offering a full illustration of her philosophical standpoint; in his opinion, it is in particular in *Daniel Deronda* that 'George Eliot comes closest to creating a Romantic resolution by showing that Deronda is able to reconcile organicist goals with the acceptance of advanced Romantic thinking and with self-realisation, an aim one usually associates with Romantic egotism' (Newton 1981: 200).

A more conventional account of the ways in which George Eliot's works demonstrate her indebtedness to the philosophical, literary and scientific currents of her time constitutes the central focus of Rosemary Ashton's brief introductory study, *George Eliot* (1983), in the Past Masters series. This short book may be a useful and reliable starting point for the study of the writer's life and work, but its brevity (under 100 pages of text) necessarily makes its critical accounts of the individual novels and stories rather rudimentary. At the same time, the constraints of space help Ashton to synthesise her points in a simple and succinct, and yet informative and precise manner:

Like Dickens, Tennyson and Hardy, but more consciously and articulately than they, George Eliot responded ambivalently to the intellectual movements and discoveries of her age. She wanted to accept Comte's optimism about the future of a secular society freed from religious and metaphysical creeds, yet, as an artist imagining the lot of the individual in society, what she saw and rendered were the personal tragedies and dislocations of those caught up unconsciously in the onward march of progress. Darwin's evolutionary theory satisfied her intellectual scepticism of supernatural beliefs and plausibly explained the origin and progress of animal and human species, yet she was disturbed at the implications for such 'emmetlike' creatures as the Dodsons and the Tullivers. Strauss demonstrated to her satisfaction the mythical origin of Biblical events, but she celebrated with warmth as well as irony the importance in the lives of ordinary people of a traditional religious creed. Spinoza and Feuerbach among philosophers, and Goethe and Scott among creative writers, most earned her respect by their humane interest in how men are affected by momentous changes and by their tolerance of that clinging to old ways which Marx, for example, despised.

(Ashton 1983: 98)

Despite its rather misleading title, Karen B. Mann's book *The Language that Makes George Eliot's Fiction* (1983) is not a study of linguistic aspects of George Eliot's work but an analysis of the way in which her use of metaphors deriving from various aspects of experience contributes to the creation of broader fictional structures such as character, plot and point of view. Although some of Mann's observations, such as her discussion of the way in which George Eliot uses metaphors relating to drama and theatre to mediate changes in the narratorial perspective of her fictions, are genuinely illuminating, the overall structure of the book, organised somewhat mechanically along thematic lines, makes it difficult for the author to relate her analyses to the specific contexts of the individual works; in consequence, her book creates the impression of lacking a clear focus and sense of direction and is, as a result, rather confusing for the reader to follow.

George Eliot's interest in the philosophical, theological and psychological thinking of her time lies at the heart of the didactic impulse of her work, investigated by William Myers in *The Teaching of George Eliot* (1984). Stressing her allegiance to the Positivist interpretation of history and sociology, to Feuerbach's conception of religion and to the psychological theories of Alexander Bain, Myers identifies the key areas of George Eliot's teaching; he focuses, in particular, on the investigation of the relationship between religion and morality in *Scenes of Clerical Life* (see Works, **pp. 32–6**) and *Adam Bede* (see Works, **pp. 36–44**), on the analysis of the theme of heredity in *The Mill on the Floss* (see Works, **pp. 44–51**), on the presentation of the evolutionary, melioristic vision of history in *Romola* (see Works, **pp. 56–61**) and on the critical exploration of the politics of class in *Felix Holt* (see Works, **pp. 61–7**). George Eliot's pronouncements on those questions are subsequently tested as Myers discusses them adopting, in turn, Marxist, Nietzschean and Freudian standpoints; these critiques are, however, in due course rejected as Myers demonstrates how, in her last two novels, George Eliot develops what amounts to her own philosophy, stressing the significance of the pursuit of fundamental moral values and the centrality of the problem of moral choice:

> There were [. . .] questions about which she had to make judgments on her own account, specifically on the relativity of truth, the origin, nature and extent of evil, the legitimacy or otherwise of extreme subjective endeavour, and the nature of freedom and choice. This she did with great difficulty, but with no less deliberation, coming in some cases to striking and even disturbing conclusions. Among the most important of these were her decision in *Middlemarch* to develop an absolute notion of sanctity, and her commitment in *Daniel Deronda* to the 'royalty of discernment and resolve'. Thus the starting point and conclusion of George Eliot's didacticism are the same: she begins with a conviction that it is morally necessary to make clear and coherent judgments about values and she ends heroically, one might almost say wilfully, putting them into effect.
>
> (Myers 1984: 230)

Elizabeth Deeds Ermarth's introductory critical study of *George Eliot* (1985) in the Twayne's English Authors series sets out as an attempt to revise some of the received perceptions of the author's life and career while at the same time offering an accessible account of her works. In trying to achieve the former objective, Ermarth underlines the significance, for the development of the writer's world-view, of the extensive study of philosophy which she undertook in relation to her work as a translator and essayist; the book concentrates, in particular, on the impact of the works of Spinoza and Feuerbach on George Eliot's understanding of culture and tradition and on the way in which her opinions on a wide range of subjects she was to investigate in her novels, from question of the morality of art to the situation of women, were reflected in her periodical essays and critical reviews. In her critical analyses of the novels, Ermarth's focus is predominantly on the dynamics of the relationship between individuals and the broad social culture they create. In her view, 'George Eliot's cultural vision [. . .] involves the constant action of individual talent on tradition, changing and altering its entire homeostatic balance at every moment. [. . .] Her culture is incomplete, ever-changing, open-ended, incarnate in its participants and their works' (Ermarth 1985: 134–5). Ermarth is particularly convincing in her study of the social and cultural fabric of the world of George Eliot's early novels; the section on *Middlemarch* (see Works, **pp. 67–8**) and *Daniel Deronda* (see Works, **pp. 80–8**), in which the main focus is on the use, in the two novels, of motifs of secrecy and confession, offers some interesting insights but does not relate very directly to the rest of the author's argument.

Mary Wilson Carpenter's book *George Eliot and the Landscape of Time: Narrative Form and Protestant Apocalyptic History* (1986) discusses the author's major works, with the exception of *Silas Marner* and *Felix Holt* but including *The Legend of Jubal and Other Poems* (see Works, **pp. 94–6**) from the rather unusual angle of their relationship to the broad tradition of Christian prophetic thought, particularly in relation to the interpretation of the Book of Revelation. Carpenter's argument focuses on ways in which George Eliot's works rewrite conventional Christian visions of history along secular and feminist lines; the central place in her argument is occupied by *Romola* (see Works, **pp. 56–61**), a complex text that represents 'George Eliot's revolution against that most formid-able authority, the "Law" of history and narrative written by the Fathers of the church' (Carpenter 1986: 102). Noting the passivity of the novel's narrative, Carpenter nonetheless stresses that ambition of its philosophical project:

> In *Romola*, George Eliot seems anxiously to try to find in her text the face of a female self not yet born – the face of a *legitimate* prophetess. The resulting 'apocalypse of history' [. . .] exhibits an 'artificial and imaginary' character – a densely allusive and symbolic art that elicits more respect than enthusiasm from the modern reader. Yet when we read it as George Eliot's most deeply studied 'landscape of time', *Romola* achieves a distinction unique among her works. At once the least and the most Victorian, and at one the least and the most her own.
> (Carpenter 1986: 103)

Highly original in the perspective it adopts, Carpenter's book may at times appear to put its argument forward along rather unexpected and unorthodox lines; it is, however, consistent in its approach and insightful in some of its interpretations, even if some of them may, to more conventionally minded readers, appear rather speculative and far-fetched.

Kerry McSweeney's volume in the Macmillan Literary Lives series, *George Eliot (Marian Evans): A Literary Life* (1991), is, despite its title, not so much a biography as a biographically contextualised introductory critical analysis of the works. The opening two chapters of McSweeney's book offer a straightforward, concise account of Marian Evans's life up to the late 1850s; from that point on, the focus of his study turns to George Eliot's writings, which are analysed in a conventional, but often insightful manner, with frequent references to their biographical, social and literary background. A good deal of attention is paid, for example, to the characteristic features of her handling of the narrative voice of the novels, in particular in *Adam Bede* (see Works, pp. 36–44), to the ambivalence of George Eliot's position on 'the woman question', with particular reference to *The Mill on the Floss* (see Works, pp. 44–51), and to the historical and political dimensions of *Felix Holt* (see Works, pp. 61–7) and *Middlemarch* (see Works, pp. 67–80). In a welcome departure from the pattern of most similar introductory studies, McSweeney's book also includes some useful comments on a number of George Eliot's poems, which are discussed in relation to some of the central themes and concerns of the novels, such as, for example, the question of the professional and artistic ambitions of women ('Armgart' [see Works, pp. 94–5]) or the artistic implications of the author's interest in the philosophy of Positivism ('O May I Join the Choir Invisible' [see Works, pp. 95–6]). Clearly structured and thoroughly readable, this is a useful if not particularly ground-breaking guide to George Eliot's work.

One of the best general studies of George Eliot's works to appear in recent years is David Carroll's *George Eliot and the Conflict of Interpretations: A Reading of the Novels* (1992). Carroll relates George Eliot's work to the Victorian interest in hermeneutics – a branch of philosophy concerned with the problem of interpretation, initially of texts, but increasingly also of all reality; in his view, 'the intensity of [George Eliot's] career as a novelist comes from her vivid, almost apocalyptic, sense that traditional modes of interpretation – making sense of the world – were breaking down irrevocably' (Carroll 1992: 4). In consequence, her novels can be seen as attempts to explore different modes of hermeneutics, ranging from the application of conventional patterns of typology, characteristic of the tradition of the analysis and interpretation of the Bible (*Scenes of Clerical Life, Adam Bede, The Mill on the Floss*), through legal or quasi-legal procedures (*Adam Bede, Silas Marner, Felix Holt*), the use of confession (*Scenes of Clerical Life, Adam Bede, Daniel Deronda*), the methods of literary and historical research (*Romola, Middlemarch*), to the methodology of science (*Middlemarch*). These modes of the interpretation of the world are studied in a variety of ways: through different modulations of the narratorial voice, through the presentation of characters, through the construction of plots, etc. In consequence, the whole fictional world of George Eliot's works becomes a process of constant interpretation and reinterpretation, reflective of the quintessentially Victorian search, in the aftermath of the loss of traditional forms of religious belief, for alternative sources of certainty and reassurance. As a result, Carroll's analysis of the novels, though originating from an attempt to argue a specific thesis, turns into a broad-ranging, inclusive discussion of the major elements of their artistic structures: an attempt to explore George Eliot's comprehensive study of the mechanisms of interpretation becomes a process of the comprehensive interpretation of the texts which George Eliot creates to carry out her investigations. Perhaps inevitably, the conclusions Carroll reaches are rather open-ended:

> Much of the narrative energy of George Eliot's fiction comes from the dismantling of these same theories of life which seek, as they must, to escape their own provisional nature. Whether they are expressed as religious truths, theodicies, family codes of practice, founding historical myths, political programmes, models of vocation, or class ideologies – all are subjected to the hermeneutic of suspicion which reveals their inner contradictions. Representation and interpretation proceed simultaneously. The fictional experiments which elicit these disconfirmations are various, but an essential feature of any comprehensive world-view in George Eliot's fiction is the inevitability of its self-deconstruction.
>
> (Carroll 1992: 313)

In the early novels, Carroll argues, the cognitive world order is re-established – 'the hermeneutic of suspicion turns into the hermeneutic of restoration' (Carole 1992: 314); in the later novels, George Eliot's vision of the process of interpretation becomes increasingly complex, with the writer and the reader finding themselves in a kind of hermeneutic circle, in which moments of genuine insight and understanding are only part of a process of the constant re-evaluation of interpretations: 'Like the reading of a text, experience in the world involves a projection of its meaning on the basis of partial understanding. The further we read the more we regress, as that understanding is extended and deepened' (Carroll 1992: 315).

A sceptical reader might perhaps consider this conclusion to a 300-page monograph to be characteristic of contemporary literary criticism in its aura of fluidity and inconclusiveness – but even if it were to be the case, it does not detract from the quality of Carroll's interpretations of George Eliot's individual novels: exemplary in their depth, attention to detail and clarity of presentation, they remain as valuable when read as free-standing critical essays as they are as part of the author's overall argument.

Alan W. Bellringer's 1993 volume in the Modern Novelists series provides a useful and informative introduction to George Eliot's fiction. Without committing himself to any specific critical agenda, Bellringer offers a number of insightful readings of all the novels and stories; some of the best sections of his study include the analysis of the complexity of the construction of the narrative voice in *Adam Bede* (see Works, **pp. 36–44**), the appreciative discussion of *Romola* (see Works, **pp. 56–61**), which he considers 'George Eliot's most ambitious novel' (Bellringer 1993: 81), and the last chapter, in which he undertakes a succinct but at the same time comprehensive overview of the history of critical responses to George Eliot's works. The book may lack a clear overall focus, as a result of which it works rather better on the level of close reading and critical analysis of individual texts than in terms of offering a sustained critical interpretation and assessment of the writer's literary career, but it remains, nonetheless, a convincingly argued, well-documented and perceptive critical study of the George Eliot canon.

A useful critical study of George Eliot by Josephine McDonagh in the *Writers and their Work* series (1997) focuses on the way in which the writer's presentation of the processes of social and cultural change is mediated through her complex method of storytelling – fundamentally realistic but acquiring, in the course of her career, an increasingly powerful dimension of symbolism. The book argues that the development of George Eliot's artistic technique away from the detailed documentary realism of her early fictions, *Scenes of Clerical Life* (see Works, **pp. 32–6**) and *Adam Bede* (see Works, **pp. 36–44**), towards the different forms of non-realistic writing in the late works, particularly *Daniel Deronda* (see Works, **pp. 80–8**) and *Impressions of Theophrastus Such* (see Works, **pp. 89–90**), is reflective of the complexity, disparateness and uncertainty of the world she attempts to describe, a world which increasingly cannot be contained within the conventionally realistic pattern of her early works. Although the relatively small scale of McDonagh's project does not offer her enough room to discuss all of the novels in detail, her selection and treatment of her material – including, for instance, a very subtle discussion of George Eliot's use of the motif of doors as an example of the integration of realistic and symbolic modes of writing, as well as an analysis of her representation of changing patterns of family life as a reflection of broader developmental processes in the life of modern society – ensure that the book's general argument is conveyed in a clear and persuasive manner, even if its general approach, by no means overly complex but nonetheless presupposing the reader's familiarity with more basic critical material about the novels, makes the volume relatively more advanced than readers of other books in the series might perhaps have come to expect.

An interesting perspective on George Eliot's work is offered by Peter C. Hodgson in his monograph on *Theology in the Fiction of George Eliot* (2001). Hodgson perceives the author of *Middlemarch* not as a committed atheist but as a person whose religious opinions

> evolved through several phases, which might be regarded as stations along a pathway of pilgrimage: evangelical Christianity, the religion of humanity, and elements of a future religion that would avoid accusation and consolation, be practical in orientation, manifest a reverence for mystery in nature and history, and in its highest form express the idea of a sympathetic, suffering, (omni)present God.
>
> (Hodgson 2001: 3)

Hodgson studies the novels in an attempt to discover in them aspects of religious experience that would be indicative of the author's own spiritual journey. Although the book strikes the reader as curiously old-fashioned, betraying the author's background as a theologian rather than a literary scholar both in his critical approach and in his stylistic mannerisms, the central argument the volume puts forward cannot be easily dismissed:

> Not always but from time to time in the world of George Eliot's fiction, human beings find it possible to go on or start over in the midst of suffering, defeat, and despair. The decisive transformations are recounted in terms that suggest religious conversion, a process of death and

rebirth, of losing and finding oneself, of creating a new kind of communal ethos defined by love and justice, which in the language of the
Bible is something like the kingdom of God. God does not appear as an
empirical object or a direct agent anywhere in George Eliot's fictional
world. But there are hints that it is the power of God, of infinite suffering
love, that constitutes the power of new predication by which redemptive
possibilities come to speech, become speech-acts, in a tragically con-
flicted world. In this respect George Eliot's fictional world envisions
something more than she herself was ever able to affirm directly. In
the praxis of writing fiction she was able to overcome personal doubt
and intellectual skepticism, and to enter a world of transformative
possibilities.

(Hodgson 2001: 150)

A succinct but at the same time comprehensive account of George Eliot's work,
bringing into focus the concerns of a diversity of contemporary critical
approaches, such as the engagement, central to the work of feminist and post-
colonial critics, with the problem of otherness, but ultimately relating those
concerns to the central ethical dimension of the novels, is offered in Pauline
Nestor's 2002 volume in the Critical Issues series. Nestor's central argument – 'in
the broadest of terms, Eliot moves throughout her fiction-writing career from a
position of confidence in the moral efficacy of self-regulation and self-awareness,
to a more modest recognition of the limits of agency and subjectivity' (Nestor
2002: 10) – is developed through an analysis of the works that manages to inte-
grate discreet but consistent attention to the biographical and intellectual context
of the writer's life, an interdisciplinary awareness of the range of issues – psychological, sociological, philosophical – addressed in the novels and close attention to
their essentially literary features. Thus, for example, Nestor's account of *The Mill
on the Floss* (see Works, pp. 44–51), concentrating on the exploration of the
novel's psychological focus, brings together the context of the philosophy of
Spinoza, whose ideal of the regulation of emotion by intellect George Eliot inter-
rogates, the concerns of feminist critics, dissatisfied with the presentation of Maggie as a martyr to the principle of renunciation and the novel's engagement with
the problems of moral and social evolution and progress – all carefully interwoven into a firmly literary-critical discussion that takes in the novel's plot, its
presentation of characters, its quasi-autobiographical qualities and its metaphorical structure. Although Nestor's treatment of her subject involves no radical
reassessment of George Eliot's work, her monograph is nonetheless one of the
most successful general studies of the writer published in recent years; it is balanced, thoroughly researched and intellectually stimulating and, at the same time,
clearly structured and pitched at a level accessible not only to specialists but also
to the relatively inexperienced general reader.

Feminist criticism

The emergence, in the 1970s, of feminist criticism inevitably generated an
important new impulse in George Eliot studies, even if, somewhat paradoxically

perhaps in view of her importance as one of the most prominent women writers in the English literary canon, she was at first treated by feminist writers and critics with a considerable degree of suspicion. Kate Millett's early comment in *Sexual Politics* – 'Dorothea's predicament in *Middlemarch* is an eloquent plea that a fine mind be allowed an occupation; but it goes no further than petition' (Millet 1970: 139) – foreshadows later criticisms of George Eliot's work made, for example, by Elaine Showalter, who, in drawing a comparison between Charlotte Brontë's rebellious Jane Eyre and George Eliot's self-destructive Maggie Tulliver, notes that 'Maggie is the progenitor of a heroine who identifies passivity and renunciation with womanhood, who finds it easier, more natural, and in a mystical way more satisfying, to destroy herself than to live in a world without opium or fantasy, where she must fight to survive' (Showalter 1977: 131). On closer analysis, the sense of unease felt by feminist critics in relation to George Eliot is not perhaps quite as surprising as it might first appear: although Marian Evans was prepared to challenge the moral assumptions of ultimately patriarchal Victorian orthodoxy in her private life, in her capacity as a writer of fiction (for which she, very significantly, adopted a masculine pseudonym) she pursued a moral agenda of a distinctly conservative kind. Even the most dynamic and independent-minded of her heroines end up either, like Dinah Morris or Dorothea Brooke, as happy wives and mothers, giving up their public roles and focusing instead on their domestic responsibilities, or, like Janet Dempster or Romola, adopting sexless quasi-maternal roles in a spirit of penitence or voluntary self-sacrifice, while at the same time those of George Eliot's women who are prepared to rebel, or at least to assert their independence, are inevitably punished, either literally, like Hetty Sorrel and, in a different way, Maggie Tulliver, or metaphorically, like Armgart or Alcharisi. It was not until the publication of Sandra M. Gilbert and Susan Gubar's seminal book *The Madwoman in the Attic: The Woman Writer and the Nineteenth-Century Literary Imagination* (1979), that feminist critics began to uncover the tensions underlying this seemingly complacent arrangement: as Gilbert and Gubar argue, George Eliot's fascination with the theme of (self-)destruction is associated precisely with her inability to articulate in her fiction, in a direct way, the tension between her rational and her emotional sides:

> For, as an agnostic setting out to write about the virtues of clerical life, a 'fallen' woman praising the wife's service, a childless writer celebrating motherhood, an intellectual writing what she called 'experiments in life' in celebration of womanly feeling, Eliot becomes entangled in con-tradictions that she can only resolve through acts of vengeance against her own characters, violent retributions that become more prominent when contrasted with her professed purposes as a novelist.
>
> (Gilbert and Gubar 1979: 479)

The first full-length study of George Eliot to adopt an explicitly feminist stance was Gillian Beer's 1986 volume in the Key Women Writers series. Not surprisingly, given earlier feminist critics' scepticism about George Eliot's feminist credentials, the book is an attempt to redress the critical balance by demonstrating that her work 'helped in some measure to bring into question assumptions about male/female polarisations, about women, and about the awkwardly pre-emptive forms "womanly" and "womanhood" ' (Beer 1986: 1), and that 'her presence at the centre of literary culture in the past hundred years is of immense worth to other women, and her achievement can be belittled only at our own cost' (Beer 1986: 1). As befits the first major study to deal with George Eliot specifically as a woman writer, Beer's book does not restrict its focus to the interpretation of the novels but considers the broader context within which they were written: some of the most valuable parts of this study are those devoted to the discussion of Marian Evans's response to the mid-to late-nineteenth-century debate about 'the woman question' (Beer 1986: 152–84) and to the position she took on the literary works of her women contemporaries (Beer 1986: 30–51). Though accepting that the novelist was not a feminist in the modern sense of the word, Beer underlines Marian Evans's familiarity with the objectives and methods of the Victorian women's movement, as well as the fact that she shared her feminist friends' concern about the lack of educational and professional opportunities for women, a view expressed most explicitly in *Middlemarch* (see Works, **pp. 67–80**). It is also in that novel that George Eliot enters most forcefully into ideological debate with her female contemporaries, rejecting both the concept of the renunciation of sexual love as an acceptable price to be paid for the achievement of social independence and the kind of simplistic determinism involved in the concept of natural law and the idea of biological motherhood as a defining aspect of womanhood. Elsewhere in her study, Beer focuses on other significant aspects of George Eliot's work as a woman writer, such as the significance of her choice of a male narrator in *Scenes of Clerical Life* (see Works, **pp. 32–6**), *Adam Bede* (see Works, **pp. 36–44**) and 'The Lifted Veil' (see Works, **pp. 88–9**), the theme of passionate feeling and renunciation in *The Mill on the Floss* (see Works, **pp. 44–51**), the question of parenthood in *Silas Marner* (see Works, **pp. 51–6**), *Romola* (see Works, **pp. 56–61**) and *Felix Holt* (see Works, **pp. 61–7**) and the emergence of a new and complex type of modern womanhood in the character of Gwendolen Harleth in *Daniel Deronda* (see Works, **pp. 80–8**). Altogether, the book is a valuable introduction to a number of issues important to a reading of George Eliot's novels from a feminist standpoint; it may not attempt to prove any specific central thesis about George Eliot as a woman writer, except for making a strong case for the validity of that particular type of approach to her work, but it certainly succeeds in re-establishing her place in the centre of the tradition of Victorian women's writing.

Jenny Uglow's study of *George Eliot* (1987) usefully combines biography and criticism: it opens with a more or less traditional account of Marian Evans's childhood and youth but, as it reaches the moment of the emergence of George Eliot the novelist, the focus shifts to the analysis of her works. The biographical chapters trace the tensions and contradictions involved in the future writer's pursuit of her intellectual ambitions against the background of the conservative environment in which she grew up and about which she remained, throughout her life, deeply nostalgic. They also recognise the complexity of her position as, on the one hand, a leading female thinker and writer prepared to rebel against the social conventions of her time and, on the other hand, a profoundly vulnerable individual in desperate need of support and reassurance from others. The book's feminist slant becomes prominent in the chapter on ' "George Eliot" and the Woman Question in the 1850s', in which Uglow discusses Marian Evans's periodical essays (see Works, **pp. 91–3**) as signalling her developing interest in some of the issues that will become the central concern of her works of fiction:

> the nature of womanhood; the fear of change; the exclusion of women from the realm of the intellect and from effective power; the alliance in oppression of women, workers and slaves which gives them a shared rhetoric of freedom and resistance; the conflict between the new drive for autonomy and the older ethic of self-sacrifice; the difficulty of achieving independence without losing the possibility of sexual passion and family life.
>
> (Uglow 1987: 80)

These themes are then discussed in relation to the novels and stories; Uglow demonstrates how, as George Eliot's career progresses, her interests in women's problems expand to include issues such as the nature of motherhood and its social and psychological implications. The book offers some unexpected insights and re-evaluations: thus, for example, *Romola* (see Works, **pp. 56–61**) is praised as 'Eliot's most striking exposition of the role of women' (Uglow 1987: 161), in which the writer, in a pattern reminiscent of her own situation in life,

> takes the maternal mission away from the docile wife and mother of the evangelical family, away from the 'specialised' morally superior but intellectually inferior womanhood idealised by Comte, and hands it over instead to the single, sensually aware but childless woman, an educated Madonna who, having learned from experience, has freed herself from the domination of men and is prepared henceforth to think for herself.
>
> (Uglow 1987: 174)

Uglow concludes by describing George Eliot's developing perception of the role of women in modern society and of the relationship between the sexes in the following terms:

> It is because of her exploration of the complementary nature of masculine and feminine qualities (within individuals of both sexes as well as within societies), and her subtle re-working of the images of the good daughter, sister, wife and mother, that her novels remain so suggestive and disturbing, particularly to women readers. She uses the metaphors of separate spheres, not to justify women's restriction to the realm of 'feeling' and domesticity, but to argue that the sympathy and sense of responsibility for others traditionally associated with 'maternity', and the passion and intuitive vision associated with 'female irrationality' should be brought to bear in the 'masculine' spheres of action and judgement. While women will be better able to achieve their full potential if they are given access to good education and to professional work, so men will grow if they are free to nurture and care – like Silas, Rufus Lyon and Daniel Deronda. If this could be achieved, society might replace a

repressive, rule-bound ethic with one that is flexible, imaginative, and able to cater for humanity in its infinite variety.

(Uglow 1987: 250)

Dorothea Barrett's study of *Vocation and Desire: George Eliot's Heroines* (1989) is an interesting attempt to bring together biographical, feminist and psychoanalytical approaches to the study of George Eliot's fiction. Barrett takes issue with the conventional perception of the writer as a Victorian sybil and sets out to demonstrate, through her analysis of the novels' central women characters, how their creator's complex and passionate personality comes across in the narrator's treatment of the female protagonists. The book stresses the ambivalent, polyphonic nature of the discourse of George Eliot's novels, stressing that 'the divisions between the radical and the conservative, the passional and the intellectual, the unconsciously betrayed and the consciously contrived in George Eliot's work are not static but dynamic' (Barrett 1989: 32), and that 'their constant struggle, their lack of ultimate resolution, is itself a victory for the radical, passional, and unconscious' (Barrett 1989: 32–3). The ensuing discussion of individual novels (all except *Silas Marner*) offers some interesting analyses and interpretations: thus, for example, Barrett calls for the recognition of the significance of Hetty Sorrel as a structural counterpoint to Dinah Morris in the fictional structure of *Adam Bede* (see Works, **pp. 36–44**), and she devotes a good deal of attention to a subtle analysis of the character of Mrs Transome in *Felix Holt* (see Works, **pp. 61–7**); there is also a useful recapitulation of the main critical points made over the previous decades by commentators concerned with George Eliot's contribution to the feminist debate. Ultimately, Barrett comes to the following conclusion:

[George Eliot's] feminism is to be found in the tension between the monumental characterizations of her heroines and the inadequate options available to them, and in the tension between their fictional lives and the actual life of their author, which is constantly present in the reflexive elements of her novels and narrators. Behind those narrators we are constantly made aware of [her] as a woman whose intellect and artistry render the bigotry of sexism self-evident.

(Barrett 1989: 178)

One of the most accessible feminist studies of George Eliot is Kristin Brady's monograph (1992) in the Women Writers series. The focus of the book is consistently on gender politics: Brady discusses the various ways in which the patriarchal structures of social, economic and cultural life of Victorian Britain influenced the writer's life, how they are reflected – and, importantly, undermined – in her works and how they continue to influence the perception of her achievement in the modern world. Brady opens her discussion with an account of the way in which patriarchal presuppositions about gender characteristics and consequent gender roles influence biographical interpretations; in this context, she identifies ways in which established biographers and critics of George Eliot, among them, in particular, Gordon S. Haight (see Criticism, **p. 111**), tend to interpret her character and life 'according to essentialist assumptions about feminine weakness and dependence' (Brady 1992: 22). From there, Brady proceeds to tell her own story of the writer's life; she does not set out to offer any new material, but she draws the attention of the reader to a number of aspects of Marian Evans's life which have hitherto been neglected – such as, for example, the impact on the teenage Mary Ann of the loss of her mother – and she discusses, in considerable detail, the complexity of her position in the predominantly masculine world of the mid-Victorian intellectual establishment, both before and after her decision to set up home with Lewes. Finally, Brady embarks on a comprehensive analysis of George Eliot's works: virtually all of her major works – all of the novels and short stories and the most important of the poems – are analysed in terms of the way in which they 'at once reflect, expose and undermine the hierarchical ideologies of patriarchy' (Brady 1992: 59). Brady defines the mechanism in which George Eliot's works display their engagement with issues of gender in the following way:

> In Eliot's fiction, such incongruities [between the explicit objectives of the text and the emotional impact it generates] appear most frequently in the self-subverting structure of her plots; in the exaggeratedly male or the ambivalently androgynous voices that tell her stories; and in the overdetermined position created for the reader by those plots and voices – a position that can lead the reader to supplement and to resist the text's apparent or explicit meaning. Often, Eliot's fictions elicit a double or a multiple reading, one which emerges from a radical disjunction between, on the one hand, the aims achieved by the conventional plot and voice and, on the other hand, the desire for a different story and treatment fostered by the narrative's detailed attention to the consequences of sexual difference in patriarchal culture: a 'gender plot' works against the grain of the conventional narrative of romantic love or personal development, exposing its privileging of the masculine.
>
> (Brady 1992: 59)

Thus, all the early novels and stories, from *Scenes of Clerical Life* (see Works, pp. 32–6) to *Silas Marner* (see Works, pp. 51–6), are seen as demonstrating different forms of the sacrifice, or silencing, of the female voice by the dominating systems of patriarchal structures; the works of the middle period, from *Romola* to *The Spanish Gypsy* (see Works, pp. 93–4), use historical distancing as their seemingly powerful feminist voices are ultimately contained and muted; finally, *Middlemarch* (see Works, pp. 67–8) and *Daniel Deronda* (see Works, pp. 80–8) describe the modern world of pre-defined gender roles which are, in themselves, a form of oppression.

Psychoanalytical criticism

Despite the intensity of George Eliot's interest in character and motivation, and despite the complexity of her psychological investigations, it was not until the mid-1970s that her novels began to generate significant interest among critics adopting, in their study of the writer, a psychoanalytical perspective. One of the first major studies in that vein was Laura Comer Emery's *George Eliot's Creative Conflict: The Other Side of Silence* (1976), a rigorously Freudian demonstration of how George Eliot's five 'middle' novels – Emery's discussion leaves out *Adam Bede* and *Daniel Deronda* – can be read as a projection of the process of the author's struggle to cope with her own desires and uncertainties, from 'the inadequately controlled fantasy in *The Mill on the Floss*' (Emery 1976: 3), where the final scene of the flood represents a moment of wish-fulfilment symptomatic of the writer's own emotional insecurities, through the defensive attempt at self-control and reintegration of personality in *Romola* (see Works, **pp. 56–61**), to the final achievement of the sense of inner balance and self-acceptance demonstrated by the clarity and coherence of the presentation of the central characters of *Middlemarch* (see Works, **pp. 67–80**). Although the focus of Emery's main analysis is firmly on the novels, she inevitably relates her findings to the background of the writer's life, as a result of which the progress of George Eliot's career as a novelist proves to reflect the process of her readjustment to a situation of social isolation (including, very importantly, the isolation from her family) that followed her decision to live with Lewes. The critical comments Emery makes about the novels themselves are often insightful – she is particularly good on the analysis of Romola's progress from her search for a father-figure to the fulfilment of quasi-motherhood and on the exploration of the emotional and moral growth of Dorothea and of the nature of her relationships with Casaubon and Will Ladislaw – but the book as a whole does not put its argument across quite as clearly as the reader might have wished: Emery's approach translates itself, in stylistic terms, into overreliance on the kind of specialised vocabulary that is likely to obfuscate the book's message for all but the relatively experienced students of psychoanalytical theory and practice ('while *Silas Marner* begins with regression and moves toward a basically Oedipal position combined with aspects of oral dependency, *Romola* moves toward a regressive orality and away from the Oedipal conflict and its anal-sadistic resolution', Emery 1976: 103–4).

A rather more accessible reading of George Eliot's fiction is offered by Diane F. Sadoff in the chapter on 'George Eliot: "A Sort of Father" ' in her book *Monsters of Affection: Dickens, Eliot and Brontë on Fatherhood* (1982). Focusing on the complexity of George Eliot's presentation of father–daughter relationships, analysed both in terms of their emotional significance and as structures of power and authority, Sadoff relates her readings to the background of Marian Evans's life, including in particular the writer's close but by no means unproblematic relationship with her father (see Life and contexts, **pp. 2–3**). Some of Sadoff's most interesting observations relate to the way in which George Eliot's construction of the narrative voice of her fictions is an important aspect of her negotiation of imaginative authority over her writing; the discussions of individual works include a useful section on *Daniel Deronda* (see Works, **pp. 80–8**), with its focus on the story of Daniel's adoption of Mordecai's national ideal as an expression of filial desire: 'While replacing filiation with affiliation, then, Eliot's book of Daniel surreptitiously confirms the authority of the Judaic patriarchs. [. . .] Eliot binds familial desire into transmissible form, into sympathy with a race of exiles seeking a homeland' (Sadoff 1982: 103).

Peggy Fitzhugh Johnstone's monograph *The Transformation of Rage: Mourning and Creativity in George Eliot's Fiction* (1994) is a readable analysis of the novels, aimed at demonstrating that George Eliot's frequent exploration of the subject of rage and aggression, as well as of denial of aggression through renunciation, can be seen as 'her constructive response to unconscious mourning over the loss of her parents' (Johnstone 1994: 3) and that 'her intellectual and creative work served to provide her with the necessary process of self-strengthening that would finally ease the depressive symptoms of her rage' (Johnstone 1994: 11). Johnstone's analysis places the novels firmly within the context of the writer's life; thus, for example, George Eliot's idealisation of Maggie Tulliver and the rationalisation of her behaviour towards men is seen as an attempt to justify her own controversial decisions in her personal life (see Works, **pp. 44–51**), while *Silas Marner* (see Works, **pp. 51–6**) is an 'attempt to master her pain of [the] loss [of her mother] by writing a story that would dramatize her mother's disappearance (the theft of Silas's gold and the death of Eppie's mother) as well as her return (the attachment between Silas and Eppie)' (Johnstone 1994: 84). The individual chapters follow different manifestations of aggressive tendencies in the novels' major characters, focusing in particular on patterns of what Johnstone describes as 'narcissistic rage', caused by a sense of underachievement and disappointed ambition, as evident in Maggie Tulliver, Tito Melema and Gwendolen Harleth, as well as on the ways in which George Eliot's idealised characters – Adam Bede, Romola, Felix Holt, Dorothea Brooke – suppress their potential for aggression in an attempt to deal with their emotional traumas. There are also some interesting observations on how the psychological mechanisms Johnstone analyses operate not only on the level of the individual but also in broader social contexts – as evident in the study of the motif of mob violence in *Felix Holt* (see Works, **pp. 61–7**) – and how their effects on individual characters combine to produce complex visions of the social reality; this is, most notably, the case in *Middlemarch* (see Works, **pp. 67–80**):

> The provincial society [. . .] is actually portrayed as a tightly knitted group of individuals, bound together by their shared sense of loss, and doomed to mediocrity. The group is seen as conspiring to inhibit the growth of any individuals, like Lydgate, who might have the potential to become extraordinary. [. . .] To judge from Eliot's portrayal of provincial society, the only way to achieve individual aspirations is to leave the group behind, as Eliot had left behind her own family and society.
>
> (Johnstone 1994: 157)

Historical criticism

By comparison with psychoanalytic criticism, a far more productive contribution to the debate about George Eliot's work has been made over the years by critics approaching her novels and stories from a variety of perspectives which could be broadly described as historicist. Some of the earliest comments in that vein were made by Arnold Kettle, who, writing about *Middlemarch* in *An Introduction to the English Novel* (1951), criticised George Eliot for what he saw as her failure to see society in dynamic terms; in his view, 'it is the very inadequacy of her mechanistic philosophy, its failure to incorporate a dialectical sense of contradiction and motion, that drives George Eliot to treat the aspirations of Dorothea idealistically' (Kettle 1951: I, 177). Two decades later, Raymond Williams, in *The English Novel: From Dickens to Lawrence* (1970) described her works as occupying an uneasy space between the conventional middle-class novel operating within traditional assumptions about social and economic hierarchy and the modern novel concentrating on the personal development of individuals:

> George Eliot's novels are transitional between that form which could end in a series of settlements, in which the social and economic solutions and the personal achievements were in a single dimension, and that new form which extending and complicating and then finally collapsing this dimension ends with a single person going away on his own, having achieved his moral growth by distancing or by extrication. It is a divided consciousness of belonging and not belonging. The social solutions – the common solutions – are still taken seriously up to the last point of personal crisis, and then what is achieved as a personal moral development has to express itself as some kind of physical or spiritual renewal; an emigration, at once resigned and hopeful, from what had originally been offered as a decisive social world.
>
> (Williams 1970: 86–7)

Some of the most interesting historicist research into George Eliot's œuvre focuses on the relationship between her work and the intellectual context of her time. One of the best studies in this area is Sally Shuttleworth's monograph on *George Eliot and Nineteenth-Century Science: The Make-Believe of a Beginning* (1984). Although the title of the book could well be seen as misleading – readers looking for information on the scientific background of the scene of the blood transfusion in 'The Lifted Veil', or on the broader context of the state of early nineteenth-century medical science in *Middlemarch*, are likely to feel disappointed – Shuttleworth does nonetheless offer a comprehensive account of the way in which the novels of George Eliot are informed by their author's engagement with some of the central intellectual debates of the Victorian era, primarily those relating to the philosophical implications of the theory of organicism, which perceived society in terms of a living organism and, in consequence, drew a parallel between, on the one hand, the mechanisms determining the dynamics of social development and, on the other hand, the natural processes of biological life. Shuttleworth pays special attention to the impact, on George Eliot's work, of the sociological studies of Comte and of the physiological and psychological research of Lewes; she investigates, in particular, the way in which their work prepared the ground for George Eliot's analysis of the ethical consequences of their organicist theories. The book's sustained analysis of George Eliot's seven novels demonstrates how the writer's initial pastoral concept of organicism, most fully expressed in *Adam Bede* (see Works, **pp. 36–44**), gradually gives way to a more complex vision, involving a profound psychological investigation of characters operating in increasingly complicated and fragmented social contexts – a vision most fully embedded in the experimental presentation of modern British and European society in *Daniel Deronda* (see Works, **pp. 80–8**). At the same time, the novelist's changing perception of organic theory finds an expression in the changing artistic shape of her works, with the integrated structure of the earlier novels gradually giving way to more complex and dynamic patterns of her later fictions. In consequence, Shuttleworth argues, George Eliot's fiction becomes the literary equivalent of the trends characterising the major directions in the development of nineteenth-century scientific thinking:

> Study of George Eliot's involvement with organicist theory suggests the complex ways in which nineteenth-century social and scientific thought were intertwined. Clearly, evolutionary theory was not the sole ground of interconnection; nor was the relationship between science and social philosophy manifest only in the realm of explicit social ideas. As we have seen, biological theories of the organic influenced not only the social theory, but also the narrative methodology of George Eliot's work. Her shift from a static to a dynamic model of the organism, and from the role of passive observer to that of active experimenter reflects the nineteenth-century decline in natural history and the rise of experimental science. This movement in the field of science found parallel expression in the development of nineteenth-century fiction. As interest in the sciences moved from the order of nature to its history, so novelists turned their attention to the historical growth of the social whole and the inner workings of the mind. With the decline of natural history, conventions in realism also shifted: the task of the novelist, like that of the scientist, was no longer merely to name the visible order of the world. George Eliot's fiction encapsulates these changes, foreshadowing subsequent developments in the Victorian novel.
>
> (Shuttleworth 1984: 204–5)

Covering some of the same ground as Shuttleworth's book, Suzanne Graver's extensive volume on *George Eliot and Community: A Study in Social Theory and Fictional Form* (1984) offers a detailed account of the way in which the novels of George Eliot explore one of the central problems of nineteenth-century sociology – the changing nature of social structures defining the relationship between the individual and the community, including in particular the evolutionary transformation of traditional local communities, fundamentally agricultural in origin and firmly rooted in the established heritage of traditional culture, into a more complex, diverse, dynamic, but at the same time highly competitive and, in consequence, alienating and atomised structure of the modern urban industrial society. These two social models, referred to in the book, after the late-nineteenth-century German sociologist Ferdinand Tönnies, as, respectively, *Gemeinschaft* and *Gesellschaft*, provide the fundamental tools with which Graver approaches her analysis of the social vision of the novels; in her opinion, George Eliot's fictional world is one of dynamic, but somewhat uneasy and therefore unstable balance between the two types of social organisation:

> While she hoped her fiction could bring together realism and idealism, neutrality and partisanship, Gesellschaft and Gemeinschaft, the prosaic and the poetic, most often it reveals the conflicts that obscure and complicate a vision of fellowship. Nonetheless, the very instabilities contribute in a vital way to the natural history she was creating. By

capturing polarities that point to antagonistic values, while evoking through the effort to overcome them a vision of wholeness, she created a body of fiction most compelling when it reveals a double consciousness, moving toward fusion while uncovering conflict as each side implicates the other both affirmatively and negatively. As a result, her most successful reconciliations are those tenuous and makeshift ones that render fragile the very principle of fellowship she struggled to affirm. Powerfully confronting both sides and creating an engaging and embattled middle ground, she held out to her readers an ideal of community while suggesting, sometimes at the same moment, the impossibility of that ideal.

(Graver 1984: 148)

Graver then goes on to explore the relationship between the social vision of the novels and their formal properties, demonstrating how the instabilities of the structure of the communities she depicts are reflected in the disjunctions in the fictional form of the three novels which, in her view, offer the fullest analysis of the complex texture of modern British society – *The Mill on the Floss* (see Works, pp. 44–51), *Middlemarch* (see Works, pp. 67–80) and *Daniel Deronda* (see Works, pp. 80–8). Based on an extensive study not only of George Eliot's fiction but also of the work of nineteenth-century philosophers and sociologists, from Feuerbach and Strauss to Comte, Mill, Lewes and Spencer, and offering a number of interesting critical insights, for example with regard to the analysis, in *The Mill on the Floss*, of the moral evolution of Maggie Tulliver and its relation to the controversial ending of the novel, Graver's monograph is, however, a worthy but laborious rather than inspired effort. Its last two chapters, focusing on the critical responses to the novels and the ways in which George Eliot's narrators address the reader, add relatively little to the central argument of the book, while its overall structure, with the main focus shifting back and forth between social theory and literary criticism, makes it rather complex and therefore relatively difficult to navigate for a non-specialist reader.

Alexander Welsh's illuminating study of *George Eliot and Blackmail* (1985) combines, in a rather unusual way, new-historicist attention to contextual detail with a reading of the novels informed by the considerations of psychoanalysis. The book opens with an account of the role of blackmail and secrecy as major motifs in Victorian literature, followed by an extensive discussion of the emergence of information culture and public opinion as major aspects of the development of nineteenth-century society. In the critical section of his book, Welsh proceeds to investigate the significance of secrecy as a factor in the creation of George Eliot's artistic persona and as an important structural and symbolic element in her novels:

Each of George Eliot's novels after *The Mill on the Floss* explores some life history that is discontinuous yet surreptitiously connected with a past. The discontinuity is social, and nothing strange to the history of the author's own times; but its replication in narrative begins to resemble, through the importance bestowed on the past, the tracing of distortions and finally a transference, the conditions that have come to be known

as 'the analytic situation'. [. . . George Eliot] was not prepared to cede
the priority of moral demands, but she gradually enlarged her study
of consciousness, told of unconscious thoughts and mental suffering
inflicted upon the self as well as upon others, and experimented with
narrative reconstructions of both shame and guilt.

(Welsh 1985: 153–4)

With the focus of its analysis expanding to include, in the extensive section on
Daniel Deronda (see Works, **pp. 80–8**), the broader question of the role of
consciousness and ideology as sources of authority in modern society, Welsh's
book moves rather far away from its starting point and, in consequence, may
appear – not surprisingly perhaps given its substantial length – somewhat diffuse
in its approach; even if it is the case, however, his study still remains a highly
enlightening account of secrecy as a significant feature of the life of Victorian
society and of George Eliot's effective use of it for the analysis of the psychology
of her characters.

An interesting brief introduction to George Eliot's novels is provided in
Simon Dentith's volume in the Harvester New Readings series (1986). Dentith
approaches George Eliot as a fundamentally realist writer, one 'who, in the terms
and categories available to her, attempts to understand and make sense of the
social history of her time and the possibilities for individual fulfilment made
available by that history' (Denith 1986: 5). His analysis of the novels combines
the exploration of some of the central concerns of George Eliot's works, such as
the doctrine of sympathy, the problem of social progress, the critique of the moral
attitudes of modern society and the subject of gender and its implications for the
socio-economic and educational situation of women, with the discussion of some
of the key aspects of the form of her fictions, including, in particular, the nature
of their realism, the increasing idealisation of their main protagonists and the
structure and complexity of their multiple levels of discourse. Throughout his
study, Dentith's approach is strictly historical: he relates George Eliot's vision of
the world to the intellectual and social atmosphere of the mid- and late nineteenth
century, noting in particular the influence on her thinking of the ideas of Feuerbach
and Comte and pointing out the significance of her own social background and its
consequences as regards her experience, knowledge and sympathies. Although
the shifting focus of Dentith's analysis may leave a less focused reader feeling
somewhat confused, the liveliness of his informal tone and the clarity of his
argument make his book a useful contribution to George Eliot criticism.

One of the most substantial studies approaching the work of George Eliot from
an explicitly Marxist perspective is Daniel Cottom's *Social Figures: George Eliot,
Social History, and Literary Representation* (1987). Perceiving her work as an
element of the broader, heterogeneous social discourse generated by the economic,
social and political reality of nineteenth-century Britain, Cottom sees George
Eliot as a quintessential Victorian liberal intellectual, demonstrating – or rather
betraying – her commitment to the epoch's established patriarchal system of
values through the construction of the fictional world of her fiction, with its
implied ideals and practices, through her focus on specific themes, such as the
problems of education, charity and democracy, as well as through the adoption of
the aesthetics of realism. Using material from George Eliot's works to illustrate

points about the social and political vision implied in her œuvre, Cottom's study, set firmly against the context of the social, economic and intellectual background of nineteenth-century Britain, belongs, in many ways, in the field of cultural history rather than literary criticism *sensu stricto*: although it does include passages of conventional literary analysis (among them, an interesting account of the treatment of the theme of class and gentility in *Daniel Deronda* [see Works, pp. 80–8]), it does not attempt a sustained discussion of the novels and stories and is, therefore, of use primarily to students of George Eliot's contribution to the development of the social and political ideology of the Victorian establishment and only to a lesser extent to those interested in her achievement as a literary artist.

Bernard Semmel's volume on *George Eliot and the Politics of National Inheritance* (1994) is a persuasive study of the social and political ideology underlying George Eliot's works. Through his analysis of the treatment of the theme of personal inheritance in *The Mill on the Floss* (see Works, pp. 45–51), *Silas Marner* (see Works, pp. 51–6) and *Felix Holt* (see Works, pp. 61–7), Semmel introduces the broader problem of the nature of heritage, individual as well as communal, and the moral and social obligations and responsibilities associated with the acceptance of one's place in the inherited order of things. Relating his discussion of George Eliot's political ideas to the context of the intellectual life of mid-Victorian Britain and focusing in particular on the way in which her works were influenced by, as well as engaged in argument with, some of the most important philosophical doctrines of the epoch, such as, in particular, modern individualistic liberalism on the one hand and cosmopolitan Positivism on the other, Semmel defines George Eliot's conservatism in the following terms:

> Eliot had become convinced that the [. . .] values of individualism and cosmopolitanism that prevailed in British liberal circles would impair both family affection and social cohesion. Only a nation, a society that she saw as based on filial sentiment, perceived national kinship, and common historical traditions – one that linked past and future in the same way in which the transmission of property from parents to children linked the generations – could provide a realistic foundation for communal solidarity. These ties would make it possible for an individual to transcend selfish egoism and to feel a deep sympathetic concern, first towards his kin and then toward the extended family of the nation. Any more ambitious ascent from egoism to harmonious identification with all of mankind, she came to believe, could not be managed until a very long time in the future.
>
> (Semmel 1994: 6)

Semmel finds this position illustrated in George Eliot's late works: he interprets *Middlemarch* (see Works, pp. 67–80) as a declaration of the writer's support for the ideal of political compromise and gradual parliamentary reform, personified in the character of Will Ladislaw, and he reads *The Spanish Gypsy* (see Works, pp. 93–4) and *Daniel Deronda* (see Works, pp. 80–8) as expressions of her belief in 'the moral necessity of an individual to identify himself with his nation by an act of will' (Semmel 1994: 117). Although the largely historical focus of Semmel's study places it on the borderline between literary criticism and the history of ideas – not surprisingly perhaps given the author's background as a historian – it is nonetheless one of the more important recent studies of George Eliot's thought, in particular as regards her complex and often ambivalent attitude towards Positivism.

Neil McCaw's monograph on *George Eliot and Victorian Historiography: Imagining the National Past* (2000) continues the discussion of George Eliot's engagement with the problem of the national past through its investigation of the way in which her England-set fictions demonstrate the influence on her writing of some of the historiographical theories current in Victorian historical thinking: the Whig concept of history, associated with writers such as Thomas Babington Macaulay, 'one in which gradual but definable progress was evident, one in which constitutional democracy and personal liberty were hallmarks, and one which illustrated clearly the continuity between an Anglo-Saxon, Protestant England past and the Victorian present' (McCaw 2000: 35), the Romantic and ultimately profoundly conservative historiography of Thomas Carlyle, perceiving the past 'as the grand arena within which the will of God was in competition with the errant moral tendencies of flawed human selves' (McCaw 2000: 66), the sceptical, empirical vision of Tory historians, rejecting the very concept of universalising grand narratives of history and, finally, the emerging proto-feminist approach. McCaw's exploration of George Eliot's works – he focuses, in particular, on *Daniel Deronda* (see Works, **pp. 80–8**) and on *Impressions of Theophrastus Such* (see Works, **pp. 89–90**) – demonstrates the complexity of her response to these theories; although he notes that her perceptions were influenced primarily by the Whig interpretation of the past, he does nonetheless underline the ambivalence of her dynamic vision of the processes of history:

> Though there is a defined ambiguity at the heart of the relationship between these fictions and the Whig historiographical discourse, it is nevertheless a highly significant relationship. The ambiguity of the way in which Eliot at times appears to adhere to this interpretation of the English past while also, and simultaneously, undermining and doubting it is further evidence of the tensions between her work and totalizing notions of history. The frequently qualified notion of progress that is apparent in the fictions, coupled with the awkwardness as regards non-orthodox religions, are both evidence of this tendency towards and withdrawal away from the totalizing Whig perceptions of history. [. . .] When viewed in tandem with the influence of Carlyle, the landscape of a George Eliot novel becomes a complex, often contradictory terrain; it is a surface awash with doubts, contradictions and competing (and yet coexistent) interpretations and perspectives.
>
> (McCaw 2000: 143–4)

Some of the methodological aspects of new historicism underlie Kathleen McCormack's discussion of George Eliot's treatment of the theme of alcoholism and other forms of addiction in her book on *George Eliot and Intoxication: Dangerous Drugs for the Condition of England* (2000). McCormack's account of her subject begins with a succinct but comprehensive summary of the ways in which alcohol and opium constituted a significant element of the social reality of Victorian Britain and of the ways in which metaphors based on the concepts of health, illness, medicines and stimulants were used to characterise that social reality – as was the case, most notably, with the description of one of the period's central social concerns as 'the condition-of-England question'. McCormack then proceeds to sift relevant biographical evidence as well as George Eliot's works for evidence of references to drink and drugs; although the exercise appears at first to be rather mechanical – the reader is treated to some very precise figures concerning the numbers of bottles of sherry purchased at various points by the future writer's father Robert Evans and to details of the Leweses' drinking routines during their Continental holidays – as McCormack settles down to the discussion of the metaphorical significance of the motifs of drinking, intoxication, addiction and medical treatment in George Eliot's works, she gradually discovers a pattern of connections relating the use of these motifs to the author's focus on the realistic presentation of her world and on the analysis of its internal structures gradually falling into a condition of moral and social instability which her metaphors of addiction and infection turn out to represent. This network of metaphors becomes increasingly prominent as George Eliot's career unfolds; it becomes linked, in particular, with the political dimension increasingly prominent in the writer's later novels, from *Felix Holt* onwards. McCormack's analysis accordingly culminates in her account of the way in which the condition of England has become what could be called a condition of Europe, or indeed a condition of the Western world:

> At the conclusion of George Eliot's last novel, the Condition of England has only spread its infection far beyond national boundaries and begun to toxify the entire continent just as a general perception is taking shape that the whole world is sick. Together with the other drug material in *Deronda*, this spread implies that, as the century went on, George Eliot had little reason to become more optimistic about the Condition of England. Far from yielding to the many remedies applied, the Condition had become *Weltschmerz*.
>
> (McCormack 2000: 198)

Post-colonial criticism

Not surprisingly perhaps, given the profoundly domestic, English focus of the majority of George Eliot's works, the post-colonial approach has not been among the most fruitful of directions in the critical debate surrounding her work. One of the few full-length books on George Eliot written from the post-colonial perspective is Nancy Henry's study of *George Eliot and the British Empire* (2002). The approach adopted in this monograph is not, strictly speaking, typical of a literary critic: Henry's book combines, on the one hand, an investigation of relevant aspects of Marian Lewes's biography, such as her experience of reading about travel and colonisation, her relationship and correspondence with her two younger stepsons, both of whom emigrated to South Africa, her extensive range of investments in companies involved in business ventures in the colonies and the extensive experience of international business and travel acquired over the years by her husband John Walter Cross, with, on the other hand, a discussion of the way in which the emergence of the advanced, imperial form of modern capitalism in the third quarter of the nineteenth century found a reflection in the themes and the metaphorical structures of George Eliot's last two prose works, *Daniel Deronda* (see Works, **pp. 80–8**) and *Impressions of Theophrastus Such* (see Works, **pp. 89–90**). Defending George Eliot – and other Victorian novelists – from the leading post-colonial critic Edward Said's charge of complicity in the ideological justification of imperialism (Said 1993: 93–6), Henry demonstrates the ambivalence of the political message of the Jewish plot of her last novel and the irrationality of adopting an anachronistic critical position based on the benefit of hindsight; instead, she perceives the author of *Daniel Deronda* as a writer and thinker ready to embrace the challenges of the modern world in what could at the time only have been seen as a progressive, forward-looking way:

> Realistic representations of the past in Eliot's fiction made room toward the end of her life for speculations about the future, for national movements that she approved and for warfare that she abhorred. The colonies were places she would never see. Like the future, they maintained an imagined quality; pieced together from texts about which she was skeptical. Cross, on his part, had been to the New World and seen its potential, and was convinced that the future of the old world – its products, commerce, livelihood, culture – would and should be bound up with the new [. . .]. In marrying him she embraced a particular kind of future for England and, perhaps unwittingly, secured a particular image of herself for posterity – ironically, the foundations of a biographical tradition that has ignored her connections to finance and to the empire.
>
> (Henry 2002: 149)

Alicia Carroll's monograph *Dark Smiles: Race and Desire in George Eliot* (2002) combines the post-colonial approach with the feminist standpoint: Carroll focuses on the ways in which the contrast between the predominantly English – Christian – Western world of George Eliot's works and her representations of outsiders – people of other races, religions, national backgrounds or cultural heritages – is invested with a strong erotic dimension, resulting in the undermining of the conventional Victorian conception of social structures and gender roles:

> Many of the recent postcolonial readings of George Eliot [. . .] have been engaged either with celebrating her work, on Judaism, for example, as progressive and enlightened, or chiding the same as essentially reifying a colonizing, hegemonic authority. [. . .] Absent from these debates is an investigation of how Eliot's eroticized others elide those margins to the right and left of the centers of hegemonic colonialist discourses; what is most remarkable about Eliot's representations is their instability. Other than their obvious recurrence, no single pattern defines or marks Eliot's representations of Otherness. Particularly in the shifting of

their gendering, Eliot's Others resist 'stable' or static meanings. Within the same novels, they may be represented as threatening erotic outsiders who must be 'purged' from the text, as unwilling captive queens, or as competent Radicals who marry into British society and attempt to resist assimilation or conversion. Eliot's concessions to and divergences from conventional stereotypes of desirous Others are essential to her negotiation of novel writing itself.

(Carroll 2002: 3)

Carroll opens her discussion with the study of the figures of 'George Eliot's would-be Gypsy queens' (2002: 28), Caterina Sarti, Maggie Tulliver and Fedalma, all of whom, in their various ways, rebel against the conventional patterns of domesticity and duty imposed on them by their native or indeed adoptive family, social, national or religious environments. Subsequent chapters focus on the ways in which, in the writer's last three novels, the erotic dynamics of the relationships between Esther Lyon and Harold Transome, Dorothea Brooke and Will Ladislaw, and Gwendolen Harleth and Daniel Deronda serve George Eliot's purpose of exploring the underlying social, cultural, political and sexual tensions of Victorian society, thus demonstrating how 'Eliot's trope of Otherness suggests that the critique of empire and Englishness, and the struggle to express desire, begins far earlier in the history of the British novel than was once thought' (Carroll 2002: 28).

George Eliot in context

Not surprisingly in view of George Eliot's unchallenged position as the most erudite of major Victorian novelists, a number of studies focus on the relationship between her novels and the literary and artistic context of her time; with her lifelong interest in literature, music and the visual arts clearly in evidence as a major factor shaping the richly allusive texture of her fiction and providing the source of many of her central metaphors, the relationship between her work and the broad heritage of Western art and civilisation is naturally a fruitful area of research.

One of the earliest works in that vein is William Baker's monograph on *George Eliot and Judaism* (1975). Although the main focus of his study is inevitably on *Daniel Deronda* (see Works, pp. 80–8), Baker offers a detailed account of its author's knowledge of Jewish history, religion and culture, including her early reading and translation of the work of Spinoza and her use of Jewish motifs in some of her works before *Daniel Deronda* – notably, 'The Lifted Veil' (see Works, pp. 88–9), *Romola* (see Works, pp. 56–61) and *The Spanish Gypsy* (see Works, pp. 93–4) – as well as in the final essay in *Impressions of Theophrastus Such*, 'The Modern Hep! Hep! Hep!' (see Works, p. 90). Baker's approach is factual rather than analytical, but his book remains valuable for all readers embarking on a closer study of George Eliot's last novel.

The theme of the impact of Judaism on the work of George Eliot is taken up again by Saleel Nurbhai and K.M. Newton in their study of *George Eliot, Judaism and the Novels: Jewish Myth and Mysticism* (2002). The focus of their analysis is on the way in which the writer's novels, particularly, though not exclusively, *Daniel Deronda* (see Works, **pp. 80–8**), demonstrate that 'for Eliot Jewish myth and mysticism provided the metaphorical and allegorical potential to enable the novel to compete in complexity and philosophical range with tragic drama and epic poetry' (Nurbhai and Newton 2000: 2). The central place in this respect belongs to George Eliot's use of the motif of the golem, associated with the fundamental myths of creation and explored, in various ways, in numerous works of early nineteenth-century literature, from Goethe's *Faust* to Mary Shelley's *Frankenstein* and Thomas Carlyle's *Sartor Resartus*. In their detailed analysis of George Eliot's treatment of different aspects of that myth, from the investigation of the nature of the very act of the creation of the golem and its relationship with its creator to the study of the complexities of the existential, ethical and aesthetic aspects of the process of the formation of the golem's identity, Nurbhai and Newton explore the implications of this aspect of the metaphorical structure of the novels for the overall social and philosophical vision of the novels; perceiving her works in a manner that attempts to reconcile the acceptance of their realist mode with the recognition of their allegorical dimension, the two critics note, in particular, the emergence of Daniel Deronda as an idealised, symbolic embodiment of the processes of social and national integration. The closing paragraph of the book summarises its interpretation of George Eliot's vision of the relationship between individual and society:

> Beneath the realist surface there is a unifying sub-structure founded upon the central myth of the golem, around which are literary interpretations of Jewish mysticism related to this myth. Her view of the relation between individual and society is ultimately golemish. The individual remains golem if he or she fails to become integrated into society, since it is only when the individual is a part of society that wholeness is possible. But equally, societies that deny certain individuals integration risk suffering the revenge of the golem. And only when there are whole societies can they interact to become composite parts of a larger whole. The golem in Eliot's work becomes a metaphor not only related to the completion of the individual and the individual's immediate community, as in the specific Jewish context of the legend, but it also – in accordance with kabbalistic thinking where it merged with her own ideas on form – becomes a symbol of the need for national and international completion.
>
> (Nurbhai and Newton 2002: 190–1)

The first major study devoted specifically to the influence of the broader artistic context of George Eliot's work on her own achievement as a writer of fiction is Hugh Witemeyer's book on *George Eliot and the Visual Arts* (1979). Carefully researched and very informative, but at the same time thoroughly readable, Witemeyer's book offers a succinct but comprehensive account of Marian Evans's interest in and knowledge of the visual arts, particularly painting, and traces the way in which her novels reflect both her commitment to the late Romantic aesthetics of pictorialism, influenced primarily by the works of the leading Victorian art critic John Ruskin, and her recognition of its limitations – in line with the theories of the eighteenth-century German playwright and critic Gotthold

Ephraim Lessing, George Eliot's novels demonstrate that for fiction to achieve a quality of dynamism unavailable to painting, 'literary description must [. . .] give way at some point to narrative and drama' (Witemeyer 1979: 41). Witemeyer then goes on to discuss the ways in which George Eliot used this pattern of pictorial representation followed by the dramatisation of the initial scene in trying to produce in her works literary equivalents of some of her favourite genres of painting – portraiture, religious and historical painting, genre painting and landscape; in each case, the visual dimension of the text turns out to carry with it significant symbolic meanings. In an interesting counterpoint, the book closes with a discussion of Frederic Leighton's engravings for the serialisation of *Romola* (see Works, pp. 56–61), the only work of George Eliot's to be accompanied by illustrations at the time of original publication.

George Eliot's interest in music and her use of musical motifs in the symbolic structures of her novels are the subject of Beryl Gray's monograph *George Eliot and Music* (1989). Though interesting in its critical insights, particularly in its extremely detailed analysis of the use of the motif of singing as a key element in the development of the relationship between Stephen Guest and Maggie Tulliver, the book does not treat its subject with the kind of comprehensiveness promised by its title. The main problem is that of balance and focus: the brief opening chapter, dealing with the relevant details of Marian Evans's biography, is followed by an extensive discussion of *The Mill on the Floss* (see Works, pp. 44–51), constituting more than half of the book and concentrating almost exclusively on the last volume of the novel; the rest of the study consists of two relatively short chapters on *Middlemarch* (see Works, pp. 67–80) and *Daniel Deronda* (see Works, pp. 80–8). It is particularly Gray's treatment of the latter novel that creates the impression of haste and cursoriness; this is despite the fact that she recognises the role played by music in the plot of the novel and in its rich pattern of symbolic allusions:

> Nowhere in George Eliot's fiction is the pattern of musical allusion more delineated – more coherently Shakespearean in the unity it gener-ates – than in her last novel. The quality and register of the voice, what is sung (and what is left unsung), who sings, who hears, what is revealed – all that can attach emotionally and dramatically to music – is of con-sequence; and, since the pattern of social movement is very complicated in *Daniel Deronda*, contact between the different strata of its society is schematically dependent on the social function of music.
>
> (Gray 1989: 100)

Rather disappointing, too, is the fact that Gray's book makes virtually no reference to the numerous poems in which George Eliot deals with the theme of music, such as 'The Legend of Jubal' and 'Armgart'; as a result, the whole study disappointingly lacks the kind of weight and authority that the quality of the insights that it does offer suggests it might well deserve.

A much more comprehensive discussion of George Eliot's use of musical allusion is provided by Delia da Sousa Correa in *George Eliot, Music and Victorian Culture* (2002). The value of this excellent study lies primarily in its careful combination of literary analysis and historical, cultural and philosophical contextualisation: da Sousa Correa opens her investigation of Marian Evans's interest in music by placing it firmly in the context of the evolutionist theory of music proposed by Herbert Spencer in his essay on 'The Origin and Function of Music' (1857), as well as against the background of contemporary debates in musical aesthetics, on which the future novelist herself commented in her essay on 'Liszt, Wagner, and Weimar' (1855). At the same time, the book underlines the significance of the association of music with the world of Victorian domesticity and with the cultural experience of women:

> Music resounds in Eliot's complex feminism: her musical women are particularly striking – from Caterina Sarti in 'Mr Gilfil's Love Story' to the prima donna Alcharisi in *Daniel Deronda*. Eliot's novels are peopled by women through whose musicality contemporary anxieties about woman's nature emerge with particular intensity. Equivocal attitudes towards both woman and music make their association in nineteenth-century literature especially interesting. Musical allusion frequently underpins issues of social power and commodification as well as of individual women's creative fulfilment. In this respect, explorations of female musical performance and response in novels by Eliot and her contemporaries confront a number of the same preoccupations that appear in journals and advice books of the time where women's musical activity was discussed as having the potential to enhance, or to detract from, their proper role. Music played a crucial role in women's education and in their domestic life. However, music could be a dangerous sensual influence. Contradictory representations of music and woman mirror one another in literature of the period: both can be agents of domestic harmony or embody sexual mayhem. Long known as the most spiritual and yet most sensual art, the ambivalent status of music was reinforced in the mid-nineteenth century by psychological theories which explained emotion, including response to music, in physiological terms and which saw women as especially at the mercy of their bodies.
>
> (da Sousa Correa 2002: 8)

It is from that angle that da Sousa Correa proceeds to analyse the significance of the treatment of musical motifs in George Eliot's works, particularly in *The Mill on the Floss* (see Works, **pp. 44–51**), 'Armgart' (see Works, **pp. 94–5**) and *Daniel Deronda* (see Works, **pp. 80–8**); her investigation traces a variety of ways in which issues of psychology, education and race are mediated through the characters' engagement in different forms of musical activity, particularly singing. A detailed, painstakingly researched, and yet thoroughly readable book, *George Eliot, Music and Victorian Culture* is certainly one of the most important recent contributions not only to George Eliot scholarship but also to the broader area of Victorian cultural studies.

One of the important directions in the development of George Eliot criticism towards the end of the twentieth century was the increasing interest in the European context of her work. Although by no means unique among Victorian novelists in setting the action of some of her novels wholly or partly on the Continent, she exceeded the majority of her contemporaries in her personal familiarity with the main countries of Continental Europe and with their literary and cultural heritage; in particular, her extensive reading of the works of classic and modern writers, mainly though by no means exclusively French and German, raises the inevitable question of possible connections, influences, interdependencies and parallels. This first major contribution to this area of research was made by Barbara Smalley, whose 1974 study of *George Eliot and Flaubert* brings together the work of two novelists frequently perceived as the pioneers of a new, self-conscious approach to the writing of fiction that would eventually result in the development of the aesthetics of modernism. Daniel Vitaglione's study of *George Eliot and George Sand* (1993) offers a systematic comparison of the two writers' religious, social and aesthetic ideas, as well as – inevitably given their controversial personal lives and their adoption of male pseudonyms – their attitudes to matters of gender; the book identifies, as one of the key areas of the French novelist's influence of the work of George Eliot, her development of the aesthetics of 'bucolic realism'. George Eliot's responses to a variety of aspects of European culture, from the Classical scholarship of the Italian Renaissance to the landscape and culture of Spain and from the politics of the Risorgimento to the modern literature of France are traced in the essays collected in John Rignall's volume of essays on *George Eliot and Europe* (1997). Andrew Thompson's monograph on *George Eliot and Italy* (1998) analyses the impact of the writer's knowledge of Italian history and culture on the metaphorical patterns of her fiction; Thompson concentrates, in particular, on the influence of Dante on the shaping of George Eliot's moral vision in her middle and later novels, from *Romola* through to *Daniel Deronda*, and on the influence of her interest in the nineteenth-century Italian national movement, the Risorgimento, on the development of her social and political ideas, particularly with regard to the problem of nationalism. The book proposes a number of illuminating and often unexpected perspectives on George Eliot's work, even if its focus on Dante, at the expense of, for example, the relatively cursory treatment of *Romola*, creates the impression that as a whole, Thompson's study is not quite as balanced and comprehensive as its inclusive and summative-sounding title suggests.

4

Chronology

Bullet points denote events in Marian Evans (Lewes)'s life; asterisks denote historical and literary events.

1819
- Mary Anne Evans (ME) born 22 November at South Farm, Arbury, near Nuneaton, Warwickshire, to Robert Evans, the manager of the Arbury estate, and Christiana Evans (née Pearson), a daughter of a local farmer
* Peterloo massacre; Byron: *Don Juan* (Cantos I–II); Scott: *Ivanhoe*

1820
- Move to Griff House, Arbury
* Death of George III and accession of George IV

1824
- ME begins her education at Miss Lathom's school, Attleborough

1825
* Stockton and Darlington railway opened

1828
- ME moves to Mrs Wallington's school, Nuneaton

1829
* Catholic Emancipation Act passed

1830
* Death of George IV and accession of William IV; July revolution in France; Comte: *Cours de philosophie positive*; Tennyson: *Poems, Chiefly Lyrical*

1832
- ME moves to Misses Franklin's school, Coventry
* First Reform Bill passed; death of Sir Walter Scott

1833
*   The Oxford Movement begun

1834
*   Poor Law Reform Act passed

1835
•   ME leaves school and returns home to help her family to nurse her terminally ill mother
*   Strauss: *Das Leben Jesu*

1836
•   Death of ME's mother
*   Dickens: *The Pickwick Papers*

1837
•   Christiana Evans, ME's sister, marries Edward Clarke, a local doctor; ME takes over the responsibility for her father's household and embarks on an extensive course of reading
*   Death of William IV and accession of Victoria; Carlyle: *The French Revolution*

1838
*   The People's Charter drawn up – the beginning of the Chartist movement; Hennell: *An Inquiry Concerning the Origin of Christianity*

1840
•   ME's literary debut: 'Farewell', a poem, published in the *Christian Observer*

1841
•   ME and her father move to Foleshill, Coventry; Isaac Evans, ME's brother, marries Sarah Rawlins, a daughter of a merchant; ME meets Charles and Cara Bray; her religious convictions undermined
*   Feuerbach: *Das Wesen des Christenthums*

1842
•   ME refuses to accompany her father to church; meets Sara Hennell

1843
*   Ruskin: *Modern Painters*

1846
•   Translation of Strauss's *Das Leben Jesu* published anonymously by John Chapman; ME begins to publish book reviews in the *Herald*
*   The Corn Laws repealed

1847
*   E. Brontë: *Wuthering Heights*; C. Brontë: *Jane Eyre*; Thackeray: *Vanity Fair*

1848
*   Revolutions in Europe

1849
•   Death of ME's father; ME's first holiday, with the Brays, on the Continent (France, Italy, Switzerland); winter in Geneva

1850
•   ME returns to England; begins to publish in the *Westminster Review*
*   The re-establishment of Roman Catholic hierarchy in England and Wales; death of Wordsworth; Tennyson appointed Poet Laureate; Tennyson: *In Memoriam*; Wordsworth: *The Prelude*

1851
•   ME moves to London, staying in Chapman's lodging house; meets Herbert Spencer and George Henry Lewes; assumes the assistant editorship of the *Westminster Review*
*   The Great Exhibition in Hyde Park

1852
•   The first of ten issues of the *Westminster Review* edited by ME published
*   Dickens: *Bleak House*

1853
•   ME begins a relationship with Lewes and moves out of Chapman's house
*   The Crimean War breaks out

1854
•   ME leaves the *Westminster Review*; translation of Feuerbach's *Das Wesen des Christenthums* published (under ME's own name) by Chapman; leaves England for Germany to live with Lewes, and adopts the name of Marian Evans Lewes (MEL)

1855
•   MEL and Lewes return to England
*   Browning: *Men and Women*

1856
•   MEL begins work on 'Amos Barton'
*   The Treaty of Paris ends the Crimean War

1857
•   'Amos Barton', 'Mr Gilfil's Love-Story' and 'Janet's Repentance' serialised in *Blackwood's Edinburgh Magazine*; MEL adopts the pseudonym of George Eliot; notifies her family of her relationship with Lewes; relations with her family severed; MEL begins work on *Adam Bede*

1858
- *Scenes of Clerical Life* published by Blackwood; MEL reveals the identity of George Eliot to Blackwood; MEL and Lewes visit Germany and Austria

1859
- MEL begins work on *The Mill on the Floss*; *Adam Bede* published by Blackwood; death of MEL's sister Christiana; MEL writes 'The Lifted Veil'; 'The Lifted Veil' published in *Blackwood's Edinburgh Magazine*; the identity of George Eliot becomes public knowledge
* Darwin: *On the Origin of Species*

1860
- *The Mill on the Floss* published by Blackwood; MEL and Lewes visit France, Italy and Switzerland; Lewes's son Charles moves to London to live with MEL and Lewes; MEL writes 'Brother Jacob' and begins work on *Silas Marner*
* Dickens: *Great Expectations*

1861
- *Silas Marner* published by Blackwood; another visit to France, Italy, and Switzerland; MEL begins work on *Romola*
* The unification of Italy; the American Civil War breaks out

1862
- Serialisation of *Romola* begins in the *Cornhill Magazine*

1863
- *Romola* published by Smith, Elder & Co.; MEL and Lewes purchase their first house, The Priory, Regent's Park

1864
- Death of MEL's half-brother Robert; visit to Venice; 'Brother Jacob' published in the *Cornhill Magazine*; MEL begins work on *The Spanish Gypsy*

1865
- Visit to Paris; Charles Lewes marries; MEL begins work on *Felix Holt, the Radical*; another visit to France
* The American Civil War ends

1866
- Visit to Belgium, the Netherlands, and Germany; *Felix Holt, the Radical* published by Blackwood; visit to Paris

1867
- Visit to the Continent (France, Spain) continued; visit to Germany; MEL writes 'Address to Working Men, by Felix Holt'
* Second Reform Bill

1868
- 'Address to Working Men, by Felix Holt' and *The Spanish Gypsy* published by Blackwood; visit to Germany and Switzerland
* Browning: *The Ring and the Book*

1869
- MEL begins work on *Middlemarch*; visit to Italy; MEL and Lewes first meet John Walter Cross; Lewes's son Thornton arrives in England, to be nursed by MEL and Lewes through the final stages of his illness

1870
- Visit to Germany and Austro-Hungary
* Forster's Education Act; Franco-Prussian war breaks out; death of Dickens

1871
- Serialisation of *Middlemarch* begins
* The unification of Germany; Germany's victory in the Franco-Prussian war

1872
- Visit to Germany; *Middlemarch* published by Blackwood
* Ballot Act

1873
- Visit to France and Germany; MEL begins work on *Daniel Deronda*

1874
- *The Legend of Jubal and Other Poems* published by Blackwood; visit to France and Belgium
* Hardy: *Far from the Madding Crowd*

1875
- The death, in South Africa, of Lewes's son Herbert
* Trollope: *The Way We Live Now*

1876
- *Daniel Deronda* serialised; visit to France, Switzerland, and Germany; *Daniel Deronda* published in book form by Blackwood; MEL and Lewes purchase a country house, The Heights, in Witley, Surrey
* Queen Victoria declared Empress of India

1877
- MEL meets Princess Louise, a daughter of Queen Victoria

1878
- The Cabinet Edition of George Eliot's works initiated; MEL begins work on *Impressions of Theophrastus Such*; meets the Princess Royal, the Crown Princess of Germany; death of Lewes

1879
- Emotional crisis following Lewes's death; *Impressions of Theophrastus Such* published by Blackwood; friendship with Cross developing; death of Blackwood
* Meredith: *The Egoist*

1880
- MEL marries Cross (6 May); correspondence with her brother re-established; honeymoon in France, Italy, Austria and Germany; move to Cheyne Walk, Chelsea; MEL (Mrs John Walter Cross) dies (22 December); buried at Highgate Cemetery

5

Further reading

Editions

In addition to the standard Cabinet Edition (1878–80), published under the editorial supervision of the author herself (see Criticism, p. 105), and the modern critical Clarendon Edition (1980–) (see Criticism, pp. 118–19), almost all of George Eliot's works are easily available in numerous good and frequently reprinted paperback editions, most of which include useful introductions and notes. The Oxford World's Classics series includes editions of the eight major fictions, as well as of 'The Lifted Veil' and 'Brother Jacob' and of *Selected Critical Writings*, while Penguin Classics offers the eight major fictions, 'The Lifted Veil' and 'Brother Jacob' and *Selected Essays, Poems, and Other Writings*. These should not be confused with the cheap Penguin Popular Classics editions of *Adam Bede, The Mill on the Floss, Silas Marner* and *Middlemarch*, which do not have the critical apparatus of the Penguin Classics editions and are therefore less useful for a serious student of George Eliot's work. The Everyman Library includes, apart from editions of the eight major fictions ('The Lifted Veil' and 'Brother Jacob' are included in the same volume as *Silas Marner*), the only modern paperback edition of *Impressions of Theophrastus Such* (1995). There are also very useful Norton editions of *The Mill on the Floss* (1994) and *Middlemarch* (1977, 2000).

Critical studies of individual texts

The only full-length study of *Scenes of Clerical Life* is by Thomas A. Noble (1965).

Although virtually all major studies of George Eliot's fiction discuss *Adam Bede* at considerable length, the only book devoted specifically to that novel is an introductory critical commentary by R.T. Jones (1968). Modern editions of the novel include good introductory essays by Stephen Gill (Penguin, 1980), Leonée Ormond (Everyman, 1992) and Valentine Cunningham (Oxford, 1996). Lucie Armitt (2000) offers an overview of critical responses to the novel.

In addition to numerous collections of study notes on *The Mill on the Floss*, there is an introductory critical guide by Roger Ebbatson (1985) as well as a monograph by Ashton (1990). For more advanced critical studies, see a useful Casebook by R.P. Draper (1977) and a New Casebook by Yousaf and Maunder (2002), as well as a volume by Bloom (1988) in the Modern Critical Interpretations series. The Norton edition of the novel by Carol T. Christ (1994) includes a useful selection of critical comments and essays; a survey of critical opinion on the novel can be found in Armitt (2000).

The popularity of *Silas Marner* as a set text on school reading lists and examination syllabuses resulted, over the years, in the production of numerous basic study guides; these are, however, of limited use to a more ambitious reader. The only monograph devoted specifically to the novel is by Swinden (1992), but there are also a few good collections of essays – in particular, the relevant sections of a Casebook by Draper (1977) and a New Casebook by Yousaf and Maunder (2002), as well as volumes by Goodman (2000) and Bloom (2002), the latter in the Modern Critical Interpretations series.

There is an important monograph on *Romola* by Felicia Bonaparte (1979) and a useful collection of essays by Levine and Turner (1998). The 1980 Penguin edition has an excellent introduction by Andrew Sanders.

There are no full-length studies or collections of essays on *Felix Holt, the Radical*; useful introductions include those by Peter Coveney (1972) and Lynda Mugglestone (1995) for two consecutive Penguin editions.

Not surprisingly, *Middlemarch* has attracted more critical attention than any other of George Eliot's novels; there are useful critical introductions by Daiches (1963), Cockshut (1966), McSweeney (1984), Neale (1989), Chase (1991) and Wright (1991), and monographs by Hornback (1988) and Thomas (1988), while Beaty (1960) offers a detailed account of the complex process of the composition of the novel. The history of the reception of *Middlemarch* is traced in a Casebook by Swinden (1972), while comprehensive overviews of more recent critical work can be found in a Modern Critical Interpretations volume by Bloom (1987) and a New Casebook by Peck (1992), as well as in Armitt (2000); there are also separate collections of essays by Hardy (1967) and Adam (1975), and a good Norton edition of the novel, with a selection of critical essays, by Bert G. Hornback (1977, 2nd edn 2000).

Rather surprisingly, in view of the important place *Daniel Deronda* occupies among George Eliot's novels, it has not as yet generated any monograph studies or student-targeted guides; the only collection of essays is by Shalvi (1976). Valuable introductions to modern editions of the novel include those by Barbara Hardy (Penguin, 1967), Terence Cave (Penguin, 1995) and John Rignall (Everyman, 1999).

Collections of critical essays

The best selection of early criticism of George Eliot's work is provided in the Critical Heritage volume by Carroll (1971); other sources include Haight (1966), Holmstrom and Lerner (1966) and Baker (1973). Hutchinson (1996) offers an extensive, four-volume selection of critical comments both from the Victorian period and from the twentieth century; other collections of essays include a Twentieth-Century Views volume by Creeger (1970) and a Modern Critical Views volume by Bloom (1986). Key essays illustrating the main directions in modern criticism of George Eliot's work are reprinted by Newton in an excellent contribution to the Longman Critical Readers series (1991). Useful guides to research are offered by Levine (1988) and Handley (1990).

Informative guides to George Eliot's work include Pinion (1981) and Purkis (1985), while Dolin's Authors in Context volume (2005) offers a discussion of the broad social, cultural and intellectual context of her literary career. The Cambridge Companion by Levine (2001) is an excellent collection of essays summarising the key aspects of George Eliot's work, while the Oxford Reader's Companion by Rignall (2000) comes close to being a definitive encyclopedia of George Eliot studies.

Bibliography

Primary texts

Scenes of Clerical Life, *Blackwood's Edinburgh Magazine*, January–November 1857; Blackwood: Edinburgh, 1858.
Adam Bede, Edinburgh: Blackwood, 1859.
'The Lifted Veil', *Blackwood's Edinburgh Magazine*, July 1859.
The Mill on the Floss, Edinburgh: Blackwood, 1860.
Silas Marner, the Weaver of Raveloe, Edinburgh: Blackwood, 1861.
Romola, *Cornhill Magazine*, July 1862–August 1863; London: Smith, Elder, 1863.
'Brother Jacob', *Cornhill Magazine*, July 1864.
Felix Holt, the Radical, Edinburgh: Blackwood, 1866.
The Spanish Gypsy, Edinburgh: Blackwood, 1868.
Middlemarch: A Study of Provincial Life, December 1871–December 1872; Edinburgh: Blackwood, 1872.
The Legend of Jubal and Other Poems, Edinburgh: Blackwood, 1874.
Daniel Deronda, February–September 1876; Edinburgh: Blackwood, 1876.
Impressions of Theophrastus Such, Edinburgh: Blackwood, 1879.

Essays, letters, journals, notebooks, translations, etc.

Essays of George Eliot, ed. Thomas Pinney, London: Routledge & Kegan Paul, 1963.
The George Eliot Letters, ed. Gordon S. Height, London: Oxford University Press, 1954–78.
The Journals of George Eliot, ed. Margaret Harris and Judith Johnston, Cambridge: Cambridge University Press, 1998.
Some George Eliot Notebooks, ed. William Baker, Salzburg: Institut für English Sprache und Literatur, Universität Salzburg, 1976–85.
George Eliot's 'Middlemarch' Notebooks, ed. John Clark Pratt and Victor A. Neufeldt, London: University of California Press, 1979.

George Eliot's 'Daniel Deronda' Notebooks, ed. Jane Irwin, Cambridge: Cambridge University Press, 1996.

Strauss, David Friedrich, *The Life of Jesus, Critically Examined*, trans. Mary Ann Evans, London: Chapman, 1846.

Feuerbach, Ludwig, *The Essence of Christianity*, trans. Marian Evans, London: Chapman, 1854.

Spinoza, Benedict de, *Ethics*, trans. George Eliot, ed. Thomas Deegan, Salzburg: Institut für Anglistik und Amerikanistik, Universität Salzburg, 1981.

Biographies

Ashton, Rosemary (1996) *George Eliot: A Life*, (London: Hamish Hamilton.

Bodenheimer, Rosemarie (1994) *The Real Life of Mary Ann Evans: George Eliot, Her Letters and Fiction*, London: Cornell University Press.

Browning, Oscar (1890) *Life of George Eliot*, London: Scott.

Crompton, Margaret (1960) *George Eliot: The Woman*, London: Cassell.

Cross, J.W. (1885) *George Eliot's Life, as Related in Her Lettters and Journals*, Edinburgh: Blackwood.

Dodd, Valerie A. (1990) *George Eliot: An Intellectual Life*, Basingstoke: Macmillan.

Haight, Gordon S. (1968) *George Eliot: A Biography*, Oxford: Oxford University Press.

Hanson, Lawrence and Hanson, Elizabeth (1952) *Marian Evans and George Eliot: A Biography*, London: Oxford University Press.

Hughes, Kathryn (1998) *George Eliot: The Last Victorian*, London: Fourth Estate.

Karl, Frederick (1995) *George Eliot: A Biography*, London: Harper Collins.

Laski, Marghanita (1973) *George Eliot and Her World*, London: Thames & Hudson.

Redinger, Ruby (1976) *George Eliot: The Emergent Self*, London: Bodley Head.

Spittles, Brian (1993) *George Eliot: Godless Woman*, Basingstoke: Macmillan.

Sprague, Rosemary (1968) *George Eliot: A Biography*, Philadelphia, Pa.: Chilton Book.

Williams, Blanche Colton (1936) *George Eliot: A Biography*, New York: Macmillan.

Critical works

Adam, Ian (ed.) (1975) *This Particular Web: Essays on 'Middlemarch'*, Toronto: University of Toronto Press.

Allen, Walter (1965) *George Eliot*, London: Weidenfeld & Nicolson.

Armitt, Lucie (2000) *George Eliot: 'Adam Bede', 'The Mill on the Floss', 'Middlemarch'*, Duxford: Icon.

Ashton, Rosemary (1983) *George Eliot*, Oxford: Oxford University Press.

—— (1990) *'The Mill on the Floss': A Natural History*, Boston, Mass.: Twayne.

Baker, William (ed.) (1973) *Critics on George Eliot*, London: Allen & Unwin.

—— (1975) *George Eliot and Judaism*, Lampeter: Edwin Mellen Press.

Baker, William and John C. Ross (2002) *George Eliot: A Bibliographical History*, London: British Library.

Barrett, Dorothea (1989) *Vocation and Desire: George Eliot's Heroines*, London: Routledge.

Beaty, Jerome (1960) *'Middlemarch' from Notebook to Novel: A Study of George Eliot's Creative Method*, Urbana, Ill.: University of Illinois Press.

Beer, Gillian (1986) *George Eliot*, Brighton: Harvester.

Bellringer, Alan W. (1993) *George Eliot*, Basingstoke: Macmillan.

Bennett, Joan (1948) *George Eliot: Her Mind and Her Art*, Cambridge: Cambridge University Press.

Blind, Mathilde (1883) *George Eliot*, London: Allen.

Bloom, Harold (ed.) (1986) *George Eliot*, New York: Chelsea House.

—— (ed.) (1987) *George Eliot's 'Middlemarch'*, New York: Chelsea House.

—— (ed.) (1988) *George Eliot's 'The Mill on the Floss'*, New York: Chelsea House.

—— (ed.) (2002) *George Eliot's 'Silas Marner'*, Philadelphia, Pa.: Chelsea House.

Bonaparte, Felicia (1979) *The Triptych and the Cross: The Central Myths of George Eliot's Poetic Imagination*, Brighton: Harvester.

Brady, Kristin (1992) *George Eliot*, London: Macmillan.

Bullett, Gerald William (1947) *George Eliot: Her Life and Books*, London: Collins.

Carpenter, Mary Wilson (1986) *George Eliot and the Landscape of Time: Narrative Form and Protestant Apocalyptic History*, London: University of North Carolina Press.

Carroll, Alicia (2002) *Dark Smiles: Race and Desire in George Eliot*, Athens, Ohio: Ohio University Press.

Carroll, David (ed.) (1971) *George Eliot: The Critical Heritage*, London: Routledge & Kegan Paul.

—— (1992) *George Eliot and the Conflict of Interpretations: A Reading of the Novels*, Cambridge: Cambridge University Press.

Cecil, Lord David (1934) *Early Victorian Novelists: Essays in Revaluation*, London: Constable.

Chase, Karen (1991) *George Eliot: 'Middlemarch'*, Cambridge: Cambridge University Press.

Cockshut, A.O.J. (1966) *'Middlemarch'*, Oxford: Blackwell.

Cottom, Daniel (1987) *Social Figures: George Eliot, Social History, and Literary Representation*, Minneapolis, Minn.: University of Minnesota Press.

Creeger, George R. (1970) *George Eliot: A Collection of Critical Essays*, Englewood Cliffs, NJ: Prentice-Hall.

Cunningham, Valentine (1975) *Everywhere Spoken Against: Dissent in the Victorian Novel*, Oxford: Oxford University Press.

Daiches, David (1963) *George Eliot: 'Middlemarch'*, London: Edward Arnold.

Dentith, Simon (1986) *George Eliot*, Brighton: Harvester.

Dolin, Tim (2005) *George Eliot*, Oxford: Oxford University Press.

Draper, R.P. (ed.) (1977) *George Eliot: 'The Mill on the Floss' and 'Silas Marner': A Casebook*, London: Macmillan.

Ebbatson, Roger (1985) *George Eliot: 'The Mill on the Floss'*, Harmondsworth: Penguin.

Emery, Laura Comer (1976) *George Eliot's Creative Conflict: The Other Side of Silence*, Berkeley, Calif.: University of California Press.

Ermarth, Elizabeth Deeds (1985) *George Eliot*, Boston, Mass.: Twayne.

Fremantle, Anne (1933) *George Eliot*, London: Duckworth.

Gilbert, Sandra M. and Susan Gubar (1979) *The Madwoman in the Attic: The Woman Writer and the Nineteenth-Century Literary Imagination*, London: Yale University Press.

Goodman, Barbara A. (2000) *Readings on 'Silas Marner'*, San Diego, Calif.: Greenhaven Press.

Graver, Suzanne (1984) *George Eliot and Community: A Study in Social Theory and Fictional Form*, London: University of California Press.

Gray, Beryl (1989) *George Eliot and Music*, Basingstoke: Macmillan.

Haight, Gordon S. (1940) *George Eliot and John Chapman, with Chapman's Diaries*, London: Oxford University Press.

—— (ed.) (1966) *A Century of George Eliot Criticism*, London: Methuen.

Haldane, Elizabeth S. (1927) *George Eliot and Her Times: A Victorian Study*, London: Hodder & Stoughton.

Handley, Graham (1990) *George Eliot: A Guide through the Critical Maze*, Bristol: Bristol Press.

Hardy, Barbara (1959) *The Novels of George Eliot: A Study in Form*, London: Athlone Press.

—— (ed.) (1967) *'Middlemarch': Critical Approaches to the Novel*, London: Athlone Press.

Harvey, W.J. (1961) *The Art of George Eliot*, London: Chatto & Windus.

Henry, Nancy (2002) *George Eliot and the British Empire*, Cambridge: Cambridge University Press.

Hodgson, Peter C. (2001) *Theology in the Fiction of George Eliot*, London: SCM Press.

Holmstrom, John, and Lerner, Laurence (eds) (1966) *George Eliot and Her Readers*, London: Bodley Head.

Hornback, Bert G. (1988) *'Middlemarch': A Novel of Reform*, Boston, Mass.: Twayne.

Hutchinson, Stuart (ed.) (1996) *George Eliot: Critical Assessments*, Robertsbridge: Helm Information.

Johnstone, Peggy Fitzhugh (1994) *The Transformation of Rage: Mourning and Creativity in George Eliot's Fiction*, London: New York University Press.

Jones, Robert Tudor (1968) *A Critical Commentary on George Eliot's 'Adam Bede'*, London: Macmillan.

—— (1970) *George Eliot*, London: Cambridge University Press.

Kettle, Arnold (1951) *An Introduction to the English Novel*, London: Hutchinson.

Kitchel, Anna Theresa (1933) *George Eliot and George Lewes: A Review of Records*, New York: John Day.

—— (1950) *Quarry for 'Middlemarch'*, Berkeley, Calif.: University of California Press.

Leavis, F.R. (1948) *The Great Tradition: George Eliot, Henry James, Joseph Conrad*, London: Chatto & Windus.

Levine, Caroline, and Turner, Mark W. (eds) (1998) *From Author to Text: Re-reading George Eliot's 'Romola'*, Aldershot: Ashgate.

Levine, George (1988) *An Annotated Critical Bibliography of George Eliot*, Brighton: Harvester.

—— (ed.) (2001) *The Cambridge Companion to George Eliot*, Cambridge: Cambridge University Press.

MacCabe, Colin (1979) *James Joyce and the Revolution of the Word*, London: Macmillan.

Main, Alexander (ed.) (1872) *Wise, Witty, and Tender Sayings in Prose and Verse, Selected from the Works of George Eliot*, Edinburgh: Blackwood.

Mann, Karen B. (1983) *The Language that Makes George Eliot's Fiction*, London: Johns Hopkins University Press.

Martin, Carol A. (1994) *George Eliot's Serial Fiction*, Columbus, Ohio: Ohio State University Press.

McCaw, Neil (2000) *George Eliot and Victorian Historiography: Imagining the National Past*, Basingstoke: Macmillan.

McCormack, Kathleen (2000) *George Eliot and Intoxication: Dangerous Drugs for the Condition of England*, Basingstoke: Macmillan.

McDonagh, Josephine (1997) *George Eliot*, Plymouth: Northcote House.

McKenzie, K.A. (1961) *Edith Simcox and George Eliot*, London: Oxford University Press.

McSweeney, Kerry (1984) *'Middlemarch'*, London: Allen & Unwin.

—— (1991) *George Eliot (Marian Evans): A Literary Life*, Basingstoke: Macmillan.

Millett, Kate (1970) *Sexual Politics*, New York: Doubleday.

Myers, William (1984) *The Teaching of George Eliot*, Leicester: Leicester University Press.

Neale, Catherine (1989) *George Eliot: 'Middlemarch'*, Harmondsworth: Penguin.

Nestor, Pauline (2002) *George Eliot*, Basingstoke: Palgrave.

Newton, K.M. (1981) *George Eliot: Romantic Humanist*, London: Macmillan.

—— (ed.) (1991) *George Eliot*, Harlow: Longman.

Noble, Thomas A. (1965) *George Eliot's 'Scenes of Clerical Life'*, London: Yale University Press.

Nurbhai, Saleel and Newton, K.M. (2002) *George Eliot, Judaism, and the Novels: Jewish Myth and Mysticism*, Basingstoke: Palgrave.

Paris, Bernard J. (1965) *Experiments in Life: George Eliot's Quest for Values*, Detroit, Mich.: Wayne State University Press.

Paxton, Nancy L. (1991) *George Eliot and Herbert Spencer: Feminism, Evolutionism, and a Reconstruction of Gender*, Oxford: Princeton University Press.

Peck, John (ed.) (1992) *'Middlemarch': A New Casebook*, London: Macmillan.

Pinion, F.B. (1981) *A George Eliot Companion: Literary Achievement and Modern Significance*, London: Macmillan.

Purkis, John (1985) *A Preface to George Eliot*, London: Longman.

Rignall, John (ed.) (1997) *George Eliot and Europe*, Aldershot: Scolar Press.

—— (ed.) (2000) *The Oxford Reader's Companion to George Eliot*, Oxford: Oxford University Press.

Roberts, Neil (1975) *George Eliot: Her Beliefs and Her Art*, London: Elek.

Sadoff, Diane F. (1982) *Monsters of Affection: Dickens, Eliot and Brontë on Fatherhood*, London: Johns Hopkins University Press.

Said, Edward (1993) *Culture and Imperialism*, London: Chatto & Windus.

Sanders, Andrew (1978) *The Victorian Historical Novel, 1840–1880*, London: Macmillan.

Semmel, Bernard (1994) *George Eliot and the Politics of National Inheritance*, Oxford: Oxford University Press.

Shalvi, Alice (ed.) (1976) *Daniel Deronda: A Centenary Symposium*, Jerusalem: Jerusalem Academic Press.

Showalter, Elaine (1977) *A Literature of Their Own: British Women Novelists from Brontë to Lessing*, Guildford: Princeton University Press.

Shuttleworth, Sally (1984) *George Eliot and Nineteenth-Century Science: The Make-Believe of a Beginning*, Cambridge: Cambridge University Press.

Smalley, Barbara (1974) *George Eliot and Flaubert: Pioneers of the Modern Novel*, Athens, Ohio: Ohio University Press.

Sousa Correa, Delia da (2002) *George Eliot, Music and Victorian Culture*, Basingstoke: Palgrave.

Stephen, Sir Leslie (1902) *George Eliot*, London: Macmillan.

Stump, Reva Juanita (1959) *Movement and Vision in George Eliot's Novels*, Seattle, Wash.: University of Washington Press.

Swinden, Patrick (ed.) (1972) *George Eliot: 'Middlemarch': A Casebook*, London: Macmillan.

—— (1992) *'Silas Marner': Memory and Salvation*, New York: Twayne.

Thomas, Jeanie (1988) *Reading 'Middlemarch': Reclaiming the Middle Distance*, Ann Arbor, Mich.: UMI Research Press.

Thompson, Andrew (1998) *George Eliot and Italy: Literary, Cultural and Political Influences from Dante to the Risorgimento*, Basingstoke: Macmillan.

Uglow, Jennifer (1987) *George Eliot*, London: Virago.

Vitaglione, Daniel (1993) *George Eliot and George Sand*, New York: Peter Lang.

Welsh, Alexander (1985) *George Eliot and Blackmail*, London: Harvard University Press.

Williams, Raymond (1970) *The English Novel: From Dickens to Lawrence*, London: Chatto & Windus.

Witemeyer, Hugh (1979) *George Eliot and the Visual Arts*, London: Yale University Press.

Woolf, Virginia (1925) *The Common Reader*, London: Hogarth Press.

Wright, T.R. (1991) *George Eliot's 'Middlemarch'*, London: Harvester Wheatsheaf.

Yousaf, Nahem and Maunder, Andrew (eds) (2002) *George Eliot: 'The Mill on the Floss' and 'Silas Marner': A New Casebook*, Basingstoke: Palgrave.

Index

Related titles from Routledge

George Eliot's English Travels
Composite characters and coded communications
Kathleen McCormack

George Eliot's more than fifty long and short journeys within England took her to sites scattered around the country. Revising the traditional notion that George Eliot drew her settings and characters only from the areas of her Warwickshire girlhood, Kathleen McCormack demonstrates that these journeys furnished the novelist with a wide variety of originals for the composite characters and settings she would so memorably create.

McCormack traces the way in which George Eliot gathered material during her travels and drafted long sections of the novels while away from her London home. McCormack reaches the fascinating conclusion that the novels were a form of coded communication between the author and people in her life, including other prominent Victorians such as Edward Burne-Jones, Robert Lytton and Barbara Bodichon.

Presenting fresh biographical information and original insights into George Eliot's writing strategies, *George Eliot's English Travels* promises a decisive shift in our understanding of one of the most important figures in Victorian literature.

ISBN 13: 978–0415–36022–7 (hbk)

Available at all good bookshops
For further information on our literature series, please visit:
www.routledge.com/literature/series.asp
For ordering and further information please visit:
www.routledge.com

Related titles from Routledge

THE NEW CRITICAL IDIOM

Series Editor: John Drakakis, University of Stirling

The New Critical Idiom is an invaluable series of introductory guides to today's critical terminology. Each book:

- provides a handy, explanatory guide to the use (and abuse) of the term
- offers an original and distinctive overview by a leading literary and cultural critic
- relates the term to the larger field of cultural representation

With a strong emphasis on clarity, lively debate and the widest possible breadth of examples, *The New Critical Idiom* is an indispensable approach to key topics in literary studies.

'*The New Critical Idiom* is a constant resource – essential reading for all students.'
– *Tom Paulin, University of Oxford*

'Easily the most informative and wide-ranging series of its kind, so packed with bright ideas that it has become an indispensable resource for students of literature.'
– *Terry Eagleton, University of Manchester*

Available in this series:

The Author by Andrew Bennett
Autobiography by Linda Anderson
Adaptation and Appropriation by Julie Sanders
Class by Gary Day
Colonialism/Postcolonialism – Second edition by Ania Loomba
Comedy by Andrew Stott
Crime Fiction by John Scaggs
Culture/Metaculture by Francis Mulhern
Difference by Mark Currie
Discourse by Sara Mills
Drama / Theatre / Performance by Simon Shepherd and Mick Wallis
Dramatic Monologue by Glennis Byron
Ecocriticism by Greg Garrard
Elegy by David Kennedy
Genders by David Glover and Cora Kaplan
Genre by John Frow
Gothic by Fred Botting
Historicism by Paul Hamilton
Humanism by Tony Davies
Ideology by David Hawkes
Interdisciplinarity by Joe Moran

Intertextuality by Graham Allen
Irony by Claire Colebrook
Literature by Peter Widdowson
Magic(al) Realism by Maggie Ann Bowers
Metre, Rhythm and Verse Form by Philip Hobsbaum
Metaphor by David Punter
Mimesis by Matthew Potolsky
Modernism by Peter Childs
Myth by Laurence Coupe
Narrative by Paul Cobley
Parody by Simon Dentith
Pastoral by Terry Gifford
The Postmodern by Simon Malpas
The Sublime by Philip Shaw
The Author by Andrew Bennett
Realism by Pam Morris
Rhetoric by Jennifer Richards
Romance by Barbara Fuchs
Romanticism by Aidan Day
Science Fiction by Adam Roberts
Sexuality by Joseph Bristow
Stylistics by Richard Bradford
Subjectivity by Donald E. Hall
The Unconscious by Antony Easthope

For further information on individual books in the series, visit:
www.routledge.com/literature/nci